READING AND WRITING INSTRUCTION IN THE TWENTY-FIRST CENTURY

READING AND WRITING INSTRUCTION IN THE TWENTY-FIRST CENTURY

Recovering and Transforming the Pedagogy of Robert Scholes

EDITED BY
ELLEN C. CARILLO

UTAH STATE UNIVERSITY PRESS
Logan

© 2021 by University Press of Colorado

Published by Utah State University Press
An imprint of University Press of Colorado
245 Century Circle, Suite 202
Louisville, Colorado 80027

All rights reserved

 The University Press of Colorado is a proud member of the Association of University Presses.

The University Press of Colorado is a cooperative publishing enterprise supported, in part, by Adams State University, Colorado State University, Fort Lewis College, Metropolitan State University of Denver, Regis University, University of Colorado, University of Northern Colorado, University of Wyoming, Utah State University, and Western Colorado University.

ISBN: 978-1-64642-118-3 (paperback)
ISBN: 978-1-64642-119-0 (ebook)
https://doi.org/10.7330/9781646421190

Library of Congress Cataloging-in-Publication Data

Names: Scholes, Robert, 1929–2016, honoree, author. | Carillo, Ellen C., editor. | Hesse, Douglas Dean, writer of afterword.
Title: Reading and writing instruction in the twenty-first century : recovering and transforming the pedagogy of Robert Scholes / edited by Ellen C. Carillo ; afterword, Douglas D. Hesse.
Description: Logan : Utah State University Press, [2021] | Includes bibliographical references and index.
Identifiers: LCCN 2021015379 (print) | LCCN 2021015380 (ebook) | ISBN 9781646421183 (paperback) | ISBN 9781646421190 (ebook)
Subjects: LCSH: Scholes, Robert, 1929–2016—Criticism and interpretation. | Rhetoric—Study and teaching—Education (Higher) | Reading—Education (Higher) | English language—Study and teaching—Education (Higher)
Classification: LCC PE1404 .R37345 2021 (print) | LCC PE1404 (ebook) | DDC 808/.04270711—dc23
LC record available at https://lccn.loc.gov/2021015379
LC ebook record available at https://lccn.loc.gov/2021015380

The University Press of Colorado gratefully acknowledges the support of the University of Connecticut toward the publication of this book.

Cover art by Joseph A. Gerber

To Robert Scholes (1929–2016)

CONTENTS

Acknowledgments ix

Introduction
 Ellen C. Carillo 3

PART 1. TRANSFORMING SCHOLES'S "CANON OF METHODS"

1. Reading's Many Branches: Robert Scholes's "Canon of Methods"
 Paul T. Corrigan 23

2. Now More Than Ever: Developing *Crafty Readers* in Writing Classes and across the Curriculum
 Alice S. Horning 38

3. Periodical Textuality: A Case for Contextualized Reading Practices in First-Year Writing
 Christopher J. La Casse 54

4. "Learning and Teaching": A Heuristic for Prioritizing Teacher-Learning in English Education
 Jessica Rivera-Mueller 72

5. Excerpt from "A Fortunate Fall?": The Rise and Fall of English
 Robert Scholes 85

PART 2. EXTENDING SCHOLES'S SCHOLARSHIP ON DISPOSITIONS AND HABITS OF MIND

6. From Argument to Invitation: Promoting Empathy and Mutual Understanding in the Composition Classroom
 Kelsey McNiff 117

7. "Everyday Theory": Robert Scholes and the Ethics of Reading
 Christian Smith 133

8. Truth, Propaganda, and Textual Power: A Pedagogy for Combatting Cynicism in the Post-Truth Era
   Kenny Smith   145

9. "The Transition to College Reading"
   Robert Scholes   157

PART 3. THINKING ABOUT DISCIPLINARY ISSUES ALONGSIDE SCHOLES

10. How Scholes Helped English Departments Confront the Death of the Author, the Loss of Readers, and the Emergence of Intertextual Literacies
    Thomas P. Miller   167

11. Will Writing Studies Abandon Literacy Education Too?
    Emily J. Isaacs   182

12. "Not a Neat Conspiracy, but a Muddle": A College-to-Career Quality Enhancement Plan in the Spirit of Robert Scholes
    Lynée Lewis Gaillet and Angela Christie   196

13. Attending to the Tactical: Robert Scholes and the Legacy of White Language Supremacy
    Robert Lestón   212

14. "The English Apparatus"
    Robert Scholes   226

15. Presidential Address 2004: The Humanities in a Posthumanist World
    Robert Scholes   239

Afterword
   Douglas D. Hesse   253

About the Contributors   261
Index   265

ACKNOWLEDGMENTS

First, I'd like to acknowledge the contributors to this collection. I appreciate their hard work, positive attitude, and willingness to revise their chapters throughout the process of developing this manuscript. It was a real pleasure to watch the volume coalesce around their smart and innovative takes on Scholes's scholarship. I am also grateful to Sean Latham for sharing the many personal and professional details about Robert Scholes that enriched the introduction in innumerable ways. I thoroughly enjoyed working once again with Rachael Levay at Utah State University Press. I hope we continue to make a habit of working together. I am indebted to the great team at the press for always doing a fabulous job of preparing my manuscripts and elevating my scholarship: Laura Furney, Dan Pratt, Beth Svinarich, and Jennie Turcios. I would also like to thank the anonymous reviewers whose comments helped the contributors and me clarify and nuance our engagement with Scholes's scholarship.

I would also like to acknowledge the University of Connecticut's Scholarship Facilitation Fund, which covered the cost of gaining permission to reprint Robert Scholes's own writing in this volume. Permission to reprint excerpts from *Textual Power* and *The Rise and Fall of English* was granted by Yale University Press; permission to reprint "Presidential Address 2004: The Humanities in a Posthumanist World" was granted by the Modern Language Association; and permission to reprint "The Transition to College Reading" was granted by Duke University Press.

And, finally, my gratitude goes to Robert Scholes for his wisdom, which continues to guide and inspire so many of us.

READING AND WRITING INSTRUCTION IN THE TWENTY-FIRST CENTURY

INTRODUCTION

Ellen C. Carillo

> *I'm a teacher first and a critic or interpreter or semiotician or whatever second. And pedagogy is rooted in a certain amount of faith in the political process as it has been developed in this country: far from perfect, mind you, and based on assumptions about the ability of people to learn enough to make their own decisions, which are very idealistic assumptions. I'm still trying to help realize that enterprise by teaching reading and writing on a large scale at the highest possible level. My interpretive methods are based on their teachability more than anything else.*
> —"An Interview with Robert Scholes"
> (Bagwell 1983)

Robert Scholes, Andrew W. Mellon Professor of the Humanities Emeritus at Brown University, passed away on December 9, 2016, leaving behind an intellectual legacy focused broadly on textuality, which allowed him to impact a range of fields, including literary studies, composition and rhetoric, education, media studies, and the digital humanities. For more than four decades Scholes wrote prolifically on literary modernism, structuralism, semiotics, reading and writing pedagogies, the profession of English, and the future of the humanities.

Putting together this collection of essays to honor Scholes's memory and to explore and extend the continued relevance of his work exposed how impactful his scholarship was and is. Depending upon whom you ask, Scholes might be lauded as a die-hard semiotician, a pioneer in the digital humanities before such a thing even existed, a beacon of hope for those committed to humanities education, or an invaluable resource to those teaching writing and rhetoric at the secondary and postsecondary levels.

I came to know Scholes's work in that latter capacity as I was introduced to his scholarship as a graduate student of English in the early 2000s at the University of Pittsburgh. As far as I know Scholes did not directly influence the creation of the degree there, which is actually a PhD in critical and cultural studies, but his philosophies about the work of English certainly influenced its curriculum where we studied broad questions about language and textuality as they apply equally across media and to everything from high literary modernism to fan cultures and from science fiction to archival textbooks. After earning my graduate degree, I ended up at the University of Connecticut teaching a course called Writing Through Literature, the subtitle of the third and following editions of Scholes's co-authored unorthodox textbook, *Text Book*. Both the textbook and the course encourage instructors to, in Scholes's (1985, 16) own words from *Textual Power*, "stop 'teaching literature' and start 'studying texts.'" Scholes's pedagogical philosophies, it would seem, have trailed me now for more than half my life.

My introduction to Scholes came at about the time he published the short commentary titled "The Transition to College Reading" in *Pedagogy: Critical Approaches to Teaching Literature, Language, Composition, and Culture* in 2002—rather late in his career. This piece has become a profound touchstone in my own work in the field of writing studies, and my specific area of expertise, the teaching of critical reading at the postsecondary level. I rarely hold a workshop or deliver a presentation that does not include his remarkable insight in that piece about why reading largely gets neglected in the college classroom: "We normally acknowledge, however grudgingly, that writing must be taught and continue to be taught from high school to college and perhaps beyond. We accept it, I believe, because we can see writing, and we know that much of the writing we see is not good enough. But we do not see reading. We see some writing about reading, to be sure, but we do not see reading. I am certain, though, that if we could see it, we would be appalled" (2002, 166).

Invariably this quote elicits an audible gasp of recognition from audience members as they acknowledge the simple and seemingly obvious truth in Scholes's observation about the invisibility of reading, an observation that for decades has nonetheless escaped those of us teaching at the postsecondary level. It was this commentary that led me to track down Scholes's earlier award-winning book *Textual Power* (1985), as well as his other books, including *Protocols of Reading* (1989), *The Rise and Fall of English: Reconstructing English as a Discipline* (1998), *English After the Fall: From Literature to Textuality* (2011), and *The Craft of Reading* (2008). While I also came to know and admire his work on literary modernism, structuralism and semiotics, periodical studies, and the many other areas in which he published, it was Scholes's pedagogically inflected scholarship that I found especially compelling. It turned out that I was not alone.

As I shared the news of Scholes's death with colleagues in and beyond English, it was remarkable to hear about the multitude of ways Scholes's work impacted others. And so, I began thinking about what a collection that would honor this impact might look like. While it would be impossible to offer anything more than a glimpse into Scholes's legacy it ultimately seemed fitting that the glimpse would be of his pedagogical scholarship. Scholes consistently underscored his commitment to teaching and its priority above all else, to which the epigraph that opens this introduction attests: "I'm a teacher first and a critic or interpreter or semiotician or whatever second," Scholes explains. Scholes's chosen subjects were reading and writing, and his "interpretive methods" were "based on their teachability more than anything else" (Sean Latham, personal communication, May 5, 2019). Describing Scholes's priorities similarly, longtime friend and regular collaborator Sean Latham noted:

> I think that's what it all came down to for Bob: giving students the tools they needed to be both good readers and good writers . . . Bob believed our job is to teach writing and reading of all kinds while meeting the students where they are in order to connect their interests to a larger more complex set of histories and traditions. Science fiction, video games, magazines—these were all interests that led him closer to what he thought the students themselves were reading and what they wanted to do with texts.

Scholes's commitment to giving students the tools they needed to pursue their interests even if those interests didn't align with how English defined itself at the time seems paramount to understanding Scholes's investment in his students and in teaching. Of course, in the decades since Scholes began working with students on science fiction, magazines, and video games these artifacts have become more acceptable objects of study, but to undertake this work when he did was revolutionary and helps explain why his scholarship is still relevant today.

THE CONTEMPORARY RELEVANCE OF SCHOLES'S SCHOLARSHIP

Scholes's scholarship remains not just relevant, but a great deal of his pedagogical scholarship is eerily prophetic in how it anticipated the teaching challenges that have emerged as a result of our highly divisive climate. Shortly after 9/11 and writing about the English teacher's responsibility to challenge xenophobia, for example, Scholes (2002, 167–68) explained the importance of giving students the opportunity to consider themselves and their experiences in relation to others, an ability he believed Americans lack: "After 11 September 2001 we have begun to learn, perhaps, that this deficiency is serious." He goes on to describe how English instructors must help students develop reading practices "in which strength comes, paradoxically, from subordinating one's own thoughts temporarily to the views and values of another person." In a time when fear is used to encourage divisiveness and we have seen an increase in hate crimes against marginalized groups, Scholes's call for English instructors to take the lead in helping create more empathetic student-citizens could not be more relevant or important.

In addition to arguing that reading should be conceptualized as a tool to cultivate openness and related dispositions, the subject of the second part of this collection, as many as three decades ago, Scholes (1985, 15) recognized the role of education in teaching student-citizens how to push back against the nefarious powers of texts: "The students who come to us now exist in the most manipulative culture human beings have ever experienced. They are bombarded with signs, with rhetoric, from their daily awakenings until their troubled sleep." "The worst thing we can do," warned Scholes, "is to foster in them an attitude of reverence before texts" (1985, 16). In a culture where the very concept of "alternative facts" exists and in which disinformation and "fake news" move at warp speed, a reverence before texts is especially dangerous not only for individual students but for a healthy democratic society that depends upon its citizens' abilities to read, write, and think critically.

Unlike other scholars who were circulating theories of literacy around the same time, Scholes was thinking about students' literacy practices in relation to their roles as citizens in a democracy. He was concerned, in other words, about the challenges that American culture posed for students as democratic citizens. It is perhaps this specific context that has allowed Scholes, rather than other scholars, to become the touchstone on this issue. The publication of David Bartholomae and Anthony Petrosky's *Ways of Reading* was certainly an important moment in the history of literacy instruction, as was Christina Haas and Linda Flower's study on the reading practices of graduates and undergraduates. Peter Elbow's "Doubting/Believing Game" and Geneva Smitherman's *Talkin and Testifyin* were also important contributions to discussions surrounding literacy. But in our current moment in which our democracy has been threatened, Scholes, who was thinking about literacy within the context of democracy, has emerged as the touchstone. Still, readers will find in this volume references to some of these contemporaries of Scholes who were writing about similar subjects. For example, Kelsey McNiff describes her use of Elbow's Believing/Doubting Game in her classroom, and Robert Lestón looks closely at Bartholomae's 1993 essay "The Tidy House: Basic Writing in the American Curriculum."

Scholes's scholarship has by no means eclipsed that of these equally important scholars, also evidenced by Jason Maxwell's discussion of Scholes alongside Wayne Booth and Peter Elbow in *The Two Cultures of English: Literature, Composition, and the Moment of Rhetoric*, addressed below. But the context in which Scholes offered his pedagogical scholarship perhaps resonates at this moment more than similar scholarship from the same time because of the recent attacks on democracy, including the insurrection at the United States Capitol on January 6, 2021.

Because so much of what Scholes discussed in his pedagogical scholarship—including his work on the English curricula—continues to resonate, contemporary writing instructors and administrators have found themselves compelled to return to his scholarship. For example, shortly after the Association of Departments of English (ADE) released its report titled "A Changing Major: The Report of the 2016–17 ADE Ad Hoc Committee on the English Major," subscribers to the writing program administrator's listserv (WPA-L), including prominent figures in the field, invoked Scholes's ideas as they discussed the report. Doug Hesse (2018), who has contributed the afterword to this collection, wrote:

> There is an important distinction between "what ADE says" and "what individual English departments believe/do." There are certainly enlightened/progressive English department [*sic*] and there are certainly calcified ones, and for several of the former, enlightenment came years ago, even if many ignored their efforts. The example I know best was Illinois State University, in the period from 1985 to 2005, which had a robust English Studies perspective that embodied ideas given widest voice in the work that Bob Scholes was publishing. . . . If I were inventing an English department today, I'd build it around text-making: having students practice how texts are made and analyze how texts make readers, ideas, social formations, all of this informed (informed, not dominated) by how making has happened historically out of different kinds of stuff and circumstance, toward different purposes and consequences, all with a focus on students as text-makers for the present and future.

Joel Wingard (2018) responded to Hesse with the following: "I hear Bob Scholes in your coda, Doug, about building an English department from scratch. A department that is about the consumption and production of texts, aka literacy." Similarly, Andrea Lunsford (2018) commented, "This discussion sends me back to Bob Scholes's work—especially *Textual Power* and *The Rise and Fall of English*."

This return to Scholes's ideas from decades ago as English currently tries to imagine a place for itself and its major in the twenty-first century suggests just how pioneering Scholes's thinking was. Decades ago,

Scholes recognized the importance of thinking broadly in terms of both teaching and scholarship, regularly warning colleagues in English of the risks of specialization: "Every move toward greater specialization leads us away from the needs of the majority of our students and drives a larger wedge between our professional lives and our own private needs and concerns" (1998, 82). Now, as English departments across the country continue to face huge drops in the number of majors, Scholes's (1985, 16) ideas about reorganizing English departments around "all kinds of texts, visual as well as verbal, polemical as well as seductive" are being invoked as possibilities. "The exclusivity of literature as a category must be discarded," Scholes (1985, 16) wrote in *Textual Power*. A little more than ten years later, Scholes (1998, 36) would further explain the need to "deconstruct our traditional organization [and] . . . to reconstruct our efforts as students and teachers of English around the notion of textuality. Under this sign," explained Scholes, "there is no difference between the theory of composition and the theory of literature—and there is precious little difference between theory and teaching at all, since the practice of teaching is based upon the teaching of theory, and this theory itself rests upon the shared stance of students and practitioners of reading and writing—textuality." The expansive conceptualization of the work of English that Scholes proffered, one founded on a theory of textuality that encompasses both literature and composition (including creative writing) and involves the study of all texts as opposed to just literature, would seemingly hold great promise, but as Emily J. Isaacs points out in this volume, Scholes's vision never really came to fruition and now, with the rise of independent writing studies departments, is not likely to gain much traction.

Disciplinary issues aside, Scholes has also remained an important reference for those teaching writing and literature. In an October 2018 thread on the WPA-L about Scholes's *Text Book*, which Scholes co-authored with Nancy Comley and Gregory Ulmer, subscribers to the WPA-L detailed how they have used this book. Stephen Fox (2018) noted, "I used *Text Book* in our first-year literature course several times. I thought it was a smart book, and the students responded pretty well as I recall. I like the way it has students writing in genres as part of understanding those genres as readers." Matt Hollrah (2018) added, "I've never used it in a traditional Comp class, but I have used it several times in our English Cornerstone course as a way to frame the field as one focused on texts, their production and interpretation."

Scholes is also regularly invoked in scholarly monographs and professional journals. Most recently, in *The Two Cultures of English: Literature,*

Composition, and the Moment of Rhetoric, Jason Maxwell (2019) situates Scholes as a key actor in the theory revolution and one of the prominent figures, alongside Wayne Booth and Peter Elbow, who sought to unify composition and literature in meaningful ways in the late twentieth century, helping to create the parameters of what would come to be the "comp-lit wars," which still characterize English today. In *Pedagogy: Critical Approaches to Teaching Literature, Language, Composition, and Culture,* one of the few journals that publishes articles of interest to those teaching both composition and literature (among other subjects), Scholes's scholarship is regularly cited. In two pieces in separate issues of *Pedagogy,* Paul T. Corrigan (2017, 2018), whose chapter opens this volume, calls on Scholes as he reviews books about teaching literature as well as when he considers what the scholarship on the teaching of literature tells us about the state of the discipline. In her recent article in *Pedagogy,* Laura Schechter (2018, 65) invokes Scholes's scholarship on close reading to help support her argument for teaching multiple English translations of the same text in order to allow students to "consider the multiple hands—author, translator, editor, printer, publisher, and reader—that shape and mediate each work." In their introduction to a special issue of *Pedagogy* on reading, guest editors Mariolina Rizzi Salvatori and Patricia Donahue (2016, 7) connect their impetus for developing the special issue to the dearth of scholarship on reading and directly to Scholes's point "that in English studies, a discipline based on reading, 'we see some writing about reading, to be sure, but we do not see reading.'" In that special issue, Tara Lockhart and Mary Soliday (2016, 23–24) describe Scholes as the inspiration for their multiyear study of seventy-six undergraduate students' reading practices across disciplines and Stephanie Moody (2016, 120) similarly invokes Scholes to argue for the need to make the affective reading practices of readers of romance novels more visible in order to allow for an exploration of these readers' moments of critical engagement. Even more recently, editors Victoria Bazin, Sue Currell, and E. James West of *Radical Americas* (2018), a peer-reviewed open-access journal published by the University College of London, introduce their special issue by pointing to Scholes and Latham's pioneering work that helped to make the very field of periodical studies, the subject of the special issue, both visible and legitimate.

The essays in this volume, including La Casse's own chapter that draws on Scholes's work in periodical studies, contribute to these contemporary discussions inflected by Scholes's scholarship. This collection is intended to serve as both a tribute to Scholes and a resource for contemporary secondary and postsecondary instructors and administrators.

Those teaching writing and critical reading at the postsecondary level will find guidance for doing so as the contributors in parts 1 and 2 draw on and extend Scholes's scholarship to meet our present needs, and in Scholes's (1998, 68) own words, to "offer our students . . . the cultural equipment they are going to need when they leave us." Those in education will find support for preparing preservice teachers in these pages as well. Department heads, administrators, and English faculty will find chapters about the future of English generally, and writing studies specifically, as contributors in part 3 think alongside Scholes about disciplinary issues.

GIVING VOICE TO CRITIQUES OF SCHOLES'S WORK

While a tribute to Scholes and a source of support for contemporary instructors and administrators, this collection also addresses the areas in which Scholes's theories fall short. As with any scholar, Scholes was writing within a very specific period, and it would be unwise to assume that Scholes's ideas and theories could simply be imported into our contemporary moment, no matter how relevant. Emily J. Isaacs, for example, laments the impossibility of achieving Scholes's vision of unified English departments in light of the rise of independent writing studies departments. Scholes, of course, could not predict how this shift would challenge his visions of unification. Nor could Scholes predict that specialization would reach new heights *within* the factions he was seeking to unify. If the desire to reconstruct English still exists, we will need to look beyond what Scholes offers us because the landscape of English has changed so drastically since he was writing.

The methods we must help our students cultivate for engaging texts have also necessarily changed. While Scholes was ahead of his time with his focus on media and interdisciplinarity, there are moments in his scholarship that suggest a short-sightedness that one might not expect. In calling for the development of a canon of methods to share with students, for example, Scholes describes the need to turn to "the ways of reading we have already learned to use in our studies of English literature and culture" (Scholes 2001, 215). Scholes's reliance on English as the sole source of methods for engaging texts, as well as his neglect of key scholars on reading, such as Louise Rosenblatt, is problematic. Paul T. Corrigan considers these shortcomings in the opening chapter in this volume.

Like Corrigan, contributor Kelsey McNiff finds herself needing to extend Scholes's scholarship, which simply calls for helping students to develop "the rhetorical capacity to imagine the other's thought, feeling, and sentiments" (Scholes 2002, 168), but does not offer a plan for doing so. What Scholes fails to give us in "The Transition to College Reading" McNiff outlines in her chapter.

While McNiff takes up one of Scholes's calls, Robert Lestón warns us about heeding another one of Scholes's calls, this one to our profession. Scholes advocates for "developing better bourgeois subjects—better than ourselves, that is, as well as better than they might be without our teaching" (1998, 67), while Lestón challenges us to "find ways to allow those students who will never be bourgeois to transform it into something more accommodating."

Returning to Scholes's scholarship with the kind of critical eye modeled by these and other contributors is an important step toward making visible some of the shortcomings of Scholes's ideas and thereby creating a path toward expanding and extending his ideas to address the current needs of our students and our profession.

SCHOLES'S CONTRIBUTIONS: A BROADER OVERVIEW

Because this collection is limited to considerations of Scholes's pedagogical scholarship, I want to spend some time detailing Scholes's varied contributions—both scholarly and professional—in order to create a fuller picture of Scholes's work than the chapters herein allow.

Scholes authored or edited some forty books (Latham 2015, 257), including scholarly monographs, textbooks, and essay collections. His scholarship has appeared in roughly fifty different journals and edited collections over the years, including such diverse publications as the *Yale Review*, *Shakespeare Quarterly*, *PMLA*, *Quarterly Review of Film*, *Iowa Review*, *College English*, *American Journal of Semiotics*, and *Pedagogy: Critical Approaches to Teaching Literature, Language, Composition, and Culture*. While Scholes's contributions might seem eclectic—he worked across media, historical periods, on so-called "low" and "high" cultural artifacts, and on disciplinary and professional trends—Latham recognizes a thread connecting all of these interests: "[Scholes] remained a semiotician and maybe even a kind of structuralist all his life. To him, there were interesting things to read and interpret everywhere, from the pages of great books like *Ulysses* to his famous reading of a crude bumper sticker in *Semiotics and Interpretation*."

Throughout his scholarship, Scholes used semiotics and structuralist theories of language to study (and to invite students to study) texts, very broadly understood. As early as 1966, just about five years after finishing his PhD at Cornell, Scholes, with co-author Robert Kellogg, began demonstrating what that expansive notion of "text" meant for literary studies. Challenging more traditional conceptions of "capital L" Literature, *The Nature of Narrative* studies, among other genres, science fiction. Of course, in the decades since the publication of this foundational study of narrative history, science fiction has emerged as a legitimate genre within literary studies, but that was not the case in 1966. As Latham (2015, 259) points out in his tribute to Scholes in the *James Joyce Quarterly*, Scholes did something similarly bold shortly thereafter in *The Fabulators* (1967) and *Structural Fabulation: An Essay on Fictions of the Future* (1975) in that he "placed science-fiction writers like Vonnegut alongside postmodern experimentalists like Barth and Iris Murdoch. He was among the first to treat a genre many still considered pulpy trash as a serious imaginative literature."

While Scholes was modeling through his scholarship and his talks on science fiction what an expansion of the work of English might look like, he was also becoming a leading theorist of structuralism. In *Structuralism in Literature: An Introduction*, Scholes (1974) outlines the evolution of structuralism, presenting American readers with the first full-length discussion of this intellectual framework and method of criticism (Editors' Bookshelf 1975). Structuralism, as Scholes details, is at its center concerned with relationships. Scholes (1974, 11) explains that structuralism "seeks to explore the relationship between the system of literature and the culture of which it is a part," the "relationship between the language of literature and the whole of language" (1974, 13). Having received positive reviews in at least ten publications, including the *Times Higher Education Supplement*, *Modern Language Quarterly*, and the *French Review*, this book secured Scholes's position as a major literary theorist and critic, and his next book, *Semiotics and Interpretation*, which was similarly lauded for its accessibility, offered an introduction to semiotic theory and led Martin Green of *The Literary Review* (1982) to hail Scholes as "among our best interpreters of literary theory."

The lucidity with which Scholes wrote about complex subjects such as structuralism and semiotics became a hallmark of his work, and he regularly reminded his readers of the value of accessibility. "We make a mistake," wrote Scholes in *The Crafty Reader*, "if we equate the difficult and the obscure with the valuable—a mistake frequently made, especially by teachers and professors of literature" (2001, xvi). This sentiment apparently informed his teaching as well. Latham, whose first introduction to Scholes was as a graduate student at Brown, explains that Scholes "wrote to be understood—and taught me to do the same. I came to grad school as a bright-eyed theorist eager to write the densest, most complex prose I could. To his great credit, Bob suggested I could do better by writing things people could actually read and understand."

In fact, one of Scholes's many inventive projects came about in an effort to help students understand one of the most difficult genres for students: poetry. In 1976, decades before digital humanities emerged as a field, Scholes worked with computer scientist Andries (Andy) van Dam on an early digital humanities project. The NEH-funded project titled "An Experiment in Computer-Based Education Using Hypertext" involved exploring how hypertext could be used as a pedagogical tool to help teach poetry to undergraduates at Brown University where Scholes began teaching in 1970 after a short stint at the University of Virginia and a longer one at the University of Iowa.

While in the Department of English and Comparative Literature at Brown, Scholes helped create the semiotics program that went on to become the Department of Modern Culture and Media, of which he served as the first chair. In addition to his 1976 project on hypertext, at Brown he founded the Modernist Journals Project with Latham and Mark Gaipa in 1995. The Modernist Journals Project, the first digital archive of the little magazines of literary modernism, continues to be used by students and scholars worldwide.

While at Brown, Scholes began thinking more broadly about the discipline of English and its need for restructuring. In the mid-1980s, Scholes began writing extensively about English as a discipline. As Thomas P. Miller and Emily J. Isaacs both note in their chapters in this volume, he did so largely from outside English, as he had by that time founded and moved into the Department of Modern Culture and Media. As discussed earlier in this introduction, in *Textual Power* Scholes (1985, 16) develops a theory of textuality that sought to reunite the fields of literary studies and composition. Scholes had hoped that textuality could serve as a larger umbrella under which all in English could reside "with the consumption and production of texts thoroughly intermingled." He enacted the pedagogy that emerged from this theory in *Text Book* and further developed his ideas about how textuality could be used to reorganize the discipline of English in *The Rise and Fall of English* and then *After the Fall*. In *The Crafty Reader*, published just a few years after *The Rise and Fall of English*, Scholes develops his idea that reading can be taught because it is a craft rather than an art, and in that book Scholes models what "crafty reading" looks like. Scholes's ideas about texts—"valuable texts are to be found in all media, and in many genres within those media" (2001, xv)—infuse his model readings, including of works by Norman Rockwell and J. K. Rowling. Alice S. Horning's chapter in this volume focuses on this lesser-known book, arguing that "the need for crafty readers continues to expand as more information comes at all of us from more sources at ever higher speed."

Although Scholes's work continues to resonate today, it registered as pioneering when it was written, earning Scholes both the Modern Language Association's Mina P. Shaughnessy Prize in 1986 and the National Council of Teachers of English David H. Russell Research Award for *Textual Power*. He received the Francis A. March Award for Distinguished Service to the Profession of English from the Association of Departments of English (ADE)/MLA in 2000 and was awarded the Research Society for American Periodicals Book Prize for his final book, *Modernism in the Magazines* (co-authored with Clifford Wulfman) in 2011. Among other support for his research, Scholes earned three National Endowment for the Humanities (NEH) grants, a Mellon grant, and served as a Guggenheim fellow from 1977 to 1978.

During his long career, Scholes also took on various leadership roles in professional organizations relevant to his expansive interests. He served as president of the Modern Language Association in 2004, and his presidential address "The Humanities in a Posthumanist World" (Scholes 2005), in which he reflects on the state of the humanities and proposes a plan to move ahead, is included in part 3 of this volume. He also served as president of the Semiotic Society of America from 1989 to 1990 and was elected a fellow of the American Academy of Art and Sciences in 1998.

A year later, in 1999, Scholes officially retired from teaching formal classes but continued to work with graduate students and regularly published articles and full-length monographs. In fact, the majority of Scholes's scholarship to which authors in this collection refer was written during his "retirement."

AN OVERVIEW OF THIS COLLECTION

Divided into three parts, this volume seeks to illuminate the contemporary relevance of Scholes's pedagogical scholarship while extending and transforming it so that it is even more relevant to those with a stake in teaching, and specifically teaching students in English, English Education, and Writing Studies at the postsecondary level.

Part 1, "Transforming Scholes's Canon of Methods," explores how practices and methods, and particularly methods for reading, are a centerpiece of Scholes's pedagogical scholarship. Reflecting on his role as an educator, Scholes explains in *The Crafty Reader*, "As a teacher I have for years seen a major part of my task as helping students see reading as a craft, a set of methods or practices that can be learned, a skill that can be improved by anyone willing to make an effort" (2001, 139). The chapters in this section speak to the continued relevance of those methods while also exploring how they can be adapted to meet the needs of twenty-first-century students.

Paul T. Corrigan's chapter opens the section by cataloging "the many ways of reading Scholes advocates," as well as "the tenets grounding his work." Alice S. Horning considers how some of the methods and practices that Corrigan catalogs provide a guide for instructors who must help students become "crafty readers" so they can "find, understand, and evaluate sources for use in their own writing" as "more information comes at all of us from more sources at ever higher speed." Like Horning, Christopher J. La Casse explores how Scholes's scholarship can be used to support students' reading abilities. La Casse details how he uses Scholes and Clifford Wulfmann's book *Modernism in the Magazine* to ground a first-year writing research assignment focused on interpreting periodicals, which creates many opportunities for students to hone and practice their critical reading skills. The final chapter in this section shifts our attention away from teaching undergraduates a canon of methods for approaching texts and toward teaching graduate students, and specifically preservice teachers, a canon of methods. Jessica Rivera-Mueller extends Scholes's argument in his article "Learning and Teaching," and, drawing on her own work as an English teacher educator, describes how she has adapted his argument to create a heuristic for prioritizing teacher-learning in English Education. Scholes's own "A Fortunate Fall?," chapter 5 from *The Rise and Fall of English*, closes the chapter with a look at precisely how Scholes conceptualized this canon of methods and its role in the restructuring of English around his theory of textuality.

Part 2, "Extending Scholes's Scholarship on Dispositions and Habits of Mind," is comprised of chapters that consider how Scholes's scholarship speaks to the field of writing studies' current interest in habits of mind and dispositions. In 2011, representatives from the Council of Writing Program Administrators, the National Council of Teachers of English, and the National Writing Project jointly developed The Framework for Success in Postsecondary Writing, which lists eight habits of mind—curiosity, openness, engagement, creativity, persistence, responsibility, flexibility, and metacognition—described as "ways of approaching learning" that are "essential for success in college writing." Since then, scholars have been paying more attention to the qualities that students need, in addition to the cognitive abilities, to be successful in their academics and beyond. As the chapters in this section invoke Scholes, they consider a range of affective qualities that he promoted alongside the more "intellectual" practices and methods he encouraged instructors to teach their students.

In the opening chapter, Kelsey McNiff explores how Scholes's work prompted her to "meditate on the relationship between the composition classroom and citizenship education," including the place of "empathy as a civic virtue." In doing so, McNiff extends Scholes's scholarship by considering how to encourage empathy through the practices of reading and writing. Also concerned with the ethics of reading, Christian Smith considers Scholes's work on reading within the context of contemporary discussions of contemplative pedagogies in composition studies. His exploration emphasizes "the ethical questions of literacy instruction in the face of a 'post-truth America.'" Kenny Smith is similarly invested in helping students meet the challenges posed by the circulation of disinformation. Smith's chapter discusses how Scholes inspired the revision of his approach to teaching civic literacy, especially his teaching of journalistic discourse. His revised approach is inflected by Scholes's criticism of poststructuralist theory and the limitations of its ideas about referentiality, which Smith argues are necessary for understanding journalism in the post-truth era. Scholes's "The Transition to College Reading," a touchstone for many of the chapters in this section, closes out part 2.

Part 3, "Thinking About Disciplinary Issues Alongside Scholes," opens with Thomas P. Miller's chapter, which provides important historical context for understanding Scholes's contributions and their continued relevance, including the ways in which "the integrated forms of literacy and learning that Scholes helped to articulate have become a vital part of current educational reforms." Specifically, Miller details how "reading and writing have become interactive processes that integrate data, images, and other media and information" resulting in literacy becoming "redefined as information literacy, media literacy, digital literacies, and technological literacies." Miller maintains that Scholes's "work can help us engage with the integrated forms of literacy that we need to plug into if we are to make productive use of the historic changes that are unfolding before us." Also looking ahead, but perhaps a bit more pessimistically than Miller, Emily J. Isaacs's provocative chapter on the future of writing studies recognizes Scholes's vision for unifying composition studies and literary studies as theoretically compelling but explores the implications of the failure of his vision—namely the development of writing studies and stand-alone writing studies departments. Although Scholes's vision centered on rebuilding English studies as a discipline "devoted to textual studies, with the consumption and production of texts thoroughly intermingled" (1985, 16), Isaacs maintains that "consumption (literary analysis) and production (composition) never arrived at equal footing within English departments." She wonders, then, "on what grounds would anybody think the new discipline [of writing studies] and accompanying academic departments would be different?" While Isaacs's chapter considers stand-alone writing studies departments, in the chapter that follows, Lynée Lewis Gaillet and Angela Christie return us to the English Department to explore a college-to-career quality enhancement plan inspired by Scholes. They describe how the quality enhancement plan (QEP) they developed for their institution is inflected by Scholes's theories of learning, including the "commonalities across the diverse concentrations of literary studies, creative writing, and rhetoric and composition divisions" that Scholes so desperately wanted to bring together. Robert Lestón's chapter, "Attending to the Tactical: Robert Scholes and the Legacy of White Language Supremacy," on the other hand, contends that Scholes's theories of learning do not meet all of our current needs. He notes that "even if Scholes's rhetorically-oriented curriculum continues to address the needs students face in particular contexts . . . the fact of the matter remains that Scholes does not go nearly far enough for the current environment." As such, Lestón advocates for a "tactically-oriented" approach to teaching that finds ways to allow students to transform the curriculum and, by extension, the institution, into something more accommodating. This section on disciplinarity closes with two of Scholes's pieces that address disciplinary trends in English. His earlier work, chapter 1 from *Textual Power*, "The English Apparatus," lays the groundwork for his argument for restructuring English that he would develop over the next two decades. In his 2004 MLA presidential address, "The Humanities in a Posthumanist World," the final piece in this section, Scholes makes this point even more forcefully, telling his colleagues in English, "We should seek to broaden the range of our studies instead of allowing that range to shrink to a specialization. . . . We teachers of language and literature need to be less narrowly focused on particular periods or genres and broader in our grasp of literary and linguistic history. And also, for good practical reasons, we need to become broader in our grasp of other cultural fields, starting with those closest to us, such as philosophy and the visual arts and media."

It's hard to say if each chapter in this volume goes as far as Scholes would have liked in terms of integrating "other cultural fields," although Gaillet and Christie share a compelling model of this kind of interdisciplinary work in the form of their quality enhancement plan, and many of the other chapters draw on a range of fields beyond English including communications, philosophy, psycholinguistics, and education. Collectively the chapters also showcase pedagogies that deliver "a better balance between production and consumption" (Scholes 1998, 149). In the spirit of Scholes's own scholarship, then, this volume aims "to open up possibilities, to empower" (Scholes 1998, 149) as we pursue "a more spacious idea of literacy" (Scholes 2011, 139), continuing to remind ourselves all the while that "the business of English departments is to help students improve as readers and writers" (Scholes 2011, 84).

More than two decades ago, Scholes (1998, 84) also reminded us "that to function as a citizen of these United States one needs to be able to read, interpret, and criticize texts in a wide range of modes, genres, and media." "What our students need to function in such a world, then," explained Scholes, "is an education for a society still struggling to balance its promises of freedom and equality, still hoping to achieve greater measures of social justice, still trying not to homogenize its people but to allow for social mobility and to make the lower levels of its economic structure tolerable and humane." The chapters in this volume explore what this work might look like in our contemporary culture that is "more fully and insistently textualized" (1998, 84) than that which Scholes was describing in the late twentieth century. "To understand the needs of our students we shall have to face more squarely than we usually do our present cultural situation" (1998, 84), wrote Scholes. The contributors to this volume take up this important work.

REFERENCES

Bagwell, J. Timothy. 1983. "An Interview with Robert Scholes." *Iowa Journal of Literary Studies* (4): 13–20. http://ir.uiowa.edu/cgi/viewcontent.cgi?article=1077&context=ijls.

Bazin, Victoria, Sue Currell, and E. James West. 2018. "Reading the Radical American Periodical." *Radical Americas* 3(1): 18. https://doi.org/10.14324/111.444.ra.2018.v3.1.018.

Corrigan, Paul T. 2017. "Teaching What We Do in Literary Studies." *Pedagogy: Critical Approaches to Teaching Literature, Language, Composition, and Culture* 17 (3): 549–56.

Corrigan, Paul T. 2018. "The State of Scholarship on Teaching Literature." *Pedagogy: Critical Approaches to Teaching Literature, Language, Composition, and Culture* 18 (3): 415–32.

The Editors' Bookshelf. 1975. *The Journal of Religion* 55 (4): 489–98. http://www.jstor.org.ezproxy.lib.uconn.edu/stable/1201726.

Fox, Stephen L. 2018. "'Text Book' by Scholes/Comley/Ulmer?" *WPA-L*, October 10.

Green, Martin. 1982. "Pursuing Semiotics." *The Literary Review* 26 (1): 139.

Hesse, Doug. 2018. "ADE Report on the English Major." *WPA-L*, July 19.

Hollrah, Matt. 2018. "'Text Book' by Scholes/Comley/Ulmer?" *WPA-L*, October 10.
Latham, Sean. 2015. "Robert Scholes 1929–2016." *James Joyce Quarterly* 52 (2): 257–60.
Lockhart, Tara, and Mary Soliday. 2016. "The Critical Place of Reading in Writing Transfer (and Beyond): A Report of Student Experiences." *Pedagogy: Critical Approaches to Teaching Literature, Language, Composition, and Culture* 16 (1): 23–37. doi 10.1215/15314200-3158557.
Lunsford, Andrea. 2018. "ADE Report on the English Major." *WPA-L*, July 20.
Maxwell, Jason. 2019. *The Two Cultures of English: Literature, Composition, and the Moment of Rhetoric*. New York: Fordham University Press.
Moody, Stephanie. 2016. "Identification, Affect, and Escape: Theorizing Popular Romance Reading." *Pedagogy: Critical Approaches to Teaching Literature, Language, Composition, and Culture* 16 (1): 105–23. doi 10.1215/15314200-3158557.
Salvatori, Mariolina Rizzi, and Patricia Donahue. 2016. "Guest Editing as a Form of Disciplinary Probing." *Pedagogy: Critical Approaches to Teaching Literature, Language, Composition, and Culture* 16 (1): 1–8. doi 10.1215/15314200-3158557.
Schechter, Laura. 2018. "'On the Outside Facing the Wooded Ridge': Close Reading Translations and Interpretive Diversity." *Pedagogy: Critical Approaches to Teaching Literature, Language, Composition, and Culture* 18 (1): 51–68. doi 10.1215/15314200-4216930.
Scholes, Robert. 1967. *The Fabulators*. Oxford: Oxford University Press.
Scholes, Robert. 1974. *Structuralism in Literature: An Introduction*. New Haven, CT: Yale University Press.
Scholes, Robert. 1975. *Structural Fabulation: An Essay on Fictions of the Future*. Notre Dame, IN: University of Notre Dame Press.
Scholes, Robert. 1985. *Textual Power: Literary Theory and the Teaching of English*. New Haven, CT: Yale University Press.
Scholes, Robert. 1998. *The Rise and Fall of English: Reconstructing English as a Discipline*. New Haven, CT: Yale University Press.
Scholes, Robert. 2001. *The Crafty Reader*. New Haven, CT: Yale University Press.
Scholes, Robert. 2002. "The Transition to College Reading." *Pedagogy* 2 (2): 165–72.
Scholes, Robert. 2005. "Presidential Address 2004: The Humanities in a Posthumanist World." *PMLA* 120 (3): 724–33.
Scholes, Robert. 2011. *English After the Fall: From Literature to Textuality*. Iowa City: University of Iowa Press.
Scholes, Robert, Nancy R. Comley, and Gregory L. Ulmer. 2001. *Text Book: Writing through Literature*. 3rd ed. New York: Bedford/St. Martin's.
Wingard, Joel. 2018. "ADE Report on the English Major." *WPA-L*, July 19.

PART 1

Transforming Scholes's "Canon of Methods"

1
READING'S MANY BRANCHES
Robert Scholes's "Canon of Methods"

Paul T. Corrigan

When I touched the ancient tree, placed my hands on its rough bark, emotion swelled inside my chest and moisture welled up in my eyes. Standing at Angel Oak's enormous trunk, among its endless limbs, under its nearly half acre of green leaves, I suddenly felt I had to change my life. How could a tree do this to me? Allergies? No, my reaction followed from and flowed back into my *reading* of the tree in that moment—that is to say, the meaning I constructed out of what was unfolding before and within me. Namely, having traveled there purposefully as if on a pilgrimage, I read the tree as a sacred entity and my being present to it as a sacred event.

Now, some time later, my training as a scholar and teacher of English allows me to step back and consider what went into that reading. Yes, the tree itself, its physical presence, influenced my interpretation, but so did the many associations I brought with me—my sense of the usual size of trees; my memories of trees I loved and climbed during childhood; the oak at the nearby plantation I had visited just hours before, upon which humans had lashed other humans during slavery; and the many books I had read that taught me the value of "standing still and learning to be astonished" by the natural world (Oliver 2006, 1). All these went into my reading. Likewise, I can also step back and see how others interpret the tree differently—how my daughters who were with me, playing in the leaves, just found the tree a lot of fun, whereas the company Allstate, featuring the same tree in an ad selling insurance, took it as a chance to make a profit.

In considering these and other factors surrounding my reading of the tree, I can come to understand more deeply and complexly both the tree and myself. In doing so, I follow Robert Scholes (1989, 19): "We do well to read our lives with the same intensity we develop from learning to read our texts. We all encounter certain experiences that seem to call for more than a superficial understanding." I likewise follow Scholes (1989, 78) as I turn, now, to add something to the "text" of the tree that was not initially there, "exceed[ing] it in some way." I am making the tree a metaphor for reading. This metaphor helps me speak of the many ways of reading that exist, varied practices for making meaning with texts, as Louise Rosenblatt (2005) would put it, that have developed in different times and places but that are all part of the same larger category we call *reading*. Such a metaphor for organizing ways of reading is one way of helping ourselves and our students practice what Ellen Carillo (2015, 2018) calls "mindful reading"—developing a metacognitive awareness of what we are doing as we read, what we could do differently, and why.

More specifically, for my present purposes, the metaphor of the tree of reading offers a structure for mapping out Scholes's work on the teaching of reading and for building on that work. In this essay, I sift through Scholes's major pedagogical works, written over a span of decades, from *Textual Power: Literary Theory and the Teaching of English* in 1985 to *English After the Fall: From Literature to Textuality* in 2011, with other monographs, articles, and textbooks in between. My purpose is to read Scholes as Scholes reads reading. I identify in these works the core tenets of Scholes's theory of teaching reading—the "roots" of the tree of reading—and I catalog the many different ways of reading that he advocates or, in some cases, warns against—the "branches." Because this essay synthesizes a large body of work, I proceed by way of cataloging more than arguing. But the heft of the resulting catalog does imply an argument about the breadth and depth of Scholes's contribution to our understanding of the teaching of reading. Meanwhile, several gaps in the catalog also give occasion for an additional argument, that we ought to build on what Scholes has left us by attending to a still broader range of ways of reading than those confined to the "limb" of critical reading.

ROOTS: THE TENETS OF SCHOLES'S THEORY OF READING

Before cataloging the many ways of reading Scholes advocates, I want to spell out the tenets I see grounding his work, his root principles, the reasons for naming ways of reading to begin with. The first tenet is simply that we should indeed *teach reading*—that we should make the teaching of reading the defining practice of our work as English teachers. "As a teacher I have for years," he shares in *The Crafty Reader*, "seen a major part of my task as helping students see reading as a craft, a set of methods or practices that can be learned, a skill that can be improved by anyone willing to make an effort" (Scholes 2001, 139). Later in that same book, he urges other English teachers to follow suit: "start taking reading seriously" (Scholes 2001, 215). He calls for nothing less than "a constant and prevailing emphasis on the process of reading" from English teachers (Scholes 1998, 169).

He justifies this emphasis in several ways. First, teaching reading represents a better model of education. A way of *doing*, teaching reading contrasts with the more common "coverage" approach: "It is not what students have been told that matters but what they remember and can *do*" (Scholes 1998, 149, emphasis added). Thus, instead of "produc[ing] 'readings' for our students," we should "give them the tools for producing their own" (Scholes 1985, 24). Second, teaching reading fulfills an overlooked need. Though "we do not see reading," he declares, "if we could see it, we would be appalled" (Scholes 2002, 166). In short, we need to teach reading because many students read so poorly—or at least not as well as they could. Third, by teaching reading, we help students make meaning in their lives, and that, thereby, lends meaning to ours: "helping students learn how to understand texts more fully" is a crucial aspect of helping them "develop better intellectual equipment" for life (Scholes 1998, 32, 142), including the "power to change the world" (Scholes 1985, 165). For this reason, during the social upheavals and struggles for social justice in the late 1960s, Scholes found justification for his life as an English professor in the fact he "taught reading and writing" (Scholes 1998, 32).

The second tenet is that all readers at all levels can grow. On one end of the spectrum, Scholes works to help first-year college and even high school students read better (Scholes 2002, 1998). On the other end, even after decades as one of the most accomplished scholars in English, a discipline based on reading, Scholes himself still wants to grow as a reader. He seeks "to make the practice of the craft . . . more open to use by those who, *like myself*, still hope to improve as readers" and "to sharpen *my own* command of the craft of reading—to become a craftier reader" (Scholes 2001, xv, emphases added). Indeed, the limits on our growth as readers are the same as the limits on our mortal lives: "we may continue to improve as readers until age begins to weaken our powers" (Scholes 1989, 18).

A third tenet is Scholes's concept of *a canon of methods*. This canon is the major way he envisions us placing the teaching of reading at the center of the discipline of English. In short, we must "replace the canon of texts with a canon of methods" (Scholes 1998, 145). Although we are all more familiar with the concept of a canon being formed around content—a set of texts that define our discipline—Scholes explains that canons have been and can be formed around methods: a set of ways of doing that define a discipline (Scholes 1998, 109, 111). He writes: "A canon of methods, unlike a set of texts, must be conceived in terms of competence. There is no point in introducing students to the writing of Jacques Derrida, for example, if they finish their study unable to deconstruct a text and unaware of the strengths—and the limitations—of deconstruction as a way of reading and writing. A canon of methods must be organized in terms of enhanced capabilities that students will take away from their studies" (Scholes 1998, 149). How would we form such a canon? By "simplifying and clarifying the ways of reading we have already learned to use in our studies of English literature and culture" (Scholes 2001, 215). By such simplifying and clarifying, we could come up with a set of "intellectual tools" students can use or "intellectual moves" students can make while reading (Scholes 1998, 149, 167). We could break reading down for students into "discrete" intellectual moves—"just as certain movements in dance or sport" are often broken down (Scholes 1985, 21).

However, if we must simplify reading, then one more tenet is that we must not oversimplify it. In *Protocols of Reading*, Scholes (1989, 2) writes: "I should say at once that I have no simple system to propose. Reading is indeed learned and taught; it is done well and done badly; but it has too much in it of art and craft to yield entirely—or even largely—to methodization. Still, education amounts to taking method as far as it will go and then finding some way to go a bit further without it." The canon of methods will not be absolute or final. It will be an open, evolving canon. "Each of us," he adds elsewhere, "must develop the craft of reading in a way that suits our needs and capabilities. There is no single method" (Scholes 2001, 242). Yet there are methods, many methods, and his work over many years has unpacked a great number of them for us. Let us turn to cataloging them now.

SOME BRANCHES: A SPRAWLING CATALOG OF READING

In surveying Scholes's work, I had initially hoped to lay out a tidy taxonomy. But I found this impossible. An early draft of the following catalog included over seventy ways of reading. Although I have tried to group closely related ideas together, the best groupings were not always obvious. I have settled on three broad categories, ways of reading related to different intellectual moves readers might perform, purposes readers might have, and types of texts readers might read—reflecting that our ways of reading vary according to what we do while reading, why we read, and what we read. Still, because such facets of reading cannot always be pulled apart neatly, the catalog remains sprawling, its categories loose, porous.

One more thing to note is that this catalog stands in contrast to an anticatalog we also find in Scholes's writing, ways of reading poorly that he cautions us against: we should not read or teach students to read with "an attitude of reverence before texts" (Scholes 1985, 16), nor with "unearned certainty" about meaning (Scholes 2001, 219), nor ignoring "the complexity of the texts themselves, their histories, and their present situations" (Scholes 2001, 219), nor to find "*the* correct interpretation" (Scholes 1985, 13, emphasis added), nor merely to find and identify literary devices (Scholes 2001, 24). We should avoid the "selective literalism" of fundamentalist reading, whether of a political or religious variety, which "force[s] closure upon" texts (Scholes 2001, 223). Instead, we should practice and teach "crafty" reading—many varieties of which appear in the following catalog.

Ways of Reading Related to Moves

The first section of this catalog includes ways of reading that Scholes advocates in which readers make particular intellectual moves—such as contextualizing, moving among layers of meaning, and writing back. These methods are actions readers perform to make sense of texts.

Reading, interpretation, and criticism. The most prominent breakdown of reading in Scholes's work entails these three parts, appearing first, as far as I can tell, in *Textual Power* (Scholes 1985, 21–35) and reappearing, in sometimes adjusted form, in most of his pedagogical books thereafter. These three terms represent a progression of reading moves where readers first see what a text says (reading), then suss out what it means (interpretation), then decide what its implications are (criticism). While interpretation takes on its usual meaning, the other two terms take on somewhat specialized emphases: "reading" has a lot to do with connecting a text to other texts, while "criticism" requires speaking from a particular group's perspective (in the way that feminist criticism, for instance, speaks from the perspective of that larger group, i.e., feminists) (Scholes 1985, 35). Scholes initially describes the progression through these three moves in terms of a shifting balance of power: "In working through the stages of reading, interpretation, and criticism, we move from a submission to textual authority in reading, through a sharing of textual power in interpretation, toward an assertion of power through opposition in criticism" (Scholes 1985, 39). In his final book, *English After the Fall,* he makes one major revision to the scheme, swapping out "reading" for "reaction" (Scholes 2011, 50–51). More attuned to how students experience texts, this revised sequence begins not with technical textual analysis but with careful consideration of a reader's initial, spontaneous response to a text and then works from there.

Reading toward and from the text. Scholes also often breaks reading into two parts or directions. In one place, he describes these in terms of "centripetal" and "centrifugal" impulses (Scholes 1989, 8). In the first, readers try to adhere as close to the text as possible, trying to get as close a sense of the writer's intention as they can (Scholes 1985, 15; Scholes 2001, 230; Scholes 1989, 51). In the latter, readers step back and consider the larger implications of the text for their own lives and values. In *The Crafty Reader*, Scholes (2001, 197) describes how the reader falls "under the control of the writer's vision" but only "temporarily." Afterward, "the reader's critical faculty comes into play." He describes elsewhere these forms of stepping in and stepping back as a dialectic between reading "sympathetically" and "unsympathetically" (Scholes 1998, 169) and between reading "respectfully" and "disrespectful[ly]" (Scholes 1989, 78). In the one, readers try "to get inside" the text and "understand the intentionality behind" it (Scholes 1998, 169). In the other, readers try to also "get somewhere . . . [to] open a new perspective on the text read, and not simply double or repeat the text" (Scholes 1989, 78).

Reading in context. "Situate, situate" acts as a refrain for Scholes (2001, 67). Putting texts in context in order to understand them better is one of the reading moves he touts most often. He writes, "A large part of the craft of reading is the ability to 'place' or 'situate' any particular text" (Scholes 2001, 139). No text exists in isolation or comes from nowhere. Looking for contexts tells readers where writers are "coming from" (Scholes 2001, 139). Reading well involves "conscious contextualizing" (Scholes 1989, 11), understanding a text through drawing on historical and cultural "background" information (Scholes 1998, 135; 1985, 43–46), the author's life and the writing's role in it (Scholes 2001, 40), the cultural and linguistic "codes" it uses (1985, 50, 33), or specific intertexts (Scholes 1989, 11) such as an author's other works (Scholes 1985, 50) and other works in the same genre. Understanding a text's place in relation to such other texts and contexts helps readers understand the text itself.

Reading deconstructively. Scholes promotes a range of deconstructive reading practices: reading with an awareness of "inconsistencies and gaps" (Scholes 2001, 217), reading in a way "open and flexible with respect to the play of meanings in any text" (Scholes 2001, 217), reading by way of establishing and then deconstructing binaries (Scholes 1985,

4, 8–9, 112–13; Scholes 1989, 31), and reading to recognize "a medley of voices" in "a single complex text" (Scholes 1998, 134).

Reading through comparison and contrast. Scholes elevates the good old method of comparing and contrasting to the level of "a proper move in any critical reading" (Scholes 1989, 80). "Comparison and contrast," he writes, "is not just some academic reflex but a fundamental part of the reading process—which is to say, the thinking process" (Scholes 1989, 80; Scholes 2001, 51).

Reading with other readers. Scholes (1998, 134) encourages readers to keep other readers in mind in several ways. We might read to "feel . . . like members of a literary culture." We might read with knowledge of what other readers have said about the specific text (Scholes 1985, 31, 38). We might read (and then write) in such a way that "knowingly enters the interpretive dialogue" with other readers (Scholes 1985, 31). And we might read with an awareness of how a single text may have multiple audiences of other readers (Scholes 2011, 19).

Reading through writing. Between editions, Scholes and his co-editors changed the title of their textbook *Fields of Writing* to *Fields of Reading* (Comley et al. 2013), mirroring how closely related reading and writing are in his mind. Reading well includes "the ability to respond, to talk back, to write back, to analyze, to extend, to take one's own textual position in relation to . . . any kind of text" (Scholes 1998, 131). Likewise, students writing the same kinds of texts they read can learn "how the medium works from the inside, to become better readers by gaining a deeper understanding of how certain texts are composed" (Scholes 1998, 139). Students "should read not only to understand but also to emulate the text they are reading" (Scholes 1998, 133). In the preface to another textbook, *The Practice of Writing*, Scholes and company (Scholes, Comley, and Peritz 2001, vii) tell students, "writing involves reading. The readings in this book . . . are there to be worked with and responded to—in writing. They are there to be transformed, imitated, analyzed, argued with, and incorporated into new writing." Similarly, his co-authored textbook, titled *Text Book: Writing through Literature*, emphasizes reading as a basis for writing more effectively and emphasizes writing in order to read more deeply (Scholes, Comley, and Ulmer 2001).

Ways of Reading Related to Purpose

This second section of this catalog includes ways of reading Scholes advocates that have to do with purposes readers have for reading—such as seeking to understand oneself or others, to resist being unwittingly manipulated, and to understand reading itself. Such purposes are methods in that reading with particular intentions shapes what readers notice in and do with a text.

Reading literature for life. Scholes (2001, 12) urges us to read and to teach reading in a way "that connects literature to life." He instructs readers "to ask how the fictional events and characters represented in [a] printed text connect to their own lives, their own hopes and fears, their own values and beliefs" (Scholes 1998, 136). "To read at all," he says, "we must read the book of ourselves in the texts in front of us, and we must bring the text home, into our thoughts and lives, into our judgments and deeds. We cannot enter the texts we read, but they can enter us. That is what reading is all about" (Scholes 1989, 6). By reading, we can change our lives: "reading, though it may be a kind of action, is not the whole action but a part of it, remaining incomplete unless and until it is absorbed and transformed in the thoughts and deeds of readers" (Scholes 1989, x). He extols "ethical" reading: upon seeing a "metaphorical connection" between himself and an unsavory character in a novel, he writes, "I must seek to change my behavior so as to eliminate, or at least reduce, the validity of that metaphor in my life as it continues" (Scholes 1989, 152). Life can help readers understand literature in turn: "To deal with what literary works have to say about the human condition requires a fair amount of human experience" (Scholes 2004, 121).

Reading the world. If Scholes urges us to read literature into our lives, he also argues that we should read our lives and the larger world like we read literature: "We may read life as well as books" (Scholes 1989, 18; Scholes 1985, 15). Our lives are permeated with texts and have a textual quality to them (Scholes 2001, 76). "We do well," he offers in one place, "to read our lives with the same intensity we develop from learning to read our texts. We all encounter certain experiences that seem to call for more than a superficial understanding" (Scholes 1989, 19). "To understand the craft of reading," he argues elsewhere, "is to understand the world itself as a text and to be able to read it critically" (Scholes 2001, 103). Different "ways of reading" are essentially different "ways of making sense of the world" (Scholes 1989, 91). But more than just making sense of the world, readers "interact with it" (Scholes 1985, 112). Reading can be part of a larger process of engaging intellectually with contemporary issues (Scholes 2011, 23) and may even offer readers "power to change the world" (Scholes 1985, 165; 2011, 52). At the least, reading can change "our way of interpreting things" (Scholes 1985, 165).

Reading politically. Reading the world sometimes takes on a specifically political bent. Scholes proposes "one of the things that literary study is *for*" is that "it opens the way to a critique of culture" (Scholes 1985, 43, emphasis in original) and a critique of ideology (Scholes 1989, 125). The politically astute reader will ask of a given text, "who is represented, who does the representing, who is object, who is subject—and how do these representations connect to the values of groups, communities, classes, tribes, sects, and nations?" (Scholes 1998, 153). We can read cultures through reading literary texts, through reading individuals' lives (Scholes 1989, 28, 31, 49), and through reading whole genres for what they reveal about a culture's ideology (Scholes 1989, 134–45).

Reading to understand others. Scholes (2011, 166) stresses that reading can help us get out of our own perspective and into the perspectives of other people and, specifically, to recognize the "otherness" of those other perspectives. Reading can help readers "imagine the other's thoughts, feeling, and sentiments" (Scholes 2011, 168). In her essay in this volume, Kelsey McNiff describes a writing course that enacts this very insight of Scholes's.

Reading for power. Texts may exert power "over" readers. But readers, Scholes asserts, may wrest back "a measure of control over textual processes, a share of textual power for themselves" (Scholes 1985, 39), for instance, by learning to resist mass media manipulations (Scholes 1985, 15–16, 73).

Reading to debate with writers. In long stretches of his works, Scholes goes toe to toe with various literary theorists and critics. For instance, in *Protocols of Reading*, he argues with Jacques Derrida for thirty pages straight (Scholes 1989, 57–87). We might read such passages to learn what Scholes concludes about this or that topic ("nihilistic hermeneutics," in this instance). At the same time, we might read the same passages to observe how Scholes reads the writers with whom he argues. Indeed, he is not simply arguing but also carefully, critically reading these other writers' works, modeling a way "to read actively, as a participant" (Scholes 1998, 137). On this same note, we should also take a look at who Scholes does or does not debate with. In particular, he cites few women scholars, which is a widespread problem in academia (Ahmed 2017) and a point he himself critiques in the work of others (Scholes 2001, 33). His work could have especially benefited from engaging the work of Louise Rosenblatt (1964, 1978, 1995, 2005), a scholar of reading who broke much of the same ground as he did but sooner and often with greater sophistication (Corrigan 2019). Just as Scholes learns from the gaps in the works of the writers he debates, we, too, may learn from this gap in his work.

Reading reading. Finally, Scholes calls for us to practice and teach the reading of reading itself. We may pay metacognitive attention to our and our students' ways of reading (Scholes 2001, 215). We may read and assign readings of texts, "so that students can see how it is done" (Scholes 1985, 30). We may read and assign theoretical texts about reading, meaning, and textuality, as Scholes and his co-authors Nancy R. Comley, and Gregory L. Ulmer (2001) do in *Text Book* to prompt students to develop ideas about narrative structure and figurative language.

Ways of Reading Related to Types of Text

This third section of the catalog includes ways of reading Scholes advocates that relate to types of texts readers might read—such as reading poetry or reading comparatively across multiple genres in order to better understand a genre or even textuality itself. These methods tune the way one reads to what one is reading.

Reading poetry. Of all types of texts, Scholes gives the reading of poetry the most sustained, detailed, and practical attention, especially in a long essay on teaching poetry in *The Crafty Reader*. In that chapter, he even includes a thorough, bullet-pointed method to walk readers step by step through reading a poem: reading for its "prose sense"; attending to words, punctuation marks, and patterns; situating the poem rhetorically, literarily, historically, and autobiographically; deciding how the poem aims to affect readers and whether one is affected in that way; determining how one feels about the poem and why; and, finally, assessing how the form of the poem influenced any of the above (Scholes 2001, 44–46). He stresses reading not just "art poems" but also personal and political poems (Scholes 2001, 34) and attending to not just aesthetics but also the rhetoric of poetry (Scholes 1989, 109–16). He considers poetry "one of the tools" he has "for coping with the world" in that he draws "strength and insight" from poems (Scholes 2005, 731).

Reading sacred texts. Scholes attends at length to the reading of sacred texts—whether religious texts such as the Bible or political ones such as the Declaration of Independence. These kinds of texts call for "a very careful kind of reading" (Scholes 2011, 54). In what amounts to a special application of his "centripetal" and "centrifugal" reading described above, he insists on reading with both the desire to understand and the freedom to criticize, trying to get as close as possible to what the writer meant to convey as well as "interrogating the reliability" of the writer, "tak[ing] note of the gaps and contradictions in the text," and "determin[ing] its proper bearing on our own values and conduct in the world" (Scholes 2001, 54, 238).

Reading genre(s). Genre shows up in Scholes's work again and again in different ways. He writes, "generic concepts help us clarify what we are doing as readers" (Scholes 2001, 185). As already noted, we can situate texts within their genres to better understand them and we can read a genre for a culture's ideology. Additionally, when he calls students' attention to specific aspects of a text's form, the idea of genre is not far away (Scholes 1985, 66). Scholes (2001, 107) even encourages readers to discover genres not previously recognized and to value genres not usually valued (such as the "private-eye novel") in order to "read certain texts with greater comprehension and appreciation." Scholes (1998, 169) stresses the importance of reading a broad range of genres (and, indeed, a broad range of media), including texts traditionally considered "literature" but also extending far beyond those: "Reading advertisements, reading films and television shows, reading political speeches, reading poems, plays, essays, stories, and everything else under the sun—this is what we should be teaching." In addition to giving great attention to poetry and sacred texts, the many genres Scholes himself reads in his works include journalism (2011, 29, 43; 1998, 140); advertising (1989, 116–20; 2011, 43); magazines (2011, 44); detective novels (2001, 138); diaries (2001, 108); science fiction, fantasy, and science fantasy (2001, 183); film (1998, 138); drama (1998, 137); opera (2011, 35); videos (1989, 120–33); and paintings (2001, 86–88, 94–100, 241). In other essays in this volume, Christopher J. La Casse describes a course on reading periodicals while Kenny Smith describes one on reading journalism, both taking their cue from Scholes.

Reading textuality. Behind Scholes's theory of reading lies his theory of textuality. It is fitting, then, that he encourages readers read to develop our own theories of textuality. By reading in a wide range of types of texts, we can discover that many "literary" qualities can be found outside of "literature" (Scholes 2011, 24). Reading widely allows us to practice *"comparative textuality"* (Scholes 2011, 91, 101), developing a deeper and fuller understanding of what different kinds of texts are and do. As one method for accomplishing this, he favors looking at "how [certain] texts . . . move from one world to another, one medium to another" (Scholes 2011, 39). By this he means stories translated from medium to medium—such as *The Man Who Shot Liberty Valance*, a short story that became a movie that became a novel.

OTHER BRANCHES AND THE TRUNK:
NEGLECTED WAYS OF READING

As the catalog above documents, Scholes preaches and practices many branches of reading, showing us something of reading's expanse. However, virtually all of the ways of reading that Scholes discusses at any length can be mapped as branches on the "critical reading" limb of the tree of reading—which, although a large category, is still but one category of reading. While this focus of Scholes's does align with the larger tendency in higher education to privilege critical thinking above all other ways of seeing and being (Clark 2009), it leaves gaps. It leaves other ways of reading unexplored. To Scholes's credit, some of these gaps are only partial gaps, ways of reading that he touches on, but barely. We can expand his canon of methods, then, by branching out into these other ways of reading and by considering how all of these different ways of reading stem from a common trunk that is the act of reading itself (Corrigan 2013/2014). Moreover, whereas Scholes (2001, 215) understandably suggests we look specifically to "the ways of reading we have already learned" in English studies, there is more to learn than what we already know. We can take his approach a step further by borrowing from other spheres of reading, such as pleasure reading and business reading. By attending to these other ways of reading, we can help students develop a more comprehensive and flexible understanding and practice of reading, so that they can adapt how they read to the widest possible range of reading situations.

Reading contemplatively. Although Scholes does comment, rarely, on the *feelings* that may attend reading (Scholes 2011, 124), he overlooks the entire tradition of reading mindfully or contemplatively, a tradition that has powerfully engaged the affective aspects of reading. Taking up contemplative reading, we can teach students to read with not just the mind but also the heart. Contemplative or mindful ways of reading are useful not only in situations where the affective experience of the text is a key part of the meaning of the text, but also in situations where initial knee-jerk affective responses could derail sound reading. Elsewhere in this volume, Christian Smith develops Scholes's comments on ethical reading into a contemplative reading pedagogy.

Reading creatively. Although Scholes does briefly mention performing texts theatrically (Scholes 1998, 137), reading texts aloud (Scholes 2002, 167), and writing poetry in response to poems (Scholes 2001, 59), creative reading is another largely neglected limb. We would do well to unpack in greater depth the many ways of creative, playful, generative reading, where the emphasis is less on what readers can *get* out of the text but what readers can *make* out of the text.

Reading for pleasure. When Scholes briefly mentions the pleasure of reading, he means that intellectual pleasure some of us experience through reading critically (Scholes 1985, 36). But what of the sort we might call beach reading? This represents another underexplored limb of the tree of reading. In some ways the opposite of critical reading, this sort of reading for pleasure has often been abandoned to those who do not take reading "seriously." But attending more to this way of reading could help us and our students not only understand one of the most common ways of reading but also, in all likelihood, learn how to get more out of it.

Reading for business. Many of us argue that the study of English imparts valuable, marketable skills (Corrigan 2018). In their essay in this volume, Lynée Lewis Gaillet and Angela Christie make a case for translating liberal arts skills into employment skills. But Scholes actually pits the values of English against the values of business, pointing out that the deeper humanity that the humanities extol is *not* always profitable (Scholes 1998, 17–20). Both positions are correct. While the deepest values of the humanities may not always be marketable, many of our skills certainly are. Ways of reading that can help students in their careers while also embodying values of the humanities represent yet another limb to explore.

Reading as an activity. I consider the act of reading as the trunk of the tree of reading. All other ways of reading come back to reading as a physical and intellectual activity, undertaken in a body and time and place, encompassing such factors as being alert and awake or not, reading in solitude or not, taking notes and asking questions or not. Scholes does at times attend to such aspects of reading—exhorting readers "to pay attention to plain things, to notice them and not let them slip by" (Scholes 2001, 67), to reread (Scholes 2001, 239), to read slowly enough to ponder (Scholes 1998, 165), to "squeeze a short passage of text until it yield[s] plausible generalizations" (Scholes 1998, 30). These stray comments are a helpful start. But to develop more fully the canon of methods, we need to look further into the teaching of these foundational practices of active reading (Corrigan 2013/2014; Carillo 2018).

CONCLUSION

The metaphor of the tree of reading offers a way for teachers and students to visualize Scholes's "canon of methods." Surveying over thirty years of his pedagogical writings, we find a great many ways of reading. Most of these can be classified as branches on the limb of critical reading.

Attending to the other ways of reading Scholes neglects, especially ways of reading from other limbs, can help us map out a fuller tree, a more comprehensive canon. The work of cataloging I have undertaken in this essay does not come merely from the academic impulse to endlessly dissect, classify, categorize, and label things. I do not want to pin and tag these ways of reading to display behind glass like a collection of dead beetles. No, naming these ways of reading helps us better see the parts of a living tree. The catalog can help us better recognize what we might otherwise miss and help us communicate those things to students.

We could not teach all of these ways of reading to our students in a single semester (or even a single degree program), but we can contextualize the ways of reading that we do choose to teach as ways of reading that grow out of a larger history of reading. As students see that how they read is not *the* way but *a* way, they may add ways to their reading repertoire. They may learn to take greater control of their own reading, choosing reading practices not mindlessly but mindfully, not by default but according to the demands and purposes for a given moment of reading. In doing so, they may, as I did with Angel Oak Tree, even choose to read incidents in their lives more deeply. In any event, they will be better equipped to make reading a bigger, more important, and more purposeful part of their lives.

REFERENCES

Ahmed, Sara. 2017. *Living a Feminist Life*. Durham, NC: Duke University Press.
Carillo, Ellen C. 2015. *Securing a Place for Reading in Composition: The Importance of Teaching for Transfer*. Logan: Utah State University Press.
Carillo, Ellen C. 2018. *Teaching Readers in Post-Truth America*. Logan: Utah State University Press.
Clark, Mariam Marty. 2009. "Beyond Critical Thinking." *Pedagogy* 9 (2): 325–30.
Comley, Nancy R., David Hamilton, Carl H. Klaus, Robert Scholes, Nancy Sommers, and Jason Tougaw, eds. 2013. *Fields of Reading: Motives for Writing*. 10th ed. New York: Bedford/St. Martin's.
Corrigan, Paul T. 2013/2014. "Attending to the Act of Reading: Critical Reading, Contemplative Reading, and Active Reading." *Reader: Essays in Reader-Oriented Theory, Criticism, and Pedagogy* 65/66: 146–73.
Corrigan, Paul T. 2018. "Jobs Will Save the Humanities." *The Chronicle of Higher Education* June 28. https://www.chronicle.com/article/Jobs-Will-Save-the-Humanities/243767.
Corrigan, Paul T. 2019. "Citing Louise Rosenblatt." *Corrigan Literary Review* February 5. https://corriganliteraryreview.wordpress.com/2019/02/05/citing-louise-rosenblatt.
Oliver, Mary. 2006. *Thirst*. Boston: Beacon.
Rosenblatt, Louise M. 1964. "The Poem as Event." *College English* 26 (2): 123–28.
Rosenblatt, Louise M. 1978. *The Reader, the Text, the Poem: The Transactional Theory of the Literary Work*. Carbondale: Southern Illinois University.
Rosenblatt, Louise M. 1995. *Literature as Exploration*. 5th ed. New York: The Modern Language Association of America.

Rosenblatt, Louise M. 2005. *Making Meaning with Texts: Selected Essays.* Portsmouth, NH: Heinemann.
Scholes, Robert. 1985. *Textual Power: Literary Theory and the Teaching of English.* New Haven, CT: Yale University Press.
Scholes, Robert. 1989. *Protocols of Reading.* New Haven, CT: Yale University Press.
Scholes, Robert. 1998. *The Rise and Fall of English: Reconstructing English as a Discipline.* New Haven, CT: Yale University Press.
Scholes, Robert. 2001. *The Crafty Reader.* New Haven, CT: Yale University Press.
Scholes, Robert. 2002. "The Transition to College Reading." *Pedagogy* 2 (2): 165–72.
Scholes, Robert. 2004. "Learning and Teaching." *Profession*: 118–27.
Scholes, Robert. 2005. "Presidential Address 2004: The Humanities in a Posthumanist World." *PMLA* 120 (3): 724–33.
Scholes, Robert. 2011. *English After the Fall: From Literature to Textuality.* Iowa City: University of Iowa Press.
Scholes, Robert, Nancy R. Comley, and Janice Peritz. 2001. *The Practice of Writing.* 5th ed. New York: Bedford/St. Martin's.
Scholes, Robert, Nancy R. Comley, and Gregory L. Ulmer. 2001. *Text Book: Writing through Literature.* 3rd ed. New York: Bedford/St. Martin's.

2
NOW MORE THAN EVER
Developing Crafty Readers *in Writing Classes and across the Curriculum*

Alice S. Horning

In the era of "fake news," students need critical reading skills in order to find, understand, and evaluate sources for use in their own writing. A number of scholars have been making this point for some time, including, in particular, Robert Scholes in his 2001 book, *The Crafty Reader*, as well as some earlier publications. Even almost twenty years ago, Scholes could see the impact of both alphabetic and other kinds of texts on reading and writing. While he was focused mainly on the reading of literature in both *The Crafty Reader* and in *Protocols of Reading* from 1989, he takes up some issues about all kinds of critical reading that are relevant to the current environment in higher education generally and in writing studies in particular. Scholes's ideas about all kinds of reading, including literature, nonfiction, nonalphabetic texts, and so forth provide a guide for a review of the field, demonstrating that very little attention is being paid to reading, despite ample evidence that students have serious reading problems not currently being addressed; data from graduate programs and faculty surveys show that neither new nor current faculty have the relevant background to work with students on reading issues while students' reading problems become increasingly clear. And the need for crafty readers continues to expand as more information comes at all of us from more sources at an ever-higher speed.

SCHOLES'S CRAFTY READERS

One of the interesting things about Scholes's approach is that while he is largely focused on reading literature, the strategies he suggests for crafty readers are entirely suited to reading all kinds of materials; it's important to note that he makes this claim explicitly in his introduction, so that his ideas apply equally to alphabetic and digital texts of all

DOI: 10.7330/9781646421190.c002

kinds (2001, xv). His explicit definition does not fit neatly into a single sentence but includes the following features: ". . . reading depends on the use of certain tools, handled with skill. . . . [T]ools must be acquired through practice. . . . [R]eading now extends beyond the written word into various other kinds of verbal and visual texts . . ." (2001, xiv–xv). The overall idea is that since reading is a craft, it is teachable and learnable, and the tools are within everyone's reach.

The opening chapter of *Crafty* discusses reading poetry, but he suggests that readers must figure out what kind of text they are reading, should read a range of material by that author including background on his or her life and work, connect this information to real life of both writer and reader, and practice these strategies, the tools of the craft. To start, reading for meaning and dealing with vocabulary are first steps that Scholes (2001, 44) recommends for crafty reading, then situating the text in its context to whatever extent possible, drawing on time, place, author background and whatever else might be relevant. Some of these points might be more important in different courses: original documents in history require an understanding of context; authors' prior studies might be important in a scientific research report. He further suggests that what we now call "rhetorical reading" (Haller 2010) should be part of the work, considering whether the text makes a persuasive argument that might result from appeals to authority, emotion, or logic. In the reader's response, it's useful to consider not only the nature of the response but the source of the reaction and the technical features of the text that give rise to it (Scholes 2001, 44–46).

It is easy to see how this approach would be superior to the "quote mining" frequently found in the Citation Project papers discussed by Jamieson and Howard (2019). The Citation Project is a major ongoing study of student writing in which a sample of about two thousand student citations of sources was collected from sixteen colleges and universities across the country, a careful sample of students' first year writing. The findings include that only 6 percent of these references entail real summary with the vast majority drawn from the first page or two of the source. Instead of students reading one or two pages of an article or the first screen of a website, Scholes's approach would move readers to a more thorough consideration of a complete piece. Crafty readers following Scholes's protocol would be working toward understanding main ideas, details, and vocabulary—the full shape of the discussion. Such an approach is not restricted to reading serious literature; it is easy to see how it might be useful for reading textbooks, original source documents, research reports, and other kinds of material in courses across the curriculum. By staying with an author's ideas, student readers would be able to see how a full argument on an issue or topic is presented and discussed. We don't see much of this kind of careful analysis in current student work. While faculty do complain about students' reading, they don't seem willing or able to take steps to address the problem or find solutions to help them become crafty readers. And a review of the way writing studies addresses the reading issue shows just why this is the case.

WRITING STUDIES AND READING

It seems clear that the field is not paying much attention to reading, given what faculty report in terms of what they are prepared to do (more below) and given the level of attention the field is paying to this issue. But Scholes did pay attention, both in books like *Crafty* and in several textbooks on reading and writing, including *The Practice of Writing* and *Fields of Writing*, both of which he co-edited. In addition, he was the recipient of the Modern Language Association's Mina Shaughnessy Prize in 1986 for *Textual Power*, a book that advocates more focus on texts and less on literary theory. It seems clear that while he was perhaps a "lit guy" in much of his work, he was interested in and concerned about the teaching and learning of reading and writing, an interest that in due course brought him to the attention of scholars in writing studies. Given his focus on reading and writing, his work provides ample reasons for paying more attention, especially to reading. I have been nursing the idea for quite a long time that writing studies is simply not doing so.

My view could easily be attributed to sour grapes, since I have tried, both alone and in consultation and with support from colleagues, to get the Conference on College Composition and Communication (CCCC) to establish a task force on reading for at least two years. This effort was turned down more than once; recently under Asao Inoue's leadership, as chair of the CCCC's Executive Committee, it is finally off the ground. In the meantime, some members of the Reading Special Interest Group that has long been running at CCCC formed an international research team that reported on various professional organizations' approaches to the reading issue at the 2019 convention in Pittsburgh. But data from a review of key features of the field supports the view that writing studies itself really isn't paying much attention to reading at all.

To look more closely at this issue, I studied the field from several vantage points. I started by looking at the conference programs for the major meetings in the field: the National Council of Teachers of English (NCTE), CCCC and the Council of Writing Program Administrators

(CWPA). There are plenty of other meetings I might have looked at, and other organizations like the International Literacy Association and the Society for the Scientific Study of Reading, but I wanted to keep my review focused on the field of writing studies and these are its major meetings. While NCTE has more sessions devoted to reading, this finding is hardly a surprise given that the organization serves teachers of preschool to college-level courses. Much of the program that is devoted to reading deals with topics related to the teaching of reading to children and to reading difficulties like dyslexia. A relatively small number of sessions are devoted specifically to reading at the college level. Of the hundreds of sessions in 2018, for instance, a total of sixteen were marked specifically for college-level faculty and had reading somewhere in the title. In 2017, that number was seventeen, and in 2016 I found fifteen, though I was not able to locate the Sunday segment of the program online for 2016. (Although the two-year college group has its own organization and journal, reviewed below, it holds regional rather than national meetings and it was not a practical project to try to review all of the programs at that level.)

Of course, NCTE is a meeting for everyone in the language arts profession, not just college faculty in writing studies. CCCC, however, is specifically for college faculty in writing studies. A review of CCCC programs for the past three years online turned up, for 2016, four whole sessions focused on reading, one all-day workshop, one post-conference workshop, and five talks in various sessions; there were also two posters on reading issues. There was also the ongoing Special Interest Group for Reading in Composition Studies, led by Ellen Carillo, Michael Bunn, and Debrah Huffman. In 2017 a manual search turned up twenty-four sessions with reading in the title, and the SIG. In 2018, that number was seventeen, plus the SIG, along with a full-day workshop led by Ellen Carillo, Cynthia Haller, and myself. So, essentially, it's the same story from both of the major NCTE meetings in the field. That is, little attention is being given to reading by either NCTE or its subgroup for college writing faculty.

Scholes pointed to this trend long ago in his *Pedagogy* article on college-level reading in 2002, included in this volume. Discussing the relative attention to reading and writing, he observed that writing is in many ways visible or tangible and thus obviously teachable at all levels. Teachers are comfortable with teaching writing ". . . because we can see writing, and we know that much of the writing we see is not good enough. But we do not see reading. We see some writing about reading, to be sure, but we do not see reading. I am certain, though, that if we could see it, we would be appalled" (quoted in Carillo 2015, 132). Scholes thought faculty were not paying enough attention to reading in 2002, and my study suggests that observation is still true now. On the other hand, one relevant development worth noting appears in the Call for Proposals for the 2019 program put together by Vershawn Ashanti Young. The 2019 call includes the return of topical clusters, including one specifically for reading:

Postsecondary Reading/Literacy
- Integrated reading and writing instruction
- Teaching reading in first-year/advanced writing
- Politics of postsecondary reading instruction
- Culture of reading in postsecondary contexts
- Pedagogical approaches to teaching reading
- Assessing reading in first-year/advanced writing
- Disciplinary literacy
- Faculty training in reading instruction
- Academic literacy
- Reading-writing connections
- (CCCC Call for Proposals 2019 retrieved from https://cccc.ncte.org/cccc/conv/call-2019)

Surely the appearance of this cluster on reading is a step in the right direction, but it is a step that has been missing for many years, and one that has vanished again in the call for proposals for 2020. Similarly, the 2019 recognition of an edited collection by Patrick Sullivan, Howard Tinberg, and Sheridan Blau called *Deep Reading* (2017) as the outstanding book of the year by CCCC is another step in the direction of more attention to reading.

The Council of Writing Program Administrators is a much smaller meeting than either NCTE or CCCC, but it is equally if not more important than the bigger ones since WPAs are the ones who run writing programs at colleges and universities, and thus are the people who direct decisions about what gets taught, how it gets taught, and who does that teaching. Here again, the results suggest that the field is not paying much attention to reading. I reviewed three years of programs—2016, 2017, and 2018. In 2016, there was one session with information literacy in its title, a talk in a concurrent session by me, and the preconference workshop on reading that year that I did with Chris Anson and Cynthia Haller. This tally works out to 0.02 percent of the roughly 128 sessions. In 2017, there were two with reading in the title, and one with information literacy, 0.03 percent of the approximately 115 sessions. In 2018, there were two posters on reading or information literacy, but more concurrent sessions with reading or literacy in the title, a total of thirteen altogether, which works out to 0.08 percent of the 163 sessions. Thus, the same lack of interest in reading appears in the WPA conference.

Turning to the professional journals, I built on the work of Debrah Huffman in 2010, when she reviewed the tables of contents of about half a dozen major journals in the field and conference programs from CCCC. She looked back about six years and found a very small percentage of articles or presentations on reading in the field in those years. I did a similar survey with a slightly different set of journals and the conference programs discussed previously; following Huffman, I looked for the words "reading" or "literacy" in titles. I looked at the tables of contents of five leading journals: *CCC*, *CE*, *RTE*, *TETYC*, and *WPA*. Aside from *TETYC*, there are almost no articles on reading or literacy in the big three NCTE publications. Table 2.1 shows the actual numbers.

These numbers speak for themselves. Of course, writing studies journals need not be publishing huge numbers of articles on reading, but when they are virtually ignoring an essential aspect of literacy development with miniscule numbers of articles addressing reading or literacy issues, it is fair to say that the field is not paying attention to reading issues. And there is abundant evidence that more attention is needed.

STUDENTS' READING SITUATION

No matter what kind of evidence is examined on students' reading situations, the same picture emerges, allowing for the fact that testing of any kind does not offer a nuanced picture of students' true abilities. Even so, although students read plenty of Facebook posts and nonalphabetic texts like TikTok, they are not reading extended nonfiction alphabetic texts that are typical in academia. Reading extended prose is just not, for most students, an activity of choice, but it will be important to their college work and, if not in their careers, certainly important to participation in our democratic society. Even more important, they really can't read in the ways that most instructors expect. That is, they can't sustain full attention to follow the main ideas and details of an extended discussion of an idea or issue with full comprehension of the vocabulary and structure of an argument, understanding of development of characters, seeing relationships among texts on a topic, and so forth. And they especially can't evaluate texts for authority, accuracy, currency, relevancy, appropriateness, and bias. Elsewhere in this volume, Kenny Smith

Table 2.1. Use of the words "reading" and "literacy" in five leading journals

Year	Total articles	Reading	Literacy
CCC			
2013	27	1	0
2014	33	0	1
2015	16	2	1
2016	20	0	1
2017	20	0	1
2018	12	1	1
CE			
2013	22	0	2
2014	20	0	0
2015	20	0	4
2016	28	2	2
2017	21	2	2
2018*	18	1	2
RTE			
2013	16	0	5
2014	13	0	3
2015	16	1	1
2016	15	1	1
2017	16	0	2
2018	15	2	2
TETYC†			
2013	21	1	2
2014	19	0	0
2015	17	3	0
2016	15	1	1
2017	15	1	1
2018	17	0	0
WPA			
2013	16	1	1
2014	11	0	0
2015	9	0	0
2016	8	0	1
2017	15	1	0
2018	13	0	2

*The January issue of CE in 2018 (v. 80 #3) included a review article on five recent books on reading.

† The fourth issue of TETYC, in 2018, was not available when this chapter was written.

provides key insights on this problem. His strategies offer valuable ways for teachers to respond to students' needs, drawing on Scholes's views as a framework. Like Kenny Smith, my work points to the need for students to become much more critical readers of all kinds of texts.

Data from a variety of types of studies reveals the difficulties of at least half or more of the students in any classroom in any kind of higher education. The quantitative data are the easiest to point to in order to support this claim. The ACT, for example, has a specific section for reading comprehension. It is a thirty-five-minute multiple choice, paper-and-pencil exercise in which students read four short passages of text on paper and answer ten multiple choice questions on each. There are lots of reasons to discount this type of test: it's timed, on paper, multiple choice, uses short passages, and so on. However, ACT tested over 1.9 million students in 2018, and the latest data shows that 46 percent of students hit ACT's minimum score of 21 (ACT 2018) for "success" in college (scale is 0–36), and success is weakly defined as earning a 2.0 GPA and returning for a second year of college study. And, admittedly informally, I asked a group of honors college students some years ago to evaluate a sample ACT exam, and they agreed that the test had real face validity as a test of comprehension, vocabulary, inference, and critical reading.

Similar score results appear in such international testing as the Programme for International Student Assessment (PISA), run by the Organisation for Economic Cooperation and Development (OECD), a group of more than thirty mostly Northern Hemisphere countries. PISA is administered to fifteen-year-olds in those countries. US students perform at average levels, with scores around 50 percent (PISA 2019). These instruments measure reading performance of very large numbers of students (600,000 in 2018) and reveal some aspects of students' reading problems. At the same time, it is useful to keep in mind that as students face more and more of these kinds of multiple-choice instruments along with teaching to such tests, they come to see reading to be about developing the tools to answer these kinds of questions rather than the more critical and global kinds of tools Scholes advocates in *Crafty*.

Qualitative studies show similar results but are in some ways more revealing of students' difficulties. Among these is the highly respected Citation Project conducted by Sandra Jamieson and Rebecca Moore Howard (2016; also Jamieson 2013). In this work, researchers gathered a sample of two thousand actual citations to references drawn from students' writing at colleges and universities across the country. They went back to the original sources to analyze exactly what the students did with the source material. Findings show that only 6 percent of the uses of sources entail a real summary of a full text, with 46 percent of quotations coming from the first page of a source and 70 percent from the first two pages. These findings support my claims about students' reading troubles described previously. They also suggest that students who have developed certain kinds of reading tools (like for answering ACT questions) can hardly be faulted for not having the tools needed to read and use sources effectively in their own writing.

More recently, the Stanford History Education Group did a similarly careful study of actual student performance, drawing on seven thousand student responses to a set of tasks in online reading among middle school, high school, and college students. The tasks were to evaluate an article found online for reliability, verify a claim made online, evaluate a website, watch a video and identify its strengths and weaknesses, and consider whether a tweet was an appropriate information source. The tasks were all online and untimed. Findings show that 50–80 percent of students were unable to perform the tasks using age-appropriate materials. The Stanford researchers were "appalled" at the results (Stanford 2016). A number of other carefully done qualitative studies approach students' reading from different vantage points and come up with the same kinds of results.

No matter how the data are collected, no matter whether they are large numbers or small ones, the findings are fairly consistent in showing that half or more of students do not read as well as they could or should; they are certainly not the crafty readers Scholes describes in his work. These Stanford results, especially taken together with a more recent Stanford study of similar type on fact checking (Wineberg and McGrew 2019), show that students could certainly benefit, in many different kinds of classes, from instruction in lateral reading and fact-checking strategies (Caulfield 2017). Lateral reading entails cross-checking information presented in one source against others, a tool that Scholes did not specifically suggest, but that would fit with the idea that reading is a teachable, learnable craft. Of course, fact checking via lateral reading is not always necessary, but if students are aware of their own purposes and goals for reading, they should be able to determine whether various critical reading strategies are appropriate.

FACULTY PREPARATION TO WORK ON READING

If students are hoping faculty will help them with reading, there are several indications that that is probably not going to happen. Many practicing faculty do not feel well-prepared to teach reading or to help students with reading problems. The evidence for this claim comes from my own admittedly limited experience consulting on campuses around the country and from a preliminary survey done by Ellen Carillo, reported in her 2015 book, *Securing a Place for Reading in Composition: The Importance of Teaching for Transfer.*

Carillo, a University of Connecticut faculty member and director of the writing program at the Waterbury campus, did her limited study under the auspices of a major grant from the CCCC organization. The study was conducted in 2012 with one hundred volunteers solicited through the online writing program administrators' discussion list, WPA-L. While many of the instructors in the study said they used some specific approach to reading in their teaching (rhetorical reading or analytic reading or some other similar term), more than half of the participants said they were "not secure" (Carillo 2015, 32) in their knowledge of reading theory and practice or their ability to teach students to read more effectively. My own smattering of evidence, drawn from more than a dozen consulting appointments on reading across the country, supports this view. Frontline writing faculty in my experience generally don't know much about reading or how to teach it. So, students are not going to get useful help from writing faculty. It seems reasonable to think that if English teachers or writing faculty don't know much about reading and aren't able to help students in those classes, then it is even more likely that experts in other disciplines are surely equally unprepared to help students become better readers. It is worth noting that the observation about reading quoted above, which Scholes made in 2002, appeared in the journal *Pedagogy*, which is not addressed to English or writing teachers, but is intended for faculty in all disciplines concerned with effective teaching.

Some of this lack of preparation is reflected specifically in writing studies graduate programs' disinterest in training future faculty to work on reading, surely true of all other fields as well. Most programs do not offer much or anything at all in the way of instruction in reading theory or pedagogy. To take a quick look at whether graduate programs offer formal coursework or other instruction in reading theory and pedagogy, I did a minimalist survey of extant programs' course offerings, looking at random at twenty-seven of the eighty doctoral programs listed by the Consortium of Doctoral Programs in Rhetoric and Composition of CCCC (CCCC 2021). For each program, I looked at the current website and list of required and/or recommended classes if available, along with program description materials. Of these, twenty-one had no required course in reading or literacy, although some did have space for electives.

Among the others, there were courses like "Theories of Literacy" or "Critical Literacy" or "Literacy Theory and Practice," but none of these seemed to address the teaching and learning of critical reading directly.

My little cursory surveys suggest, then, that PhD programs in English or writing studies around the country are not generally offering specific coursework on reading theory and pedagogy. Nor is reading part of the general view of threshold concepts or their role in graduate education. The highly regarded *Naming What We Know* by Adler-Kassner and Wardle (2015) offers five threshold concepts for composition, with discussion of them by leading scholars. Taczak and Yancey in that collection explore the relevance of threshold concepts for graduate education; neither they nor the concepts themselves appear to take up reading in any direct or explicit way. Similar concerns are raised by Jessica Rivera-Mueller in her discussion elsewhere in this volume on teacher preparation at the secondary level. While K–12 teachers almost always have at least some coursework in reading, the focus for secondary teachers is not on helping them teach the kind of critical reading students will need in college and beyond. Her approach entails considerable reading on the part of teachers and possibly also for students; though Rivera-Mueller doesn't discuss them directly, Scholes offers insights to how that reading might occur for both students and teachers.

Taken together, these points all show that there are serious problems with students' abilities to read critically on paper or online, that faculty currently in classrooms do not feel particularly prepared to address these problems, and that current graduate training programs around the country are not doing much to prepare graduate students to work on reading issues in their own classrooms or in the programs they will join after graduation. Finally, other chapters here make clear Scholes's ideas for how reading might be better integrated in K–12 classrooms as well as at the college level. The need for critical reading and thinking continues to grow in an era of online communication, twenty-four-hour news, and evidence of students' reading difficulties; the need for students to become crafty readers has never been more important in every course as well as in preparing students for participation in our democracy.

STEPS FORWARD

There are many resources for faculty who want to help students move toward becoming crafty readers. I have been asked to visit a number of colleges and universities in the United States and Australia to discuss students' reading situations and help faculty work on the problem. Generally, I suggest that all faculty can achieve their own teaching goals more effectively if they help students read assigned course material efficiently. The steps involved do not require that faculty become reading specialists. In fact, most faculty are themselves already highly effective readers, though they are largely unaware of their skills because they are so thoroughly practiced. In *Protocols*, Scholes offers some advice, dealing mainly with literary interpretation, but he suggests that reading requires not only comprehension but also incorporation of the text into readers' own systems of knowledge and understanding (1989, 9). In this way, texts need to be connected to other texts, pictures, prior knowledge, and experience (1989, 21), a point with which most psycholinguistic research would surely agree. He further suggests that reading entails and includes rhetoric, by which he says, "pleasure and power are exchanged between producers and consumers of texts, always remembering that writers must consume in order to produce and that readers must produce in order to consume" (1989, 90). In these points, he is building a case for what Haller and other scholars have called "rhetorical reading" (2010).

In his more recent book, Scholes himself provides more specific guidance for teaching reading. While neither *Crafty* nor *Protocols* is a textbook, Scholes does intend to explain the "craft," which he says involves the use of tools along with the skill to use them (Scholes 2001, xiv). With respect to digital texts or new media, Scholes makes a very specific point about the relevance of crafty reading in those venues: "New media, in any case, do not exactly replace or eliminate old ones. They take their places in a world of communication; they require realignments of that world; they borrow from the older ways of composing texts; and they change—often enrich—the older forms themselves. . . . I will assert here, and maintain throughout this book, that valuable texts are to be found in all media, and in many genres within those media" (2001, xv). Like other scholars, Scholes believes that the skills of crafty reading will be helpful whether the text appears on paper or on a screen. Beyond this point, Scholes takes his English Department colleagues to task later in the book, saying that they need to "start taking reading seriously" (2001, 213) by putting "the craft of reading at the center of their discipline, using all sorts of textual creatures, great and small, as specimens for analysis and models for imitation" (214). He says teachers of English literature should use the skills they already have, the craft, to teach students to be better readers (214–15). After a lengthy discussion of a reading of a Bible text, Scholes says that readers must stay close to the text itself, but at the same time, they should take into account both what is included and also what is omitted from any text under study (223), as well as those parts the readers might agree with along with those with which they disagree (223). But all of these features of reading are teachable and learnable, according to Scholes, because they are elements of craft.

Other sources offer several additional key suggestions that all faculty can implement easily enough, again to achieve their own goals. Linda Nilson, emerita director of the Office of Teaching Excellence and Innovation at Virginia Tech, has two very useful chapters on reading for classes across the curriculum (2016). Among other things, she points out that faculty should not "lecture the readings," thus excusing students from doing the reading themselves. It is also important to have students do something with the reading that they do—write a summary, prepare questions for other students, respond to a reading assignment with a post to a discussion board, and so forth. Any technique that leads to what she calls "reading compliance," that is, students actually doing the assigned reading, is a good thing.

I have found that asking students to work collaboratively writing twenty-five-word summaries of sections of a text is a highly engaging technique for getting them to discuss the content of a chapter or article. Bazerman outlines this approach in some detail (1995). Because of the word limit in this task, students see it as a challenge to get the key ideas in a condensed form. The discussions tend to be very focused on capturing content, exactly the kind of discussion of reading most faculty hope students will have. Posting these short summaries to a discussion board allows all class members to have access to a full summary of a reading. They can also provide an important springboard to evaluation of any text for authority, accuracy, currency, relevancy, appropriateness, and bias. Carillo's annotation strategy is yet another device to help students improve their reading (2016; 2017). Scholes points out that there isn't one right way to read (2001, 242), so all of these approaches have the potential to help students become crafty readers.

A further issue has to do with the current and continuing growth of the online environment for reading materials of all kinds. To address this aspect of reading, a recent book by highly respected reading scholar Maryanne Wolf is very helpful (2018). She proposes that current readers need to be able to read both traditional texts printed on paper and every sort of digital text we find on a screen, both alphabetic and visual. For instructors at all levels, this view means that all faculty need to help students become "biliterate," that is, able to work with both traditional and electronic forms of texts. But the fundamentals of comprehension, vocabulary, and critical evaluation do not change if the site of reading moves from page to screen or the type of text moves from alphabetic to digital. The need for sustained attention and deep reading remains and must be a target in classrooms at every level.

One more point to keep in mind is that the picture of students based on performance on various kinds of objective measures does not tell the whole story about students' reading abilities or their actual reading activity. An early report of a Pew Center study suggests that young people *are* in fact reading quite a lot (LaFrance 2014). While they don't, according to this report, necessarily see libraries as a key resource, they *do* read, and in fact read more books than older people. And we need to think about the fact that writing a college research paper (of the kind studied by the Citation Project) is not the be-all and end-all of reading for students or anyone else. However, a focus on the craft of reading as Scholes defines it is certainly essential to help everyone participate fully in a functioning democracy.

Scholes would also, I think, be in favor of Wolf's ideas and the other approaches offered by Nilson, Bazerman, and Carillo. He understood the need and saw the problem long before Facebook and Twitter took over our lives. Scholes saw the need for crafty readers and that need has only grown in the past nearly twenty years since his book was published. It's worth thinking about why this ability is and always will be useful to students and all adults. The most obvious reason is that effective, efficient reading can help students learn course material, do solid research in any field, and succeed in college and careers. Beyond this tangible reason, though, much has been written about the ways in which certain kinds of reading (of literary fiction, in particular) can help people develop empathy as they gain insight into the views or experiences of others (Chiaet 2013). But empathy can be aroused in the reading of nonfiction prose as well, as Kelsey McNiff points out elsewhere in this book. As she explains, "critical reflection" is essential to understanding others' positions on any issue. In a climate of increasing polarization, political and otherwise, such empathetic reading might help to improve people's ability to get along with one another. A fuller awareness of the nature of the information we receive, now from the vast resources of the internet, might also allow all readers to attend carefully to the ways in which "manufactured consent" via the media influences our lives (Herman and Chomsky, 2002). Finally, crafty readers have the ability not only to follow an argument with full comprehension, but also to evaluate it on the critical criteria of authority, accuracy, currency, relevancy, appropriateness, and bias; these abilities are crucial to success in and beyond school, and also crucial to sustaining a functioning democratic society. Scholes knew what he was talking about; we should attend to his wise advice and counsel.

REFERENCES

ACT. 2018. *The Condition of College and Career Readiness—National Results.* https://www.act.org/content/dam/act/unsecured/cccr2018/National-CCCR-2018.pdf.

Adler-Kassner, Linda, and Elizabeth Wardle. 2015. *Naming What We Know: Threshold Concepts of Writing Studies.* Logan: Utah State University Press.

Bazerman, Charles. 1995. *The Informed Writer.* Reissued by WAC Clearinghouse, 2011. http://wac.colostate.edu/books/informedwriter/.

Carillo, Ellen C. 2015. *Securing a Place for Reading in Composition: The Importance of Teaching for Transfer.* Logan: Utah State University Press.

Carillo, Ellen C. 2016. "Engaging Sources through Reading-Writing Connections across the Disciplines." *Across the Disciplines* 13 (1). http://wac.colostate.edu/atd/articles/carillo2016.cfm.

Carillo, Ellen C. 2017. *A Writer's Guide to Mindful Reading: Practice and Pedagogy.* Fort Collins: The WAC Clearinghouse and University Press of Colorado. https://wac.colostate.edu/books/mindful/.

Caulfield, Michael A. 2017. *Web Literacy for Student Fact Checkers and Other People Who Care about Facts.* https://webliteracy.pressbooks.com/front-matter/web-strategies-for-student-fact-checkers/.

Chiaet, Julianne. 2013. "Novel Finding: Reading Literary Fiction Improves Empathy." *Scientific American.* https://www.scientificamerican.com/article/novel-finding-reading-literary-fiction-improves-empathy/.

Conference on College Composition and Communication (CCCC). 2021. Doctoral Consortium in Rhetoric and Composition. https://ccccdoctoralconsortium.org/.

Haller, Cynthia. 2010. "Toward Rhetorical Source Use: Three Student Journeys." *WPA: Writing Program Administration* 34 (1): 33–59.

Herman, Edward, and Noam Chomsky. 2002. *Manufacturing Consent: The Political Economy of the Mass Media.* New York: Pantheon Books/Random House.

Huffman, Debrah. 2010. "Toward Modes of Reading in Composition." *Reader* 60: 204–30.

Jamieson, Sandra. 2013. "What Students' Use of Sources Reveals about Advanced Writing Skills." *Across the Disciplines* 10 (4). http://wac.colostate.edu/atd/reading/jamieson.cfm.

Jamieson, Sandra, and Rebecca Moore Howard. 2019. "The Citation Project." http://www.citationproject.net/.

LaFrance, Adrienne. 2014. "Millennials Are Out-Reading Older Generations." *The Atlantic.* https://www.theatlantic.com/technology/archive/2014/09/millennials-are-out-reading-older-generations/379934/.

Nilson, Linda. 2016. *Teaching at Its Best.* 4th ed. San Francisco, CA: John Wiley.

Programme for International Student Assessment. 2018. "2018 Results: Insights and Interpretations." PISA 2018 Results. http://www.oecd.org/pisa/publications/pisa-2018-results.htm.

Scholes, Robert. 1989. *Protocols of Reading.* New Haven, CT: Yale University Press.

Scholes, Robert. 2001. *The Crafty Reader.* New Haven, CT: Yale University Press.

Stanford History Education Group. 2016. "Evaluating Information: The Cornerstone of Civic Online Reasoning." Civic Online Reasoning. https://cor.stanford.edu/research/evaluating-information-the-cornerstone-of-cor/.

Sullivan, Patrick, Howard Tinberg, and Sheridan Blau. 2017. *Deep Reading: Teaching Reading in the Writing Classroom.* Urbana, IL: NCTE.

Taczak, Kara, and Kathleen Blake Yancey. 2015. "Threshold Concepts in Rhetoric and Composition Doctoral Education: The Delivered, Lived, and Experienced Curricula." In *Naming What We Know*, edited by Linda Adler-Kassner and Elizabeth Wardle, 140–56. Logan: Utah State University Press.

Wineburg, Sam, and Sarah McGrew. 2019. "Lateral Reading: Reading Less and Learning More When Evaluating Digital Information." *Teachers College Record* 121 (11): 1–40.

Wolf, Maryanne. 2018. *Reader Come Home: The Reading Brain in a Digital World.* New York: HarperCollins.

3
PERIODICAL TEXTUALITY
A Case for Contextualized Reading Practices in First-Year Writing

Christopher J. La Casse

> *Our English word text comes from the Latin verb texere, which means specifically "to weave," and, by extension, "to join or fit together anything; to plait, braid, interweave, interlace; to construct, make, fabricate, build." From texere also comes texum, "that which is woven, a web . . . that which is plaited, braided, or fitted together," and, when applied to literary composition, "tissue, texture, style." But the connection between textuality and weaving will take us to other places if we follow that thread (73).*
>
> —Robert Scholes, *English After the Fall: From Literature to Textuality*

Robert Scholes's words may seem prophetic today. Decades ago, he cautioned that teachers must teach writing by first teaching students to read, and now, for various reasons, critics are starting to take notice—from studies on test scores and habits of student readers to the neuroscience of the "reading brain" and reading's role in humanity's collective development (Wolf 2006; Carr 2011). To see that even English studies is prepared to start a conversation about different reading practices, one has to look no further than the "unprecedented" consecutive installments of *PMLA* (2018 and 2019) *Cultures of Reading*, which covers "robust" submissions attempting to make legible the various approaches that complicate the "deceptive simplicity" of the term "reading" (1075). As promising as this renewed reading interest may be, its place in education is still underexplored. Alice Horning's contribution in this collection offers a brief survey of conference programs in writing studies (NCTE, CCCC, WPA) as well as professional journals (*CCC, CE, RTE, TETYC,* and *WPA*), revealing that the field is "virtually ignoring an essential aspect of literacy development."

DOI: 10.7330/9781646421190.c003

Recent empirical studies have begun to illuminate the consequence of problematic reading practices, such as "surface reading" (Carr) and "quote mining" (Horning in this volume). The multi-institutional research endeavor called the Citation Project finds that less than 10 percent of students are summarizing, with most simply paraphrasing, or worse, merely copying without processing the content. As students employ reading and writing practices that circumvent basic comprehension, it is perhaps no surprise that Educational Testing Services found that only 50 percent of America's millennials reached "Level 3 in the literacy component"—suggesting that very few respondents can "identify, interpret, or evaluate one or more pieces of information, and often require varying levels of inference" (Carillo 2017, 199–200). Web-based reading habits may be one explanation, but several pedagogical and structural reasons in our public education system may also explain why students seem to have a "simplistic and mechanical understanding of reading" (Sullivan 2017, xvii).

Reasons for surface reading may be beyond the student's control or stem from misconceptions about the purpose of reading and its relationship to disciplinary ways of knowing. Testing, for one, sends the message that students should read content for recall. High stakes testing, moreover, appears to function as a form of operant conditioning, inscribing a certain disposition in students toward reading, what Elizabeth Wardle calls an "answer-getting disposition," rather than inviting students to cultivate a "problem-exploring disposition" (2012). John Bean (2011) also cautions against school cultures that privilege quizzes as well as an instructor's willingness to lecture over assigning reading. Lecturing instead of assigning reading sends the message that the material is "too difficult" to comprehend or that it is not worth the time on task: Simply remain dependent on the teacher, who will distill the assigned pages down to the gist (Bean 2011, 166). These possible causes are worth further inspection because they potentially send troubling messages to our students about reading's function.

Robert Scholes (2002) and Ellen Carillo (2009) observed that students tend to consider the content of all course texts as factual, or "correct" entities. Scholes's colleague Tamar Katz posits that students are inclined to "want to read every text as saying something extremely familiar that they might agree with" (Scholes 2002, 166). Additionally, Sonya Armstrong and Mary Newman (2011) discovered that "many students also tend to view reading as a passive activity that involves determining a single, correct meaning that is 'in' the text, but that they often can't seem to retrieve" (7). In light of these trends, educators are responsible for transforming curriculum and creating an environment that deepens reader-text interactions so that students have the means to critically engage and see the value in devoting the necessary energy to wrestle with complicated passages, follow the thread of a writer's argument, and make connections between texts and across various contexts.

There are many best practices for provoking deeper and dynamic reading practices, but my purpose here is to call for a closer scrutiny of the mediums that deliver course readings. So often students encounter literature or course materials in first-year writing (FYW) anthologies or textbooks that encourage decontextualized reading habits. Decontextualized reading fetters or stunts readerly transactions, perpetuates simplistic views of reading, discounts reading as a constructive act, and runs counter to renewed valuation of reading rhetorically and other best practices in the classroom.

RHETORICAL READING AND TEXTUALITY

Rhetorical reading and textuality are in many ways two sides of the same coin—and they enrich student reading and engagement when brought together deliberately in the classroom.

Rhetorical reading acknowledges that students do not passively receive information but instead practice strategies to construct meaning. These reading strategies might include reproducing the "rhetorical context," as students use "their own knowledge of the world, of the topic, and of discourse conventions, to infer, set and discard hypotheses, predict, and question in order to construct meaning for texts" (Haas and Flower 1988, 167). The richness and potentiality of these transactions, however, depends upon the student's knowledge—which may be limited for first-year students who have yet to benefit from the cumulative effects of their disciplinary coursework. Across various cultural artifacts, Scholes demonstrated a variety of reading practices to help students understand how language, rhetoric, and media formats quietly shape our perspective or persuade us to a way of seeing. The term *textuality*, its root word and etymology, may help educators reconceptualize much more historically embedded and interwoven readerly practices that require countless layers of "unweaving." Bringing together textuality and rhetorical reading, I argue, would mean designing curriculum in which students are attentive to the contextual and historical dimensions of texts while classroom discussions involve explicit instruction in rhetorical and dynamic reading practices. As Paul T. Corrigan reminds us in his chapter, one of Scholes's popular refrains was "situate, situate." The focus of this chapter is on perhaps the most textually rich type of cultural artifact that drew Scholes's interest late in his career and to which he believed educators had a responsibility: periodicals and magazines.

Early work on magazines, especially in modernist literary studies, fixated on their historical role as mere platforms for launching new talent; ignoring context, scholars treated magazines as anthologies, as containers for noteworthy and emergent literary works. For the field of modernism, Sean Latham and Robert Scholes (2006, 519) played a role in shifting perspectives by identifying the periodical as a significant "cultural object" in its own right. Periodicals are themselves texts that "contain subtexts" and are positioned amid overlapping contexts. Because of their seriality or periodicity, these artifacts archive the complexities and contradictions of cultural evolutions in more obvious ways than other mediums students read. The textual horizons of periodicals are not only vast. Historical periodicals, in particular, offer a defamiliarized reading terrain that provokes dynamic and reconstructive reading processes. *Periodical textuality*, for these reasons, must assume a richly contextualized, interdisciplinary, material, sociocultural, political, and, ultimately, pluralistic reading of texts. Scholars have shared their classroom experiences using periodicals to challenge their disciplinary boundaries by expanding their students' historical and cultural perspectives (Cole 2006; Churchill 2008; Scholes and Wulfman 2010). Yet those boundaries require further disruption as well as increased cross-border conversations. Extending Scholes's and others' work, this chapter weaves these threads with best practices in composition studies and into a range of fields on teaching literacy.

WHOSE READING CRISIS?

It may be tempting for educators to be "appalled" by what appears to be a widespread reading crisis, but it's important for us to consider our own liability, as instructors as well as participants of a wider educational industry and set of traditions. As conversations continue about ways to address passive or shallow reading habits, there has been surprisingly little research conducted on how the packaging of texts encourages approaches and habits of mind averse to more active forms of reader-text transactions. Most students access literature through anthologies, nonfiction through readers, and history through textbooks, which provide "structure and meaning to the complexity of the past" (Latham and Scholes 2006, 521). Anthologies, textbooks, or "readers" are necessary to our classrooms in many ways, but they potentially limit the reading horizons: how reading is *packaged* influences pedagogical goals and theories as well as students' perception of their role as readers.

In exploring using periodicals or "bland" anthologies in an American literature course, Jean Lee Cole (2006, 58) found that her students were attentive to their various interactions based on these different forms. One student discovered that she had "fostered an understanding she would never have gained from 'any textbook because it was the knowledge of the true way of life of those periods, rather than the dates and events that history books decide to remember'" (Cole 2006, 62). This seemingly unmediated access to the past is elaborated on in a series of interviews Suzanne Churchill (2008) conducted with her colleagues in modernist periodical studies. While Patrick Collier referred to periodicals as not as "epistemologically over-determined as the anthology" (Churchill 2008, 219), Ann Ardis observed that students gained a "sense of being 'in the moment' . . . that feeling of being thrown in the middle of on-going debates about art and politics rather than being asked to stand back and revere . . . the aura of great 'masterworks'" (Churchill 2008, 218). Perhaps because literature teachers usually cover periods of history, they are sensitive to how periodicals might provide situated contextual transactions that make the historical distance between reader and text more intimate or knowable. Conversely, scholarly curated mediums—in their function to canonize, legitimize, and elevate—may manufacture a sacred aura, a deferential distance between reader and text.

Not all anthologies or readers are alike; some may contain more of the editor's guiding hand than others. It is beyond the scope of this chapter to explore in any thorough way the different mediums in which students encounter reading and how that packaging influences their transaction. Yet Jerome McGann's (1991) observations on "reading editions" versus "critical editions" of literary works may provide an instructive way to consider how different textual conditions mediate and shape the reading experience. For McGann, reading editions, free of an editor's critical apparatus, promote a linear reading process that critical editions attempt to disrupt. Beyond illustrating textual variants in critical editions, critical apparatuses may appear in readers, anthologies, and scholarly editions. Some apparatuses may contain notes or annotations explaining historical figures, events, or terms while others may even reprint primary sources and scholarly excerpts or include introductions with historical and biographical contexts. A scholarly curated anthology or edition, with such an apparatus, could situate readers in a "radial reading" process that encourages them to jump from notes to appendix and other suggested materials that "expand and enrich" the textual experience (McGann 1991, 120) as these forms embody what McGann called "the most sociohistorically self-conscious of texts" (McGann 1991, 121). Editions that signal their own textuality certainly promise to promote more dynamic reading practices. Since the publication of *Textual Condition*, though, digitally archived periodicals have perhaps assumed that mantle to offer an even more historically rich and textually expansive reading experience.

The difference between reading editions and those with critical apparatuses is instructive, as it offers crude parameters to categorize various material mediums and conceptualize how paratextual and bibliographic or nonlinguistic coding may shape reading practices. How might forms resembling reading editions, editions with critical apparatuses, and periodicals differ in their abilities to mediate the reading experience and embed students in a range of transactions informed by contexts? This question is important because these mediums may, in varying degrees, either remove students from the author, context, time period, and discourse community or enhance their attentiveness to these considerations while reading. To interrogate this reader-text distance, I extend these observations made by periodical and textual studies scholars into disciplinary concerns and developments in reading pedagogies and composition/rhetoric, with the aim to consider the potential implications of decontextualized reading habits.

Readerly transactions may be limited for learners not yet socialized into their discourse communities. When reading in a new subject area, many students may experience the psychological phenomenon "cognitive egocentrism," which is not unlike Scholes's observation that students want to see something familiar in a text, which leads to reductive and oversimplified readings consistent with their preconceived notions (Bean 2011, 165; Scholes 2002, 166). Students reading dislocated texts, consequently, may not recognize they are not the primary audience and thus project assumptions into the reading. According to John Bean (2011, 165), educators must consistently recontextualize because "inexperienced readers often fail to appreciate the political biases of different magazines and newspapers or the theoretical biases of different academic journals and presses." Students therefore view sources as "inert information" and lack the guidance on how to see themselves in conversation with the author or how they might differ from the original or intended readership. The thoroughly defamiliarized territory of periodicals should give students pause. As they peer through this window, they may become aware of their estrangement from the cultural values and beliefs of a rich and complicated past, which may then help them recognize their positionality and the necessity of their own socialization into a historically removed periodical community. In addition to provoking a more mindful readerly socialization process, *periodical textuality* may function to mitigate other trends or misconceptions that arise among inexperienced readers when adjusting to unfamiliar reading terrain.

Periodical textuality, by contrast to other mediums, makes it abundantly clear that the contemporary reader is far removed from the historical or intended audience. Inexperienced readers may not work through texts strategically, changing their pace or purpose for different genres (Bean 2011, 163–64). *Periodical textuality* places great demands on readers of all abilities to vary their reading practices (described in detail later in this chapter). To cope with the abundance of information, gaps in knowledge, and diverse range of genres comprised in these unfamiliar print artifacts, students must *skim* for the gist, *pursue references* to fill gaps, and *slow down* to scrutinize, *draw connections*, *make inferences*, or *circle back* to reconsider initial interpretations. Periodicals also restore a truly authentic rhetorical situation against which to read contributions, enabling students to build a context and cognitive schema into which to assimilate new material or more fully comprehend a particular reading: they might read texts against a historical event or a contributor's position in conversation with others. In sum, then, periodicals provide the various textures that make readers aware of their historical remove as well as a roadmap toward dynamic reading and deeper understanding, as they comprehend, analyze, evaluate, and synthesize the overlapping layers of context in what might be considered reconstructive reading processes.

Forms with editorial or critical apparatuses work to a different end than reading editions, as they attempt to pilot students through allusions, references, and guided questions toward disciplinary socialization or a more immediate view of that historical time period. While these mediums are practical and necessary, they may still risk limiting the reading horizon by setting boundaries with apparatuses that artificially work to establish context and thus inherently inhibit "readings." While reading editions, or decontextualized reading practices in general, may conceal the distance between reader and text, the more authoritative scholarly curated mediums may inadvertently socialize deferential readerly manners that preserve reader-text distance. Unlike periodicals, forms with critical apparatuses may not allow for richly authentic rhetorical reading practices, full immersion into a discourse or periodical community, or the necessary dynamic, layered, and reader-led transactions.

In explaining his reasons for not advancing a theory of textuality, Jerome McGann (1991, 16) argued that "what is textually possible cannot be theoretically established." McGann's statement here may apply even more so to a periodical's textuality. The possibilities for making connections and interpretations are limitless, which is probably why Latham and Scholes (2006, 518) called for a collaborative and interdisciplinary approach to periodical scholarship. Reading for textuality in the classroom, on the one hand, liberates students from the authority of what Scholes (1985) called "fundamentalist" reading. On the other hand, this approach raises other practical concerns when students become immersed in periodical textuality's interminable threads—the "unfamiliar territory" that materializes once classes venture beyond the "canonical" and "authoritative anthologies" (Churchill 2008, 219). What follows is an explanation of approaches and various reading practices that help guide and position students to enact a range of transactions and dynamic readings of these complicated objects of study.

PERIODICAL TEXTUALITY: WAYS OF READING THROUGH THE LAYERS

A quick overview of these rich resources illustrates the range of cultural and historical artifacts available as alternative course reading materials: Research Society for Victorian Periodicals, Modernist Journals Project, Modernist Magazines Project, Virtual Newsstand of 1925, Conrad First, Pulp Making of America Collection, ArtMag, Pulp Magazine Project, and The Pulp Magazine Archive. Some nineteenth-century monthlies still in existence today provide their own databases for a small student fee. Classrooms may obtain access to digital repositories of *The New Yorker* and *The Atlantic*, giving readers a long view of a periodical's publication run. It is worth noting that periodical scholars prefer students to handle the physical artifact. Some have gone to lengths to purchase periodicals for classroom use because the object's immediacy enhances information literacy, as students are better able to distinguish between sources; the internet's "homogenized presentation" of digital archives and other material, conversely, projects a "postmodern collapsing of time" and "flattening of affect" (Cole 2006, 61). Nonetheless, online archives enable many innovative classroom opportunities.

Robert Scholes and Clifford Wulfman's book *Modernism in the Magazine* (2010), which outlines methods for engaging these complicated forms, has been an invaluable introduction in my own experience teaching periodicals. More recently, the Modernist Journals Project (MJP) continues building conversation around teaching periodicals, with sample syllabi and assignments as well as overviews like "How to Read a Magazine," which includes twelve methods and twelve reading strategies (MJP, "Teaching Tools"). The first step in periodical pedagogy is to provide descriptive work that sketches the "periodical community" (Delap 2000, 234). Both nineteenth- and twentieth-century periodical scholars in literary studies have offered strategies for teaching students to read different types of evidences to identify editorial staff, regular contributors, and readers as well as the types of content (sociopolitical and cultural leanings), business practices, materiality, and, ultimately, the periodical's positionality within wider contexts. The initial reading practice is dynamic, as Scholes and Wulfman describe the "internal" and "external" or holistic approach required to process and understand the range of evidences that help reconstruct an original audience. Since periodicals are a collage of voices, which sometimes harmonize and other times clamor in discord, readers have no choice but to account for a wide range of evidences while attempting to distinguish patterns. Explaining the rationale behind their methods, Scholes and Wulfman (2010, 150–51) write: "Because we are dealing with multiple authorship, we must read internal texts closely, and we must root around in other primary and secondary sources, too, putting these efforts together at every stage of studying a periodical."

Part of this initial detective work of rooting around also leads to inferring the periodical's position in the public sphere and identity of the "implied" reader by considering aspects like "age, gender, economic class, intellectual class, race, and politics" (Scholes and Wulfman 2010, 147). The history and prospectus of the magazine set the stage, and content can provide obvious clues; the student-researcher may also conduct what the MJP refers to as "material readings." Circulation numbers, patterns, and amount or ratio of advertising to content may capture the periodical's position in the public sphere as "center" or "marginal." Types of periodicals (genre and form) and their daily, weekly, or monthly frequency—or periodicity—often signal the editor's commitment to wider public concerns (Beetham 1990; Brooker and Thacker 2009). Since periodicals are collaborative enterprises, student-researchers can read letters and memoirs to gain important behind-the-scenes insights into the editor and regular contributors as they consider who they are, what they value, and whether they coalesce around a group identity or set of principles. In the process of recovering and constructing microhistories, students make natural connections and deepen their historical knowledge through research that is organic, as they follow up on the obscure reference, historicize issues to understand the exigency of editorials, and fill the gaps produced by ellipses or truncated commentary that the historical readership would have taken for granted. By learning to establish this first step in how to reconstruct a periodical community, students obtain a framework for thinking about audience in meaningful ways while practicing a range of reading modes.

Periodical reading is itself nonlinear, requires multiple reading lenses to discover new ways of seeing, and is a constant process of reframing and reconceptualizing. Much like writing drafts, first-year students must cope with the recursive reading habit as they sift through layers of context to sharpen their focus and deepen comprehension. In *Textual Power*, Scholes (1985, 3) notes that "concepts like genre and style are useful because they give us access to the invisible forces that share textual production." In periodicals, there are many invisible codes students must learn to read. Understanding audience, purpose, and writerly decisions across different types of texts is a common feature when studying these forms that embody various genres. The MJP's twelve methods provide different frameworks for inquiry, as many students may otherwise struggle to conceptualize the parameters of reading and researching periodicals. The MJP's ways of reading are:

- skimming/browsing
- surveying
- grazing
- sampling
- rooting around
- selective close reading
- deciphering the magazine's bibliographic code
- moving in and out
- moving between observation and inference
- seizing prematurely on particulars
- drifting (or yielding to distraction)
- circling back

Explicit instruction in, and practice with, recursive reading processes help students orient themselves in these complex forms. It is also helpful to invite metacognitive reading reflections that recognize how reading processes and comprehension are typically based on partial evidence, as readers make imperfect conjectures: only through rereading and sifting through complicated interplay of overlapping contexts do we start "complicating" our "inferences" while bringing the picture into focus (MJP). Because of their complexity and relatively uncharted territory as objects of study, periodicals invite teachers to learn, inquire, and rethink alongside their students during projects. A textually rich and collaborative reader-led classroom may serve as an important starting point if we are to make a case for explicit instruction in reading pedagogy as a foundation of general education courses. By encouraging a metacognitive awareness of reading through reflection and classroom discussion, we may start to make visible the messy "interiority" of reading practices while also promoting transferable habits of mind and coping strategies students will later need to navigate future disciplinary readerly socializations.

DEFAMILIARIZED HISTORICAL SPACES: RECONSTRUCTING AUDIENCE, READING DISCOVERIES

Periodicals offer a textured and pluralistic view of history. As Maria DiCenzo (2015, 31) notes, "history and periodical studies are inextricably linked, which is why periodicals are so valuable in telling different stories about the past in a specific period or national contexts or comparatively." Whereas textbooks, anthologies, or readers may be misperceived as comprehensive and definitive, periodicals offer seemingly limitless reading horizons. While a collection of these artifacts presents multiple windows into the past, a single issue alone is often rife with layers of complexity, inviting students to read with an openness and curiosity. Importantly, student reading discoveries can be developed into authentic contributions through writing projects. As Scholes and Clifford Wulfman (2010, 216) remind us in *Modernism in the Magazines*, "We all have things to learn about that foreign country that is the past."

As boundless as their horizons may be, periodicals are also a foreign country where one may occasionally get lost. *Modernism in the Magazines* as well as the Modernist Journals Project provide several well-designed assignment ideas that set specific parameters for how students might read and write about periodicals. Although Scholes often called for us to move beyond disciplinary boundaries, *Modernism in the Magazine* is still very much centered within the core concerns of modernist literary studies. The theme-based writing course I proposed and designed, Textual Identities, was not beholden to covering subject area content. Instead, the course sought to complement and enrich best practices in composition studies (explicit instruction in reading and writing, scaffolding assignments, peer review, and metacognitive reflections) with methods from print culture/periodical studies and a range of interdisciplinary lenses.

Throughout the semester, Textual Identities empowered students to delve into the sociocultural particularities of that "foreign" past, as they examined the intersection of periodical textuality and concepts of identity, such as representations, value norming, and prejudice. Shorter writing assignments equipped them with the means to explore the defamiliarized historical space of older magazines. We read and discussed how Eddie Bernays revolutionized consumer culture and American middleclass identities through advertising that targeted the psychological undergirding of male and female social identity constructs, which then equipped students with a critical lens for their magazine advertisement image analysis. Drawing upon concepts such as the male gaze and Martha Nussbaum's seven forms of objectification, they also analyzed a magazine's representation of women. In addition to providing lenses to empower students to interrogate textual constructs of identity, the shorter assignments also socialized students into different contextualized reading practices. In these assignments, they were asked to perform textual analyses of identities set against the backdrop of a readership and its values, which, importantly, served as early scaffolding for the research project. Shortly after embarking on the research project, one student, a dual English and philosophy major, told me that he was excited to see how the shorter assignments were meant to prepare him for the research project and how he felt he had several options and the specific tools to begin this work.

For their research projects, students had many digital archives to choose from, but several were drawn to The Pulp Magazine Project; though this archive is incomplete, the digitized pulps nonetheless provide unique access into cultural history. In class, we discussed how the pulps were produced for mass consumption and can be read as a window into the typically male perspectives and prejudices of an era. While science fiction pulp stories captured the intersection of emergent technology and imagination, the "girlie" magazines, which often tested the threshold of acceptable social mores, offered insights into male fantasies and fetishes. Sandra, an art history major, advanced an insightful critique of the February 1930 issue of *Ginger*, one of the titles from the 1920s–1930s publisher Frank Armer, who was forced to "tone down" his content after newsstand owners' arrests. The stories are often broken off at some climactic point in the seduction, redirecting readers to thumb through other enticing content before picking up the thread. Upon reading initial issues, Sandra noticed trends and patterns through an image-text analysis. Most of the stories included dynamics that positioned men in dominant roles based on race and class: ethnic and social-class dialects (*Ginger* 19), educational differences ("nitwit dame") (*Ginger* 35), sugar daddies (*Ginger* 27), plantation housekeepers (*Ginger* 10), exoticized and hypersexualized island natives (*Ginger* 41), and sexual propositions to be the lead in a "musical hit" (*Ginger* 39) populated the pages of the *Ginger* issue (1930).

Sandra was particularly interested in how working-class and racialized representations of women were often placed in demeaning and subjugated physical, social, and economic positions. She considered readership, which she had reconstructed from the evidences across the magazine, particularly the advertising, which seemed to be novelty items priced as a middle-class luxury at the time (*Ginger* 51–66). She surmised that the depression and economic anxiety for middle-class men may have made these representations especially appealing. With perhaps their own status in question, male middle-class readers would have felt reassured in these fantasies that depicted exoticized and uneducated women in subordinated roles.

Ultimately, the course aimed to more fully realize Scholes's call to teach a range of texts that practice power or influence over our collective perspectives. Its focus on identity was a move away from canonized literature, and, in fact, drew upon a range of textual artifacts. Student projects that come to mind include papers in which students used their understanding of readership to advance insightful close and contextualized readings—from a student who read *Fight Stories* as boxing matches with nationalistic undertones to the way the "how-to" advertising for technical courses (e.g., Coyne Electrical School) and home chemistry kits in *Amazing Stories* drew upon an optimistic narrative of modernity and technological progress (back matter of *Amazing Stories* December 1926). These are just a sample of students' responses to the assignment. With the continued expansion of digital archives, the possibilities for other types of projects are seemingly limitless.

Textual Identities seemed to give students even more than a set of methods, critical lenses, and reading and writing practices. Classroom conversations indicated that students held many assumptions about older generations that were becoming unsettled. Periodicals are not an entirely unmediated view of the past, but when considered together these diverse artifacts and their textualities encourage us to resist the ultimate story—a grand narrative. When given the tools to read and conceptualize the particularities of these richly heterogeneous forms, students are also able to compose original arguments. By asking students to understand how context (e.g., magazines) frames content, we can challenge them to participate in the humanities' goal of thinking across disciplines and synthesizing discourses from literature, history, philosophy, and politics to how the periodical mediates and shapes representations of race, class, gender, or a particularly divisive historical event. Upon completing the course, my student who wrote about *Fight Stories* (a senior science major) claimed he had never been challenged to think for himself before taking my course. As the instructor, I, too, enjoyed learning a great deal from my students about that "foreign country that is the past" (Scholes and Wulfman 2010, 216).

TRANSFORMING AND EXTENDING ROBERT SCHOLES'S PERIODICAL PEDAGOGY

Bringing periodical textuality into the classroom may raise questions about the aim and scope of FYW. Would the difficulty of contextual reading require more emphasis on reading to the detriment of class time spent on writing instruction? These practical concerns warrant a careful and close alignment between reading for textuality and writing course objectives. Borrowing key elements from the "Framework for Success in Postsecondary Writing" as well as the Writing Program Administrator's (WPA) "Outcomes Statement for First-Year Composition," it becomes clear how studying periodicals produces opportunities for articulating reading methods that align with best practices in writing studies, with a particular focus on what we might consider the triumvirate of current practice.

- *Rhetorical Knowledge / Audience:* Periodical reading begins with a rhetorical understanding of the readership as well as knowledge of the purpose of different genres or texts that comprise these heterogeneous forms.
- *Process:* Reading periodicals yields similar cognitive benefits and "habits of mind" that come with recursive writing processes.
- *Critical Thinking / Argumentation:* Robert Scholes argues that teaching writing begins with teaching reading. Transactions with periodicals through the lens of textuality enables students to stake a position and produce authentic, original claims. Additionally, they obtain a view of how language and contexts mediate and construct meaning.

The aim in these final pages is to make a case for this final tenet. Critically and rhetorically reading periodical textuality may serve as a gateway to critical thinking, original thought, and argumentation—and the kinds of dynamic reading practices discussed above hold great promise for empowering students to become authentic knowledge-producers in the *writing* classroom.

As of late, scholars have called the traditional research paper into question (Gaillet 2012a; Hayden 2017; Davis and Shadle 2000). The Citation Project's findings seem to suggest students are skimming sources to piece together quotations—producing what John C. Bean would term the "wandering 'all about'" paper (2011, 91). If this portrait accurately represents student reading habits, then on some level educators may be liable for students misperceiving the nature of knowledge as fixed and retrievable—which leaves little room for engaging sources in meaningful ways. Consequently, the practice of teaching critical thinking in the writing classroom may fall far short of the goal. The WPA outcomes statement, "Critical Thinking, Reading, and Composing," acknowledges "*critical thinking* is the ability to analyze, synthesize, interpret, and evaluate ideas, information, situations, and texts. When writers think critically about the materials they use . . . they separate assertion from evidence, evaluate sources and evidence, recognize and *evaluate underlying assumptions*, read across texts for connections and patterns, identify and evaluate chains of reasoning, and compose appropriately qualified and developed claims and generalizations" (CWPA 2014, emphasis added). The traditional research paper certainly seems like the most obvious type of assignment for students to practice higher-level thinking while engaging sources. Yet certain secondary source materials close off conversation, especially when students struggle to voice their own perspectives amid a scholarly conversation. Recently, scholars have shared strategies and curriculum that enables student voices to be more than a mere conduit for quoting or paraphrasing a scholar's viewpoint.

One of the most promising developments in writing studies has been the archival turn. Much like periodical textuality, archives command multiple reading practices. Instructors have found that students reading primary sources have no choice but to make inferences and value judgments about the artifacts they encounter. Reading their historicity and sociocultural significance is somehow inherent to the archival research process. Lynée Lewis Gaillet (2012b, 8) describes how archival projects require students to establish their positionality to the material, craft an original argument or narrative, and become immersed in an interdisciplinary set of discourses, thereby developing varied skills that are transferable. Similarly, Wendy Hayden (2017) finds that archival projects enable students to practice dynamic reading strategies that yield original interpretations. Archives and periodicals alike resist a grand narrative through countless textual possibilities as well as their limitations.

Because archives are curated, they are themselves objects of study: how they are assembled, what is omitted, and which parts are emphasized requires a rhetorical awareness. Similarly, periodicals are their own kind of archive or time capsule, which likewise calls upon multiple lenses of textual and contextual interpretation.

Because of their positionality in the public, multiple authorships, and genres, periodicals rank among the most interdisciplinary and textually rich archives or cultural artifacts. These forms, to be sure, are curated—but they are usually arranged in accordance with an editorial agenda and in response to their milieu. The layers of text include primary sources embodied in a curated, material context and social setting (i.e., the periodical community) that, in turn, is enmeshed in a historical web of ongoing conversations about a variety of topics. The overlapping contexts, dialogism, and contradictions of these artifacts—and their plethora of genres, subtexts, intertextualities, and references—make them ideal objects of study for textuality and a wide range of thematic or disciplinary approaches. Ultimately, rhetorical readings of a magazine's positionality and readership create opportunities to perform various contextualized readings of texts.

Curriculum that teaches periodical textuality reorients how students view, position themselves, and engage their reading material, which in turn might mitigate current reading challenges such as surface reading, quote mining, patch writing, and answer-getting dispositions. The advantages of teaching periodical textuality are numerous: this approach may dissuade student tendencies to reach for the interpretation most familiar to them or project their values without fully regarding an author's possible view or intent. From this more immersive reading experience, students can cultivate a problem-exploring disposition. These complex forms may additionally slow readers down and force them to read recursively. Reading through layers of *periodical textuality*, students may fill in gaps of their knowledge while making inferences about genre and purpose by looking for patterns, relationships, and common themes to become better acquainted with the rhetorical context and audience—a rhetorical reading enlivened by a textured access to the values of writers and readers from the past.

Scholes's seminal *Textual Power* (1985) and *English After the Fall: From Literature to Textuality* (2011) provide a lens to reenvision our teaching habits to ensure students "come into their own powers of textualization" by encouraging them to "read" the sociocultural contexts in which texts are produced—and consumed (Scholes 1985, 20). Textuality promotes reading practices in which knowledge is not merely passed from the professor to empty vessels. Rather than intimidating students with "our own superior textual production," Scholes envisioned a classroom in which students would become knowledge producers—an FYW concept and goal. The idea of *text* as a metaphor envisions our cultural world as a woven tapestry. The interwoven nature of the periodical—internally as a coherent form as well as an external web of connections—makes the epigraph that opens this chapter a useful reminder to teachers and students of the constructed-ness of these archives. The call to study the power of language and the effects of contexts is exigent, as it is easy to forget that today's information deluge is deliberately manufactured to influence readers' perceptions. In an increasingly hectic, accelerated world that privileges consumable soundbites, the stakes could not be higher for educators to teach the craft of unweaving. Periodicals comprise various types of threads, which, in essence, plait a unique tapestry—its own writing or kind of language. An interdisciplinary and dynamic reading of *periodical textuality* reveals the fine stitchwork and interstices of these intricate texts.

ACKNOWLEDGMENTS. I would like to thank my friends and colleagues for reviewing drafts and sharing their own classroom experiences teaching periodicals and promoting dynamic reading practices, including Keith Clavin, Mark Noonan, and, in particular, Mariette Ogg, for sharing her experiences using *The New Yorker*'s digital archives with her first-year writers.

REFERENCES

Armstrong, Sonya, and Mary Newman. 2011. "Teaching Textual Conversations: Intertextuality in the College Reading Classroom." *Journal of College Reading and Learning* 41 (2): 6–21.

Bean, John. 2011. *Engaging Ideas: The Professor's Guide to Integrating Writing, Critical Thinking, and Active Learning in the Classroom*. 2nd ed. San Francisco, CA: Jossey-Bass.

Beetham, Margaret. 1990. "Towards a Theory of the Periodical as a Publishing Genre." In *Investigating Victorian Journalism*, edited by Laurel Brake, Aled Jones, and Lionel Madden, 19–32. London: The MacMillan Press.

Brooker, Peter, and Andrew Thacker. 2009. "General Introduction." In *The Oxford Critical and Cultural History of Modernist Magazines*. Oxford: Oxford University Press.

Carr, Nicholas. 2011. *The Shallows: What the Internet Is Doing to Our Brains*. New York: W. W. Norton & Company.

Carillo, Ellen. 2009. "Making Reading Visible in the Classroom." *Currents in Teaching and Learning* 1 (2): 37–41.

Carillo, Ellen. 2017. "Preparing College-Level Readers to Define Reading as More than Mastery." In *Deep Reading*, edited by Patrick Sullivan, Harold Tinberg, and Sheridan Blau, 188–209. Urbana, IL: National Council of Teachers of English.

Churchill, Suzanne. 2008. "Modernists Periodicals and Pedagogy: An Experiment in Collaboration." In *Transatlantic Print Culture, 1880–1940: Emerging Media, Emerging Modernisms*, edited by Ann Ardis and Patrick Collier, 217–35. New York: Palgrave Macmillan.

Cole, Jean Lee. 2006. "History of the Book in the American Literature Classroom: On the Fly and On the Cheap." In *Teaching Bibliography, Textual Criticism, and Book History*, edited by Ann R. Hawkins, 58–64. London: Pickering & Chatto.

Council of Writing Program Administrators. 2014. "WPA Outcomes Statement for First-Year Composition (3.0)." http://wpacouncil.org/aws/CWPA/pt/sd/news_article/243055/_PARENT/layout_details/false.

Davis, Robert, and Mark Shadle. 2000. "'Building a Mystery': Alternative Research Writing and the Academic Act of Seeking." *College Composition and Communication* 51 (3): 417–46.

Delap, Lucy. 2000. "*The Freewoman*, Periodical Communities, and the Feminist Reading Public." *Princeton University Library Chronicle* 61: 234.

DiCenzo, Maria. 2015. "Remediating the Past: Doing 'Periodical Studies' in the Digital Era." *English Studies in Canada* 41 (1): 19–39.

Gaillet, Lynée. 2012a. "Archival Research in Rhetoric and Composition Studies: A Conversation with Lynée Lewis Gaillet." *Issues in Writing* 19 (1): 8.

Gaillet, Lynée. 2012b. "(Per)Forming Archival Research Methodologies." *College Composition and Communication* 64 (1): 35–58.

Haas, Christina, and Linda Flower. 1988. "Rhetorical Reading Strategies and the Construction of Meaning." *College Composition and Communication* 39 (2): 167–83.

Hayden, Wendy. 2017. "And Gladly Teach: The Archival Turn's Pedagogical Turn." *College English* 80 (2): 133–54.

Latham, Sean, and Robert Scholes. 2006. "The Rise of Periodical Studies." *PMLA* 121 (2): 517–31.

McGann, Jerome J. 1991. *The Textual Condition*. Princeton: Princeton University Press.

Modernist Journals Project (MJP). 2019. "Teaching Tools." https://modjourn.org/teaching-tools/.

Scholes, Robert. 1985. *Textual Power: Literary Theory and the Teaching of English*. New Haven, CT: Yale University Press.

Scholes, Robert. 2002. "The Transition to College Reading." *Pedagogy: Critical Approaches to Teaching Literature, Language, Composition, and Culture* 2 (2): 165–72.

Scholes, Robert. 2011. *English After the Fall: From Literature to Textuality*. Iowa City: University of Iowa Press.

Scholes, Robert, and Clifford Wulfman. 2010. "How to Study a Modern Magazine" In *Modernism in the Magazines: An Introduction*, 143–67. New Haven, CT: Yale University Press.

Sullivan, Patrick. 2017. "Introduction." In *Deep Reading: Teaching Reading in the Writing Classroom*. Urbana, IL: National Council of Teachers of English.

Wardle, Elizabeth. 2012. "Creative Repurposing for Expansive Learning: Considering 'Problem Exploring' and 'Answer-Getting' Dispositions in Individuals and Fields." *Composition Forum* 26. Accessed April 1, 2021. https://compositionforum.com/issue/26/creative-repurposing.php.

Wolf, Maryanne. 2006. *Proust and the Squid: The Story and Science of the Reading Brain*. New York: Harper Collins.

4
"LEARNING AND TEACHING"
A Heuristic for Prioritizing Teacher-Learning in English Education

Jessica Rivera-Mueller

In "Learning and Teaching," an article published in *Profession*, Scholes (2004, 123) argues that "[i]n the humanities, we learn in order to teach. It is as simple as that." In this statement and throughout his work, Scholes argues for the importance of ongoing teacher-learning. Teacher-learning is best conceptualized as an active process—rather than the knowledge or skills teachers acquire to teach—because teaching always occurs in a context. For secondary teachers, a range of stakeholders (including colleagues, administrators, students, parents/guardians, and legislators) shape the teaching context through their actions. Teacher-learning, then, is the process of making sense of a context and creating questions that propel the teacher into deeper understandings and improved practices.

Often the process of teacher-learning is prompted by conflict. As Gatti (2016, 39) explains, "[A]t its core, learning to teach is about confrontation. The preservice teacher must confront her prior experiences in school; her racial, linguistic, class, gender, and cultural identities; her beliefs about learning and development; and her grasp of her subject matter(s)." In this process, the conflicts teachers face can be conceptualized as "problems" to be worked out in some way. A teaching "problem" isn't necessarily something bad or something that's going wrong in the classroom; instead, it is something that the teacher wants to better understand or improve. From these problems, teachers craft the questions that drive their process for teacher-learning.

Because teachers' engagement with "teaching problems" provides the exigence for teacher-learning, preservice teachers' orientation toward "teaching problems" is critical for prioritizing teacher-learning. It is imperative that teachers have ways to critically analyze the values and assumptions that shape their understandings of the problems and how

DOI: 10.7330/9781646421190.c004

those understandings shape the questions that drive teacher-learning. For this reason, I find returning to the scholarship of Scholes so helpful. The two intellectual activities Scholes (2004) describes in "Learning and Teaching"—creating research and creating scholarship—provide a heuristic for discussing and engaging in the kind of intellectual work that is necessary for learning to teach in a secondary context. Drawing from Scholes's definitions of research and scholarship, the heuristic I propose is comprised of research-based problems and scholarship-based problems. Any question about teaching and learning can be conceptualized as a research-based or scholarship-based problem, so examining the distinction between these two ways of framing a problem serves as a valuable heuristic for discussing a wide range of teacher-learning.

In this chapter, I extend Scholes's work in "Learning and Teaching" by showing how his argument holds incredible relevance for the teacher educators who prepare today's secondary English teachers. Drawing from my practices as an English teacher educator, I propose that Scholes's argument offers language that can help teacher educators facilitate teacher-learning in English education and beyond. Toward that end, I begin by describing Scholes's argument and explaining how I have adapted his argument to create a heuristic for prioritizing teacher-learning. I then share an assignment I use in my Teaching Literature course to illustrate how this heuristic provides language to study the nature of teacher-learning, to pursue teacher-learning, and to identify conditions for teacher-learning. Finally, I close by reflecting upon the importance of this vision for teacher-learning.

CREATING A HEURISTIC FROM SCHOLES'S ARGUMENT IN "LEARNING AND TEACHING"

In "Learning and Teaching," Scholes (2004) challenges us to rethink how we conceptualize humanistic study. Scholes asserts that "many of our problems stem from our having accepted a misleading notion of what we do—of what we can do and what we should do—and this categorical error has led us into many of our other difficulties. Our fundamental error, as [he sees] it, comes from accepting the notion of 'research' as a part of our enterprise" (Scholes 2004, 119). His argument, much like the argument Emily J. Isaacs makes in her chapter in this volume, points to what can be lost when a discipline seeks disciplinary status. To restore the severed connection between teaching and teacher-learning, Scholes (2004) makes a distinction between the activities of research and scholarship. Scholes (2004, 120) defines research as an activity that "can be done in a field of study where there is a certain level of agreement about what the problems are and what methods can be used to solve them." Research, as conceptualized by Scholes (2004, 120), "is progressive; it involves invention or discovery of something new." He argues this kind of intellectual work is a good fit for the sciences because those fields meet the criteria of having defined problems and methods for solving those problems. In the humanities, though, Scholes believes "research has replaced learning" (2004, 119). And for Scholes, research is not equivalent to learning; instead, it "intervenes to disrupt the relation between learning and teaching that is proper to humanistic studies" (2004, 120). Scholarship, by contrast, is a notion that Scholes argues can restore this connection between teaching and learning. He explains that scholarship "is more about recovery than discovery. It is about understanding more clearly or more richly the meaning of texts or events from the past, including how we got to our present cultural situation" (2004, 123). He defines scholarship as "learning in the service of teaching" (2004, 123).

The two intellectual activities Scholes (2004) describes—creating research and creating scholarship—provide a heuristic for discussing and practicing the kind of intellectual work that is necessary for learning to teach in a secondary context. While Scholes's argument privileged the intellectual work of scholarship to bring heightened awareness to the value of teacher-learning, pairing these two activities together as a heuristic provides two ways for understanding and working with the "problems" teachers confront through their work with students. Drawing from Scholes's definitions, the heuristic I propose is comprised of research-based problems and scholarship-based problems. Research-based problems are discovery-based problems. They require teachers to figure out how to accomplish something specific. A teacher engaging in this kind of intellectual work relies upon the notions of teaching and learning that have already been worked out and applies the methods or searches for the methods to address problems based upon shared understandings. Rooted in Scholes's definition of research, this mode of teacher-learning is based in a shared understanding of what counts as an important problem in teaching and makes use of principles for teaching and learning that have been established to address such problems. Scholarship-based problems are recovery-based problems. They require teachers to uncover something deeper about the problem. Teachers engaging in this kind of intellectual work seek to understand the complexity of the problem. Rooted in Scholes's definition of scholarship, this mode of teacher-learning is based in a teacher's activity as a teacher-scholar, an activity shaped by a teacher's ability to place educational theory and practice in conversation and create deeper understandings of teaching and learning.

Both scholarship- and research-based problems are useful for teacher-learning. For example, action research, an activity in which classroom teachers gather and analyze data to study a question related to their teaching, is a form of teacher-learning that emerges from research-based problems. When a teacher's question is conceptualized as a research-based problem, the teacher-learning that emerges is progressive; it seeks to discover a new insight or approach to teaching and learning. This form of teacher-learning is often valued in secondary contexts, but we also need ways to discuss the kind of teacher-learning that happens when teachers seek to recover or uncover deeper understanding of teaching and learning. The Storri website sponsored by Teachers College at Columbia University is a good example of teacher-learning that is rooted in scholarship-based problems. On this site, teachers share their "wobble" stories, narratives that describe moments in teaching when their belief systems wobbled. According to the site, a wobble is something that compels teachers "to pay attention, to stop and think, to raise a question, to open [themselves] to other perspectives" (Storri n.d.). Through these stories, the site aims to "help others learn about the messiness of classrooms, the joy of learning, and the importance of drawing meaning from the moments that challenge us. By collecting these stories, [they] provide other angles on classrooms, ones that show the inter-workings between students and teachers" (Storri n.d.). Paired together, research-based problems and scholarship-based problems form a heuristic for discussing this important range of teacher-learning.

APPLYING THE HEURISTIC TO ESTABLISH A CONCEPTION OF TEACHER-LEARNING

To illustrate how the research-scholarship heuristic can enhance teacher education, I will share a project that I use in my Teaching Literature course. The project is a collaborative one that invites pairs of preservice teachers to study some aspect of teaching literature and design a unit of instruction based upon their learning. As part of the project, they also teach one of the lessons from their unit and reflect upon their delivery of the lesson. The central activities of the project—designing, delivering, and reflecting upon instruction—are common activities in teacher education, and the project's emphasis on students' own questions about teaching aligns with the work of other

English teacher educators who have been developing inquiry-oriented approaches to teacher education (Simon 2015; Staunton 2008; Fecho, Price, and Read 2004). However, applying the heuristic to these activities enhances students' experiences. With the heuristic, students are able to engage in teacher-learning *and* participate in meta-thinking that supports the development of a vision for teacher-learning. In particular, the research-scholarship heuristic provides language for studying the nature of teacher-learning, pursuing teacher-learning, and identifying conditions for teacher-learning.

The core pieces of the project position preservice teachers as ongoing learners, and the research-scholarship heuristic makes visible how the project offers a range of learning opportunities. As I'll illustrate below, the way students study their questions about teaching literature will relate to how they've framed their questions. By identifying their questions as either research-based or scholarship-based problems, preservice teachers can understand how they perceive their questions, which allows them to more purposefully discuss and investigate how their choices shape their learning. Ideally this intellectual work also enables preservice teachers to identify perspectives that may be missing from their own understandings. Framing a question as a research-based problem will lead to different ends than studying a question as a scholarship-based problem, but it is important that preservice teachers understand how *both* kinds of projects are valuable and important for teacher-learning.

When I introduce the project to preservice teachers, I describe it as an opportunity to study some aspect of teaching literature that will help them design a unit of instruction for a secondary class that they imagine teaching. I suggest that the unit could be about an issue (e.g., a literary lens, humor as a pedagogical tool, or student motivation); a topic (e.g., gender, science, ethics, or sports); or a particular writer, short story, group of poems, or form of literacy. The first step of the project involves selecting a question for study. I support this initial thinking by asking preservice teachers to compose a brief proposal for their project. In this proposal, I ask everyone to identify the following: their topic and question(s) about that topic, what they already know about the topic and the sources (primary and secondary) that inform their knowledge, what they would like to know, and the places (primary and secondary) they imagine themselves locating this information. In essence, I ask preservice teachers to identify the problems that they find most compelling to study. I then discuss the proposals with preservice teachers in individual conferences. These meetings allow me to gain a firm sense of everyone's thinking and passion, knowledge that I use to create the peer partnerships. When the partnerships have been assembled, the preservice teachers are ready to begin inquiring into their topics through the study of primary and secondary sources. The purpose of finding and studying these sources is to help preservice teachers study their questions and shape their aims for the unit.

To support preservice teachers' overall development of this project, I divide the project into three major phases: studying their questions, planning the unit, and planning the teaching demonstration. For each phase of the project, I use successive class meetings to model the work in the phase and allow for in-class work time. The first phase focuses on studying the identified problems. In my own modeling, I explain that this phase generally includes a recursive process of identifying the questions associated with the topic and narrowing/addressing those questions. With my own examples, I demonstrate how personal conversations and professional resources can shape our thinking on given questions. Using a talk-aloud strategy, I invite students to listen to my internal dialogue, illustrating the ideas that I find compelling, complicated, or (mis)aligned with my pedagogical beliefs. I end this class meeting by sharing the possibilities I'm considering for my unit. To model the creative and tentative part of this process, I always describe multiple possibilities. This phase of the project is one of the most important because I ask preservice teachers to create the aims for their units based upon their learning in this phase.

In the second phase, I help preservice teachers learn and practice curricular design by identifying the desired results for their unit, the acceptable evidence that will show students have achieved these results, and the plans for instruction that will help students achieve these results. Because I model this process, I show preservice teachers how I engage in this work, which often includes making maps and memos, sometimes even creating drawings to figure out how I want to shape the unit. I explain my preferences and choices to make visible how the process of designing instruction can be incredibly fun, creative, and challenging. By making my process visible, I aim to show preservice teachers that they will have their own way of creating a unit that helps students accomplish the aims that are rooted in the teacher-learning that they've arrived at through their exploration of their problems.

In the third phase, I model the teaching demonstration that I have created from my unit and the debriefing session that follows. I then discuss the steps that will help them prepare their own teaching demonstration. At the conclusion of the project, each team submits the following:

- a cover letter that clearly defines the unit's desired results—what secondary students should know, understand, and/or be able to do at the end of this unit—and explains how the daily lessons prepare students to create the acceptable evidence,
- a prompt for the acceptable evidence (e.g., essay prompt, class project, etc.),
- ten daily lesson plans that prepare secondary students to create the acceptable evidence,
- any additional supplementary materials that support the instruction (e.g., research guide for a research day in the media center), and
- an annotated bibliography that includes citations and summaries for the seven to ten sources informing the unit.

Individually, students also submit a reflection following the teaching demonstration that describes their collaborative process, their learning from the project, and their questions moving forward. This process of designing, delivering, and reflecting upon instruction is common across English methods courses. I propose, however, that the research-scholarship heuristic for teacher-learning that is inspired by Scholes can enhance such work in the three specific ways that are outlined below.

Understanding the Nature of Teacher-Learning

First, the research-scholarship heuristic offers preservice teachers a way to think about the ongoing nature of teacher-learning. While it's well-established that teachers need to engage in ongoing learning throughout their careers, it can be challenging to help preservice teachers come to terms with this reality. Often, preservice teachers feel compelled to completely master their content and/or the "right" way to teach. In my experience, these desires come from a good place; students simply want to be the best possible teachers at the outset of their careers. It can be overwhelming, then, for preservice teachers to confront the complexity of teaching and learning and the necessity of ongoing learning. Using the language of problems, though, to construct a conception of teacher-learning makes the process more manageable and imperative.

For example, framing the above project's questions as research-based and scholarship-based problems allows preservice teachers to see and appreciate how teacher-learning supports pedagogical aims in specific contexts. Rather than creating a unit about Shakespeare that would demonstrate full knowledge of his work and/or the "right" way to teach the subject, preservice teachers can use the research-scholarship heuristic's conception of teacher-learning as an activity of working out problems to consider what they need to learn for successful teaching in a specific context. Teacher-learning as a process of working out problems, rather than acquiring already-determined content or skills, highlights the critical role classroom teachers have in seeing and attending to the questions and concerns that matter for student learning. The research-scholarship heuristic makes visible how pedagogical possibilities emerge when teachers' questions drive their learning-to-teach process.

The research-scholarship heuristic also highlights the situated nature of teacher-learning. In the above project, for example, conversations about the influence of stakeholders on local educational practice can occur during the initial stage when preservice teachers are moving from identifying their topics to creating the questions that will guide their study. By identifying their questions as either research-based or scholarship-based problems, preservice teachers can understand how they and/or different stakeholders can perceive these questions differently. While some stakeholders may believe a question should be studied as a research-based problem, others may believe the question is best studied as a scholarship-based problem. These labels provide a way to discuss and negotiate these varying perspectives. Working in partnerships creates a good context for such conversations, as it offers an opportunity for reflexivity. Preservice teachers have to make countless decisions as they craft their units, and working with a partner provides moments when they can question and press each other to articulate how and why they have reached particular conclusions. These conclusions offer important glimpses into their pedagogical assumptions, beliefs, and values. This practice is important because secondary teachers rarely have complete control over their pedagogical decisions. Text selection and learning objectives are two common factors that can be determined for teachers. However, teachers can still engage in meaningful teacher-learning when they consider the problems they would like to work out in the context of these choices.

Pursuing Teacher-Learning

Locating conversations about teacher-learning in how teachers conceptualize teaching problems, as the research-scholarship heuristic encourages us to do, also reveals how and why teaching problems are not settled and offers language for pursuing teacher-learning. In making the distinction between research-based and scholarship-based problems, preservice teachers can see how to craft different kinds of questions to drive their learning process. For example, the above project begins with each partnership identifying the topic they are mutually invested in studying and articulating questions to study this topic. Using the research-scholarship heuristic allows preservice teachers to consider how their questions for exploring this topic might shift under the two different kinds of teacher-learning. The language allows them to talk through two distinct paths for teacher-learning. This is an important opportunity for expanding preservice teachers' framework for studying teaching problems. Much like Kelsey McNiff demonstrates in her chapter in this volume, students work within the "frameworks of knowledge" that they possess. To open new thinking, we often need to provide new frameworks. For example, if the team members view their topic as a research-based problem, they can form questions of application. In such instances, preservice teachers can begin this process by articulating the core problem their unit addresses, as well as their hopes for the unit. In their exploration of primary and secondary sources, their beliefs may grow, of course, but the primary aim for their teacher-learning will be figuring out how to apply these beliefs. If preservice teachers determine their topic is a scholarship-based problem, they can form questions about the nature of the problem. This path for exploration will result in more richly defined pedagogical beliefs that they can use to shape the aims for their unit. I have seen, for example, preservice teachers develop more robust understandings of assessment through this focus. In one project, a team of students designed a unit with *Divergent*, a dystopian science-fiction novel, as the central text to help their secondary students think more critically about the theme of assessment practices in their own lives. In doing so, the preservice teachers gained more robust understandings of how they want to shape assessment practices for their future students.

Throughout this process, the research-scholarship heuristic also allows preservice teachers to gain an up-close look at the connection between educational practice and theory. As a teacher educator, I often discuss the integral connection between theory and practice, arguing that all practices have theoretical underpinnings, and all theories have practical implications. I aim to help preservice teachers see how this dynamic is always present—even if it is not acknowledged. The research-scholarship heuristic, however, offers language that allows preservice teachers to feel these connections in their experiences. As preservice teachers move through the three phases of the above project, they have the opportunity to revisit the framing of their question and pay attention to the moments when it may shift between research-based inquiry and scholarship-based inquiry. Many preservice teachers consider this move as they transition from the activity of creating curriculum in the second phase of the project to delivering and reflecting upon their instruction in the third phase. Preservice teachers who first approach their question from a scholarly mindset sometimes find themselves moving to a research mindset and vice versa. With the help of the research-scholarship heuristic, preservice teachers can see why this range of teacher-learning is necessary. In particular, they can begin to see how both kinds of problems can work in conjunction with each other to help a teacher address *and* further clarify the pedagogical questions that they find most pressing.

Identifying Conditions for Teacher-Learning
Another useful outcome from using the research-scholarship heuristic is helping preservice teachers gain critical language for seeing and processing the range of conditions for teacher-learning they may encounter in their future teaching positions. In contexts where teaching is especially standardized, teacher-learning is rarely discussed. Instead, most of the emphasis is placed on what students learn and how data can support these findings. Student learning, of course, is extremely important. But the teacher-learning path is distinct and important, too. By making a distinction between teacher-learning and student-learning, as the research-scholarship heuristic allows us to do, we gain a fuller picture of what happens through the process of pedagogy.

Some of my favorite conversations from the above project focus on these questions. These conversations usually occur as preservice teachers move from the first to the second phase of the project. In this moment, preservice teachers are crafting the desired results or learning goals for their unit. Based upon these choices, preservice teachers design their assessment and daily instruction. This process is established to help preservice teachers practice what is known as backward curricular design, an approach that asks teachers to create their goals and assessments before planning daily instruction. The approach stresses the importance of planning the assessments first to ensure that the daily lessons purposefully help students achieve the stated aims. In practicing this process, many preservice teachers discover that they want to learn how to teach toward aims that can't easily be measured. Aims such as a greater appreciation for the subject, character development, or citizenship traits aren't easily measured or visible in the course of a semester or year, let alone a unit. Preservice teachers wonder, then, how they can prioritize these important aims in the context of creating observable learning goals. The research-scholarship heuristic offers an answer by helping preservice teachers see how student-learning and teacher-learning are distinct activities. Many times, these activities become conflated, and we can lose sight of teacher-learning. While some questions can easily fit within a narrow focus on student-learning, other questions cannot. As a result, the kinds of activities teachers participate in to sponsor student-learning (e.g., creating curricular maps, data analysis reports, or daily lesson plans) may not help teachers pursue the kinds of questions that are most important for their learning. Teacher-learning, in these instances, may require different or additional kinds of professional engagement than the ones that are required by the teachers' school districts. For example, teachers may find that they want to form a book club to study an important issue with colleagues. Because the research-scholarship heuristic focuses on teacher-learning, preservice teachers can better see work that might otherwise remain invisible. Ideally, preservice teachers can also understand how both student- and teacher-learning can be distinct and occur simultaneously.

The research-scholarship heuristic can also make visible the extent to which teacher-learning may or may not be supported in an institutional context. Because the research-scholarship heuristic positions preservice teachers to make choices about how a problem is conceptualized, preservice teachers can understand how opportunities for teacher-learning are erased when teachers are excluded from this process. In these environments, teachers are technicians, rather than learners, because their job is to teach in sanctioned and (often) standardized ways. The pedagogical aims and practices have already been worked out and determined by someone other than the teacher. According to this logic, teachers do not need ongoing learning because they are simply conduits for instruction. Teachers may require training to become updated on the newest approach, but teachers' own pedagogical questions do not have a place within this paradigm. The foundational premise of the research-scholarship heuristic—that teachers are decision-makers who identify and study teaching problems—provides a clear sense of what is missing in these highly technocratic environments. This critical understanding of teacher-learning can also help preservice teachers distinguish "professional development" from "professional learning," as Allison Skerrett, Amber Washington, and Thea Williamson (2018, 117) encourage us to do in arguing the following: "We do not believe there exists an ultimate binary between professional development, such as opportunities offered by districts and schools, and professional learning opportunities outside these school-sanctioned engagements that teachers themselves create or pursue. We believe that professional development from schools and districts, depending on how they are designed, their content, organization, and forms of engagement offered to teachers, can also be generative sites for teacher learning." The distinction the authors make highlights the tension that can occur between the programs, structures, or activities that are established—and often required—by school districts to help teachers grow as professionals and the actual process of teacher-learning, which further emphasizes the need to construct robust visions for teacher-learning in English education.

CONSTRUCTING A VISION FOR TEACHER-LEARNING IN ENGLISH EDUCATION

Understandings of and expectations for teacher-learning vary across contexts, so it is important that preservice teachers have an opportunity to develop a strong conception of teacher-learning. Most important, preservice teachers need to see their own role in framing the problems that will drive their learning-to-teach process. Therefore, constructing a vision for teacher-learning that encompasses both research-based and scholarship-based problems can help preservice teachers productively engage with the situations that they will inevitably encounter and wish to address. Some of those situations will be ones that are recognizable in the field of education and can be addressed with accepted notions and practices. Other situations, however, will require teachers to push on conventional understandings in order to push the field's notions and practices further.

This vision for teacher-learning is especially important in contexts that operate with limiting notions of teacher-learning. When the complex nature of teaching is oversimplified, teacher-learning can also be minimized. Teachers have fewer opportunities to pose and pursue their own questions about teaching and learning, ones that are informed by their own expertise and passion. As Sieben and Johnson (2018, 109) note, too often the process of professional development for secondary teachers in schools involves top-down structures where "teachers' voices and goals are decidedly absent." In teacher education, then, it is important to offer a robust vision for teacher-learning that teachers can pursue throughout their careers.

REFERENCES

Fecho, Bob, Kim Price, and Chris Read. 2004. "From Tununakto Beaufort: Taking a Critical Inquiry Stance as a First Year Teacher." *English Education* 36 (4): 263–88.

Gatti, Lauren. 2016. *Toward a Framework of Resources for Learning to Teach: Rethinking US Teacher Preparation.* New York: Palgrave Macmillan.

Scholes, Robert. 2004. "Learning and Teaching." *Profession* 118–27.

Sieben, Nicole, and Lindy Johnson. 2018. "Professional Development Pathways through Social Justice Frameworks." *English Education* 50 (2): 108–15.

Simon, Rob. 2015. "'I'm Fighting My Fight, and I'm not Alone Anymore': The Influence of Communities of Inquiry." *English Education* 48 (1): 41–71.

Skerrett, Allison, Amber Washington, and Thea Williamson. 2018. "Generative Principles for Professional Learning for Equity-Oriented Urban English Teachers." *English Education* 50 (2): 117–46.

Staunton, John. 2008. *Deranging English/Education: Teacher Inquiry, Literacy Studies, and Hybrid Visions of "English" for 21st Century Schools.* Urbana, IL: NCTE.

Storri. n.d. Accessed December 1, 2018. https://edblogs.columbia.edu/storri/.

5
EXCERPT FROM "A FORTUNATE FALL?"
The Rise and Fall of English

Robert Scholes

> *Eftsoon so too will our own sphoenix spark spirt his spyre and sunward stride the rampant flambe. Ay, already the sombrer opacities of the gloom are sphanished! Brave footsore Haun! Work your progress! Hold to! Now! Win out, ye divil ye! The silent cock shall crow at last. The west shall shake the east awake. Walk while ye have the night for morn, lightbreakfastbringer, morroweth whereon every past shall full fost sleep. Amain.*
>
> —Joyce, *Finnegans Wake*

The concept of a fortunate fall, the *felix culpa* of Medieval Christian thought, in which the original sin of Adam and Eve was seen as fortunate because it led to the Redeemer, was modernized by James Joyce early in *Finnegans Wake* as a *faenix culprit* (23), a guilty figure rising like a phoenix from the ashes of its funeral pyre, perpetually, without redemption, like Finnegan at his wake, Finn again and again. In the later passage from the [*sic*] same book quoted as the epigraph to this chapter, the phoenix has metamorphosed into a Westernized Sphinx, a version of Hegel's Germanic culture, contaminated, perhaps, by Nietzsche's blond beast (Haun/Hun), that has triumphed over the dark Mediterranean power of Spain (sombrer . . . sphanished) in the name of progress, and is now poised, in its own darkness, "to shake the east awake." We could continue unpacking the layers of meaning in this text—this creature of darkness (Haun, divil) seems to be impregnating the east with his phallic church spires and enlisting it into his footsore progress—but my intention here is not to explicate Joyce's text but to use his splendid language as a way of thinking about the problem of English studies at the present time. For the field of English, as I have tried to demonstrate in earlier chapters, has been powerfully connected both to the Hegelian concept of history as a progress toward absolute knowledge and to the imperial projects of England and the United States. Which means that the awakening of the East—and the South—which is also called multiculturalism, may cause English as we have known it to be "sphanished" as well.

As I see it, the many possible fates of English can be clarified by seeing them in terms of two possible directions in which English as a field of study might go. One of them came up in a conversation I had recently with a graduate student who remembered a former teacher saying, "English may go the way of Classics—and it can't happen soon enough." Which means, as I interpret it, that the speaker, and others of his persuasion, would like to see English as a small, elite field of study, devoted to the past, and without responsibilities for general education or the teaching of writing. No "service courses," no uninterested students fulfilling requirements, just dedicated scholars and students who want to emulate them in pursuit of a humanistic education that is its own reward. One can see the beauty of it, for those privileged enough to partake of such intellectual pleasures, but Tennyson's "Lotos-Eaters" come to mind. (Even Tennyson has his intellectual uses—I should be the last to deny it. My afternoons spent mooning over his pages were not entirely wasted.) Still, if the field of English were to become such an elite preserve, much of the work of English would still remain to be done—and perhaps that foenix culprit Rhetoric would arise again to undertake the work.

The second direction, the other way to go, would be for English faculties to rethink their enterprise as a discipline—that is, to construct a discipline out of what has been merely a field, organized, like a burial ground, around the textual tombs of the great dead, with particular acolytes pronouncing elegies over the most prominent monuments. I shall not pursue this metaphor, which was explored so richly in the context of French literary study by Jean-Paul Sartre half a century ago (Sartre, 22–28), except to say that I am not going to propose that we desecrate the tombs and liquidate the elegists. If we can reconstruct this field as a productive discipline, there will be places aplenty for the great English texts—but not for monuments, because the texts that still speak to us are not dead. The question is, how can we begin, in the midst of our difficulties and squabbles, to reconstruct our field as a discipline. My answer, to put it in grossly oversimplified form, is to replace the canon of texts with a canon of methods—to put a modern equivalent of the medieval trivium at the center of an English education. I have already presented this "trivial proposal" in chapter 4 [of *The Rise and Fall of English*], in terms of what English departments might contribute to general education, but I also would like it understood that such a core of courses would make a superb preparation for a concentration or major in the discipline of English. In this, my final chapter, I will try to clarify what I mean by reorienting English from a field to a discipline, and then I will address some of the practical problems faced by English departments at the present time.

ENGLISH AS A DISCIPLINE

As a field of study in the United States, English has been organized around the literary history of England and America. Other Anglophone literatures—even Canadian—have held, at best, a peripheral place in this organization. And somewhere near the center, but almost obscured now, lies a philological organization of the field in terms of the history of the English language, from the Anglo-Saxon of the first Germanic invaders of the British Isles, through the Middle English that developed from a mixture of Anglo-Saxon and Norman French after 1066, to the more modern modes of the language, including the one canonized as the "American Language" by H. L. Mencken in the first half of the twentieth century. In practice the field is organized in the form of survey courses—usually separate surveys of British and American literature—arranged chronologically, plus courses in literary periods or major authors, often supported by requirements for English majors to study texts from earlier periods. The ideal English major emerges from this program of study in possession of a thin but clear sense of English and American literary history as a narrative (the Story of English), with some periodizing concepts (Renaissance, Romanticism, and so on), and with a somewhat deeper knowledge of a few authors and texts. The average English major graduates with an even thinner and muddier command of this narrative: that "little learning" which Alexander Pope believed was worse than none.

English majors these days all learn some critical concepts and perhaps a bit of literary theory, but if you ask them what makes any particular text a work of "literature," you will rarely get a satisfactory response. If it's in the courses, it's literature, if not, not—which is pretty much the way Roland Barthes dealt with this question some decades ago. English majors generally write better than other students, and one hopes that their studies had something to do with this. There is no reason to think it didn't, but most English majors chose the field because reading and writing came easily to them in the first place. I am suggesting that the way our present configuration of the English curriculum plays out in practice is discouraging, even dispiriting. English departments are not doing the old job very well, leaving aside the question of whether it is the right job to be doing. When I have seen the job done about as well as possible, as in the old English Semester at the University of Iowa, it has left me feeling that we might have given our students something more worthy of the splendid efforts they had made. My response to this feeling has been almost three decades spent trying to envision the old field of English reconstructed as a discipline of textuality.

What I mean by a discipline of textuality has been adumbrated in the previous chapters and assignments, but now is the time to organize those scattered glimpses into something more systematic. I would like this discussion to be practical enough for actual attempts to embody it in programs, yet not so specific as to suggest that there is only one right way to undertake the project. To that end, rather than speaking in terms of courses and reading lists, I will present the elements of the discipline under four distinct though overlapping headings: theory, history, production, and consumption. These may well be studied in courses that emphasize one or another, but they can never be isolated, one from the other. My basic assumption here is that these four elements of textuality deserve roughly equal weight in the organization of the discipline, though I see theory as constituting the disciplinary core.

Theory

By theory I mean a canon of methods to be used in studying the other three aspects of textuality: how to situate a text (history), how to compose one (production), and how to read one (consumption). Theory, which has existed since ancient times, now consists of grammar, rhetoric, dialectic, poetics, hermeneutics, semiotics, grammatology, and other modes of understanding textuality. If English is to be a discipline, theory must be at the center of our teaching. We learned—or should have learned—something like this from Northrop Frye more than forty years ago, and I must acknowledge, here as elsewhere, my great debt to him. But for Frye, theory was still in the service of an aesthetic project, a form of poetics. My project is more rhetorical, with textuality, rather than literature, as its principal object. And I have argued, here as elsewhere, that this shift is crucial to any reconstruction of the discipline. Putting theory at the center of our discipline, however—even theories of textuality—does not mean treating works of theory as we are used to treating literary texts. It would be easy to turn the study of theory into a set of Great Theories, Great Theoreticians,

Great Books all over again—and this is precisely what has happened in many schools that now require a course in "literary theory." This, in my judgment, is a mistake. Even worse, it is just the kind of mistake that we English teachers can hardly help but make, and it leads to the kind of mistake that students can hardly help but make. We put a "theory" course in the curriculum. The students "take" the course. Been there, done that, on to the next course. We do this because we have been thoroughly indoctrinated in "coverage" as the organizational basis of our field. To change English from a field to a discipline, we shall have to change the way we think at a fundamental level. This can only be painful, especially at first.

A canon of methods, unlike a set of texts, must be conceived in terms of competence. There is no point in introducing students to the writing of Jacques Derrida, for example, if they finish their study unable to deconstruct a text and unaware of the strengths—and the limitations—of deconstruction as a way of reading and writing. A canon of methods must be organized in terms of the enhanced capabilities that students will take away from their studies. The end of such studies should be what I have called, in another context, textual power. Now, any attempt to organize a curriculum around students and their abilities is likely, at the present time, to run into criticism on the grounds that they are being taught skills instead of being given the knowledge that they need. This line of argument is familiar to most of us as an aspect of E. D. Hirsch's effort to promote a national curriculum in this country. There are, I believe, some strong arguments to be made for a national curriculum, though my curriculum would be different from Hirsch's. The opposition between skill and knowledge, however, is a red herring. And it leads to Hirsch's greatest error, the equation of coverage with knowledge. Knowledge that is not usable and regularly used is lost. The knowledge that we retain is the knowledge that we can and do employ. There is an important educational principle in the old saw about things that go in one ear and out the other. What we take in through our eyes and ears must emerge from our hands and mouths if we are to hold on to it. It is a curious property of information that we keep it only if we give it away. Material "covered" in classrooms and not incorporated into the communicative lives of students simply fades away.

A canon of methods, then, must be presented to students in the form of intellectual tools that they can use effectively. I outlined a set of basic courses in textual methods in chapter 4, in the form of a new trivium, suitable for the general education of all students. Such a set of courses—or some other set that deals with the modes of thought and expression involved in those courses—would serve very well as the intellectual basis of English as a discipline.

With this kind of general education behind them, students specializing in English would already be well on their way toward mastering a canon of methods when they begin their more specialized work. If such a set of general education courses cannot be instituted—for whatever reasons—an English department could easily establish some version of them as part of its own core of study. This, at any rate, is one illustration of what I mean by putting theory and a canon of methods at the center of the discipline. Additional courses with more particular topics can easily be imagined as part of the full panoply of courses in methods offered within the discipline. The aim should be to open up possibilities, to empower. The graduates of English programs should have found the method or methods that work best for them as readers and writers—and they should know the virtues and the limitations of their preferred critical and interpretive methods. In practice, this means a reorientation of courses around the work of students, with a better balance between textual consumption and production. It is not what is covered that counts but what is learned. It is not what students have been told that matters but what they remember and what they can do. The New Critics understood this, as did their great opponent, Northrop Frye. Which brings me to another important point about literary theory and a canon of methods.

As I pointed out in chapters 2 and 4, when our culture lost its faith in the historicism of Hegel—and that of Marx—we were left open to the domination of fashion. That is, if human history is not an ordained or determined progress toward truth and freedom, or toward a classless society, it can easily be seen as an essentially meaningless succession of cultural and political styles. If human existence is not a progressive dialectic organized by the Absolute (Hegel) or History (Marx), then it is all too easy to see it in terms of cultural relativism or even solipsism. In the great world of public affairs, this leads to the aggressive construction of false absolutes, whether religions or nations, along with the awareness that power settles all questions. The victors write history. The vanquished, if they are lucky, read it. In the little world of English departments, the failure of historicism leads, on the one hand, to teaching that is dangerously close to political indoctrination and, on the other, to "research" that is mainly an attempt to write about literary works in currently fashionable modes of analysis. Both of these problems are serious and complicated. They are also closely related. Let us try to trace their interrelation.

Modern culture—that culture in which we live and learn and teach—is characterized by the loss of faith in historicism and, along with that, a loss of faith in universal values of all sorts. In literary studies, this means that the idea of literature itself, as a kind of text found with common features in all human cultures, can no longer be taken for granted. Cleanth Brooks saw the problem fifty years ago and discussed it in a brilliant essay appended to *The Well-Wrought Urn* ("Criticism, History, and Critical Relativism," 215–51), in which he argued for a poetical quality that transcends the social and historical specificity of particular times and places. Northrop Frye, also, who was completely at odds with Brooks on the subject of whether taste is a part of literary criticism or a social epiphenomenon, nevertheless believed in a universal "order of words" and in the recurrence of archetypes and generic structures across languages and cultures. Their views, and others like them, are now dismissed out of hand by many teachers of English—especially among the younger generation of teachers. At the same time there are plenty of English teachers, of my generation but also younger, who still presuppose the special status of literature and the universality of verbal art.

As you know, if you have been with me through these pages, I cannot accept uncritically the idea of literature as a uniquely privileged form of transcendental textuality. On the other hand, I believe that what Roman Jakobson and other structuralists call literariness is indeed a pervasive if not universal feature of verbal texts, found in epic poems and bumper stickers, jokes and tragic drama, films and dreams, conversation and declamation, East and West, North and South. For the study of theory in a discipline called English, this situation means that the question of universal literary values should be very squarely on the table, with the stakes clearly delineated. Understanding the category of literature as a problem—and a problem with a history—is part of what every serious student of English should know.

By going back to Brooks and Frye, I mean to make another point about the way literary study is currently being conducted. The operation of critical fashions works to make older modes of theory and analysis not simply old but obsolete. Fashion works by replacing and forgetting. The historicist dialectic works by negating, preserving, and reconstructing, so that the new always contains traces of the past—which spares us from repeating it, or, as Marx suggested, causes us to repeat tragedy as farce. Fashion, in criticism as in clothing, forgets and repeats, endlessly and aimlessly. What we need, if the old absolute guarantees of the historical dialectic are no longer believable, is a way of taking responsibility for the dialectic ourselves, replacing the endless cycles of fashion with a possible progress for which human beings must take responsibility. If we no longer find it possible to believe in Truth, we must nevertheless find our way to truthfulness, which means both being honest about what we are doing and recognizing that the truths of the past should not be thrown out like garbage or turned over to some intellectual Salvation Army but rather kept until they can be renewed or replaced by something more truthful. To put this in simple and concrete terms, it means that theory, as our disciplinary core, must be careful about preserving its own past to avoid repeating it, whether as fashion or as farce. If, as I believe is the case, the New Critics said some important and durable things about poetry, we had better ensure that these things are not lost to our students and ourselves. And the same holds true for other advances in theory made by the Aristotelians of Chicago, the formalists of Petersburg, the structuralists of Prague, and so on. If we must be "post"-structuralist, it is up to us to make sure that we are dialectically—rather than merely fashionably—"post."

We need to recover, then, something of the historicist dialectic, even if we must play the directive role ourselves in the absence of the Absolute. But what about the replacement of the transcendental and literary in our classrooms by the political? This is a direct result of an awareness that not only history but literature as well is mainly written by the victors and the dominators or those who seek their favor, and this is true in the polite world of letters as well as in the larger world of political conquest. As one of Jane Austen's heroines so graciously says to a man who is denigrating the intelligence and achievements of women, "The pen has been in your hands." Indeed it has, and when pens came to be more generously distributed the podium was still closely guarded—which has made the scene of various struggles for representation shift from the places of publication to such places of interpretation as the classroom. Every English department in the United States is now in some phase of a struggle over how "minority" literatures in English—ethnic American, postcolonial, gay/lesbian—are to be represented in the curriculum and who, if anyone, is to teach them. One result of this struggle has been the development of courses in specialized literature taught by specialized faculty to specialized students. In such courses passions often run high. The Cuban-American community, to take just one example, is deeply divided on certain issues. But are they "literary" issues?

In a curriculum oriented to English literary history, such courses remain marginalized, and their proliferation is seen as a drain on the basic mission of covering the masterpieces of British and American literature. In a curriculum oriented to English textuality, however, such courses would have a vital function. What better place to apply and test modes of reading and writing than among texts that stir the passions? And what better way of refining those passions and guiding them into productive channels than the analytical discipline of textual theory? As a discipline, English needs both the cool rigor of theory and a passionate commitment to particular texts and ideas. Even as individual readers, we need them both. The political enters the study of English primarily through questions of representation: who is represented, who does the representing, who is object, who is subject—and how do these representations connect to the values of groups, communities, classes, tribes, sects, and nations? This happens, now, because in our culture people are aware that representation is an issue. This is not some aberration of the schools. It is the operation within them of the forces that permeate our whole culture. Eliminating the political is the fond hope of those nostalgic for the cultural homogeneity of Billy Phelps's classroom. But we cannot do it, now, and still be responsible educators. Responsibility here must take the form of establishing a disciplinary framework strong enough to allow the political full play in the study of textuality. By being responsible in this way, we will not suppress the power and beauty of language that have always been our concern. We will simply resituate them in a more rhetorical and less literary discipline of thought and study.

The political in the classroom, of course, sometimes takes the form of advocacy by teachers that can be offensive, if not repressive. This is by no means as widespread as certain critics of the academy have claimed that it is. On the other hand, it should not be surprising that ill-paid part-time teachers and graduate students facing dubious futures might hold political views different from those of the wealthy and powerful who sit on the governing bodies of colleges and universities. About this situation, which is real enough, I have two things to say. One, which I would address to those in power and those concerned about possible leftist indoctrination, is this: Don't worry. As the example of Althusser in Assignment 2 demonstrates so clearly, what students learn from teachers has more to do with how they teach than with what they teach. If indoctrination in schools really worked, Soviet-style communism would still prevail in Eastern Europe. But it doesn't. Which does not mean that bad teaching should be tolerated. Still, I would rather have my children educated by smart, caring people whose political values are different from mine than by dolts who agree with me politically. Finally, one must realize that the most oppressive indoctrination often results in the most powerful resistance.

The second thing I have to say on this question is addressed to those involved in the discipline of English. There is plenty of room for advocacy in this discipline, but no room at all for indoctrination. A discipline for which rhetoric is a central concern must be a discipline in which arguments on varying sides of important issues are admitted and considered—with one exception. If tolerance and a fair hearing for different views are at the core of the discipline, then arguments against tolerance and fairness are out of order and cannot be tolerated. Though I admit that one can never be absolutely impartial or perfectly just, I still believe, with C. S. Lewis, in the honest examiner who can give high marks to a strong argument, even while disagreeing with the conclusions. Now, more than ever, the graduates of our schools and colleges will live in worlds different from those in which they were born and went to school. A discipline called English must help them prepare for unknown conditions. The best preparation we can give our students will be the highest level of competence as readers and writers, producers and consumers of the various texts they will encounter. Tolerant, skeptical, interested in the truthfulness of a text and in the pleasure it may offer—this is the kind of graduate I believe we should be trying to produce. But what of learning, what of the past, what about history? What, indeed?

History

As I have suggested, the present structuring of English around the literary history of England and America is both loose and ineffective. My suggestion here is that the discipline of English be organized differently and, at the same time, that history be attended to more seriously and effectively within the discipline. Students, it is widely agreed, know less about both history and geography (that forgotten discipline) than they used to know. From the point of view of English, history is necessary in order to situate works in the cultural contexts that originally shaped their forms and their meanings. Historical (and geographical) knowledge is necessary for the reading or consumption of texts from other times and places—and all of English, as opposed to American, literature is now foreign in this sense. But literary history is also necessary for reading modern and contemporary works. To take two of the clearest and strongest examples of this, Virginia Woolf's *Orlando* is barely intelligible and scarcely enjoyable for a reader who can't follow Orlando's progress through English culture from the Renaissance to modern times; and "The Oxen of the Sun" chapter in Joyce's *Ulysses* requires knowledge of an even greater collection of English prose styles for anything approaching full comprehension and appreciation. Joyce's book, of course, demands a wide knowledge of popular culture as well. Even such recent American works as Pynchon's *Gravity's Rainbow* demand historical knowledge for competent reading.

History, then, both social and literary, has to be part of a discipline called English. To this I would add that the histories of the other arts—especially works composed, exhibited, or performed in England and America, or influential on Anglophone writers—have something to contribute here. We thus approach a paradox if not a downright contradiction. How can we actually get more and better historical study into the curriculum while reconstructing the discipline around theory rather than literary history? The question is more than fair: it is crucial. My answer, though not simple, will be as clear as I can make it. First of all, to get serious about history means insisting that students concentrating in English take a responsible set of courses in the related historical disciplines: political history, intellectual history, art history, music history, history of science and technology, taught by faculty in those disciplines. This will undoubtedly mean a larger set of requirements for the major, though not more courses taught by the English department. This, in itself, would be a healthy counterstroke to the inclination of students to multiply the number of their majors, so that they finish with more credentials but with less learning and less usable knowledge. That is, they finish without a disciplined knowledge of any field of study. An English major with serious external requirements would make a genuine contribution to the reversal of the trend toward a "shopping mall curriculum"—a course of study without focus or concentration.

The idea is simple. Students should be free to choose their specializations. But that choice should represent a commitment to orienting their education around their chosen discipline. That is, instead of fulfilling in a halfhearted way an arbitrary set of "distribution requirements," students might satisfy the proper concern about the breadth of their education by a set of courses in various fields oriented to their major commitment—and given coherence by that orientation. We do so many things backward in education. We are always asking students to get certain requirements out of the way *before* they do something else. What I am suggesting is that the *need*—and, if possible, the desire—for certain kinds of knowledge be established in the minds of students before they begin to acquire it. In the present case, I would say, "Choose your area of interest and then get the broad educational background that will support your specialized study." As members of a discipline, an English faculty should be able to insist that students take a configuration of courses in other disciplines that will allow them to attain the competence and confidence that they seldom achieve at present. Obviously, this sort of thing will have to be negotiated with administrations and other faculties—but the results are bound to justify the trouble. And it is clear that what we are doing now is not good enough.

The second step in getting serious about the historical side of English as a discipline means rethinking the way history is approached within the English curriculum. And here I wish to propose, once again, reversing the way we have done things in the past. Thinking about the place of history within the English curriculum must begin by recognizing that history itself has not stopped during the two centuries in which English moved from the margins of humanistic education to near the center of it. In these centuries, developments in printing techniques, along with the invention of photography, film, and television, have resulted in a similar move by popular culture from the oral enclaves of the "folk" to the center of modern culture. It is this history, and the changes it has worked within the more traditional forms of textual production, that must organize the historical dimension of English studies. I am saying—insisting, if you like—that the old survey courses, which begin at the beginning and follow a narrow line of "masterpieces" until the end, no longer serve their purpose. It is not simply that the line is too narrow, though it is, but that this material does not reach students effectively because they do not know why they need it. I would go further. In many cases, it is not what they need most.

This is a complicated matter. I ask your patience while I try to address some of the complications. First of all, we must admit that there is no good argument against any kind of knowledge. Is it good to know *The Faerie Queene*? You bet it is—much better to know it than not to know it. It is better to know all six books, and the two Mutabilitie Cantos as well—not to mention Spenser's shorter poems, his role in the subjection of Ireland, his awareness of Italian models, and so on—than just to know Book One. But a curriculum is always a trade-off between knowledge and time. The question posed by every curriculum is "What knowledge is most crucial for students to have at this point in their education, and how much of that knowledge can they really acquire in the time and format available?" Both aspects of this question are important. That is, (1) what do students most need, and when are they readiest to learn it? and (2) how much of what they need can they be expected to learn in any given course or set of courses?

The historical knowledge that students of the discipline of English need the most is an understanding of the cultural changes that have taken place during the past two centuries, the centuries in which the modern media arose and came to dominate the cultures of the world. Such a knowledge, I am convinced, would enable students to discover that developments of great importance had preceded these two centuries, and would give them both motivation and direction in seeking out courses that would answer to their desire to understand the modern world more fully. Let me be as clear as I can be about this point. I think that the historical goal of English as a discipline should begin and end with where we—our students and ourselves—are now. What are the texts, the events, the ideas, and the forces that have made our present world and continue making it every day? How are we to understand this world—and which texts can tell us the most about it or currently have the most to do with shaping it? These are the questions that must be asked at the beginning of our historical inquiry and continue to be heard throughout that inquiry.

To put it simply, we must begin where we are, at the end, and start asking how we got here. In terms of a curriculum to sustain the historical dimension of the discipline of English, this means that most introductory courses should not be literary surveys that start at the "beginning" but rather courses in the culture of the modern period that accommodate the rise of the new media and situate traditional literary works among the texts of these upstart media. Beyond this I would like to see historical options for students in the form of courses that seek to connect earlier times and texts to our modern situation. At the level of ideas and values, what we think of as modern culture emerged from a struggle between Enlightenment notions of individual freedom and rationality, on the one hand, and challenges to those notions by the Romantic poets and by thinkers like Nietzsche and Freud, on the other. A course that explores this process, through a range of texts from the eighteenth to the twentieth century, can be very appealing to students who are committed to understanding modern culture and have some grounding in that culture from their introductory courses. I have personally taught such courses, including one that traced the rise and fall of aestheticism from the first uses of the term in the eighteenth century to modern portraits of artists in literature and other media, and I have found the subject matter, if well arranged, to be so powerfully engaging as to triumph over the most indifferent instruction.

The desire to learn is a fundamental human characteristic. Given half a chance, students take to historical learning avidly and gratefully. But our schools often manage to discourage such desires by courses that are poorly conceived, leading to knowledge that does not seem either interesting or useful. We can do better, and do so easily, if we will only drop a few preconceptions, like the need to cover everything and to start all historical studies at the earliest possible moment. We will also, of course, need to stop arranging syllabi of masterpieces like ducks in a row and start designing courses around topics and questions that connect the past to our present cultural situation.

Production

This is the part of English that is usually put beyond the pale (as "creative" writing) or down in the dungeon (as "composition"). Yet just the other day I sat in a room full of English professors and heard them complaining about the writing of their students. As I hope I made clear in chapter 1, this is not a new complaint. What was most dispiriting about the conversation I attended, however, was that it seemed to presuppose writing to be a mere tool, something students ought to have picked up along the way. This is, to put it as mildly as my indignation will let me, not helpful. The ability to write well in a range of expressive modes ought to be a major and explicit goal of any discipline called English. This means that courses in which writing is a central concern should be given a serious place in the English curriculum—and that the writing of students should be given serious attention in every English course. In the standard English major, neither of these conditions prevails in the actual practice of teachers, whatever the departmental literature may claim to be the case. Most departments, however, would not even claim that they accept writing courses as the equal of reading courses in their curricula, because reading is actually called literature, while writing is just writing.

The way the invidious binary literature/composition plays out in English departments has been the object of my attention in an earlier book (*Textual Power*, chapter 1), so I will not go over that ground in any detail here. The key to solving the problem, however, is in the recognition that what the structuralists call literariness is a part of ordinary language and, in particular, is visible in most good writing. The condition I described in chapter 1 of this book, in which students studied orations in order to become orators, cannot be repeated on the grand scale of contemporary education, no doubt, but it can still serve us as a useful model. Better reading and better writing go hand in hand. One of the uses of the best writers from the past (not the only one, but one) is that they provide models of syntactic and semantic possibilities. From Hooker, Donne, Swift, Johnson, Austen, Pater, Woolf, and Joyce we can learn something about life, to be sure, but we can also learn a lot about the possibilities of English prose. Students who are encouraged not only to read the major texts of the past but to pastiche and parody their styles will do a better job of getting inside the heads of those writers, and they will themselves become better writers because they have done so.

We are living, as some of our most acute thinkers keep reminding us, in an age of parody and pastiche. What is often called postmodernism is cultural production in which appropriation of the past plays a major part. Think of a production, now available on video, of Igor Stravinsky's modern opera *The Rake's Progress*, in which the narrative is derived from a sequence of engravings by the eighteenth-century English artist William Hogarth, presented in a production using a stunning visual setting designed by the contemporary painter David Hockney, with a libretto in which the modern poet W. H. Auden pastiches neoclassical writing even as Stravinsky pastiches the musical styles of Handel and Mozart. In an age like ours, pastiche and parody are the natural way into our cultural heritage. We should make better use of this route in making this heritage available to our students.

Production, in this age, must also mean film, video, and digital composition, for all of these use the verbal language as well as the languages of images and tones. An English department cannot do everything, of course, but literary study that cuts itself off from the performing and media arts risks going the way of classics. It was not a mistake for the rhetoric department at Berkeley to incorporate the study of film and television. To such departments the future will belong—or to English departments wise enough to embrace rhetoric and the media themselves and to find ways of connecting these contemporary texts to their more traditional concerns. In particular, writing for these media, and writing in hypertextual digital modes, should be seen by English departments as ways of maintaining their necessary connection to the culture around them—if they wish to play a major role in that culture.

That having been said, I want to add that "creative writing" faculties are now often a very conservative element in English departments. Think about it. You have faculties largely trained in modes of writing that are themselves becoming marginalized. Often, they espouse avant-gardist attitudes that are now ritualized gestures, paying tribute to a futurist or dadaist moment that is long gone. And they disdain what I have heard creative writing professors refer to as genre Fiction—something they consider beneath their attention. No matter that some of the most exciting work in fiction now appears in the form of crime, espionage, and techno-fiction. So they go on offering courses in traditional modes of "creative" writing, including the now traditional avant-gardist sorts of experimental fiction. In this situation a genre like the essay, which has an excellent pedigree and is still flourishing, often falls through the cracks, being neither "creative" nor academic, though it is a useful mode for developing writers.

As I hope I have made plain, by giving production a larger place in the discipline of English, I do not just mean allowing credit for traditional courses in composition or creative writing within the English major. I am asking for a rethinking of what writing and other modes of linguistic production have to offer students, and a reconstruction of the courses themselves. Those who teach students how to write poetry, fiction, and drama have never expected all their students, or even most of them, to become professional writers of stories, poems, and plays. They have always believed, however—and many have said this to me—that their students would be better readers of literature because of their attempts to write it. And they are right, I have no doubt. What is necessary, now, is for the discipline as a whole to accept this position and to rethink the role of writing in English studies with few preconceptions beyond the goal of producing the most literate students possible. This will mean, as I have been arguing, both new kinds of courses and a new relation between reading and writing in the courses being taught.

Consumption

It is no accident that what English departments consider their principal reason for being comes last in this list of four functions, and under a heading that suggests either the old name for a dreaded disease or the driving force behind a market economy. This ungracious heading also displaces attention from the quasi-sacred textual object, Literature, to the process by which such objects are assimilated or ingested: consumption. All this is deliberate, tendentious, and possibly unfair. It is also necessary, for the notion of literature as something to be professed, something that carries its own transcendental justification, is deeply embedded in the thinking of English teachers, to the point where it seriously inhibits reconstructing the discipline. Throughout this book I have been giving reasons why I believe this way of thinking about texts is no longer useful, but it is so deeply ingrained that I fear even one more attempt to dislodge it may not be sufficient. Let me try once again. I will attempt to make my point in a manner sufficiently different from my earlier efforts to afford some mild amusement for those who have already taken it.

What sacred texts offer within their own cultures can be described as the Truth, or the Way. They tell believers how things are—and how to live. Secular texts cannot offer the same consolations with the same absolute conviction. To read the Bible as literature is to secularize it. To read *Middlemarch* (to name a work with serious ethical aspirations, written by a woman who knew her Bible, as well as many other things) is to read a text that aspires to a certain kind of authority: the right to generalize about human nature, to say "we" and make it stick. This is not a despicable power, but, since the author is neither God nor inspired by a divinity, we are not obliged to believe what the author tells us nor to act as she advises us. If we do believe, and if we do try to act as she suggests we should, it is because of the power of the examples and arguments she puts before us. No despicable power, as I said, but a rhetorical power, not a fundamental power. The intellectual situation that I am attempting to describe is an ancient one, the divine in opposition to the secular, the absolute opposed to the relative, the True text as opposed to the Rhetorical one.

For our purposes, what is most interesting about this opposition is the place of the literary text in relation to the sacred and the secular. Plato, in a certain mood, was quite ready to push poetry over to the rhetorical side and exile it from his ideal state. Aristotle, who held his nose in order to produce a handbook of rhetoric, nevertheless found a secular use for poetic drama—it purged pity and fear from the minds of citizens, thus enabling them to use those minds for thinking about civic matters. Romantic aestheticians and their followers have tried to push poetry or literature back toward the sacred, as partaking of the oversoul, the primary imagination, or universal archetypes. From this we should learn that literature, sometimes called poetry, has no fixed place but changes its position and function as cultures change. English departments rode Pegasus to a position of academic prestige and relative affluence, but now, in our time, Pegasus has begun to look like other extremely large creatures with wings, that run very fast but can't get off the ground. The myths tell us that such creatures put their heads in the sand to avoid unpleasant or threatening sights. But what do myths know?

In the age of mass media, literature has, as Walter Benjamin put it, lost its aura. We can either pretend, ostrichwise, that this has not happened, or decide what to do about it. As you might expect, I am all for doing something about it. Indeed, I welcome the opportunity. This is the chance, this is the moment, to change reading from a passive to an active process. This is the moment to replace priestly exegesis and passive coverage with attention to reading as a process. The idea is not new. In 1818 the young John Keats, in a letter to his friend Reynolds, urged reading only a few things, perhaps a single page, and letting that lead to "a voyage of conception." Keats called this process a "delicious, diligent Indolence," and went on to describe it in a lovely metaphor:

> Now it appears chat almost any Man may like the spider
> spin from his own inwards his own airy Citadel
> —the points of leaves and twigs on which the spider
> begins her work are few, and she fills the air with
> a beautiful circuiting. Man should be content with
> as few points to tip with the fine Web of his Soul,
> and weave a tapestry empyrean full of symbols for
> his spiritual eye, of softness for his spiritual touch, of
> space for his wandering, of distinctness for his luxury. (Keats, 79)

Keats, through his Romantic vocabulary of soul and spirit, is talking about reading as a creative process, and his metaphor is the metaphor of textuality, the spider weaving her web, creating something new, which is strung from a few leaves and twigs already in place but is nevertheless unique and beautiful. The human reader, like the spider, should create a "tapestry" that depends upon a few previous texts but is the reader's own creation, offering solace and stimulus. The play of Keats's own mind, as he reaches for difficult concepts here, leads him to weave a web of paradox and oxymoron—especially in the root concept of "diligent Indolence," which animates the whole passage. The New Critics would be quick to tell us that this is a sign of the presence of poetry itself, and the structuralists would call it literariness. And they would be right.

Such concepts, and others like them, ought to be a part of the reading equipment of all readers, and especially of those readers who are trained in the discipline of English. I am suggesting that Keats offers us more than one thing from which we can learn in this passage. The simple message that a few texts well-pondered may be more valuable than many texts consumed thoughtlessly—that is just one of the things we can learn from the passage. Another is the rhetorical power of images, like that of the spider. Others are the poetical power of the paradox, and the rhetorical power of oxymoron. To read this passage fully, of course, would be to look for the intertextual twigs and leaves from which it hangs, to see where this vocabulary of soul weaving comes from, to explore the other letters and the life of Keats, to see, for instance, how he was, in fact, reading quite a lot in those days, especially Shakespeare, and constantly dropping allusions into his letters. To read the letters of Keats is to wish to know him better. And to know him better, it is clear, one must know Shakespeare as well.

What am I trying to say about the consumption of texts, otherwise known as reading? Let me try to boil my thoughts down to a few twigs and leaves, or, as Ezra Pound would put it, an abc of reading.

a. The process of reading should take precedence over the coverage of texts in the English curriculum. By process I mean learning how to read closely and carefully, how to situate a text in relation to other texts (intertextuality), how to situate a text in relation to culture, society, the world (extratextuality). Let me give some very simple examples of this. I recently saw two bumper stickers. Admittedly, bumper stickers are a very modest form of textuality, but reading them requires, in little, many of the skills required for texts of greater consequence. One of these bumper stickers, on an old VW Beetle, read this way: "God is coming, and Is She Pissed!" Inelegant? Yes. Vulgar, even blasphemous? Certainly. But, like much blasphemy, theologically interesting. In reading this text five moves are crucial. One is the intertextual move, in which the reader connects this text to many others that announce the end of the world or the Second Coming. This begins as another such eschatological statement. The second move is also intertextual but at a less specific level. The feminine pronoun, "She," comes as a shock because of all those other Judea-Christian texts in which "He" is used, and all those visual texts that represent God as distinctly male. The third move is to note the shift of register in the last word, which makes the whole second clause idiomatic, vulgar, and arresting. "Pissed" is short for "pissed off," which is colloquial for angry. Which brings us to the fourth move, the move to interpretation, in which we consider the significance of what we have already noted and seek the meaning (or most prominent meanings) of this little text. The vulgarity is mainly an attention getter, meant to shock us. It works because the notion of an angry God has been very pervasive in Jewish and Christian thought (think of Jonathan Edwards's representation of him, for instance). Reducing the divine wrath to the level of urine is funny because of the incongruity. Is there a contrast between this liquid and the fires of hell—or is that going too far with interpretation?—questions to be debated. Finally, the text invites us to assume that thousands of years of being represented by the wrong gender might indeed be a justification for a bit of pique. The fifth move, extratextual but still a part of reading, is to consider the place of the text in the world—in this case an ancient Beetle, a sixties car, a feminist text, which leads to guesses about the owner—possibly wrong ones—and to the reasons for this particular display. Learning to read is all about the ability to make intellectual moves like these—and to make them on texts more complicated and difficult than this one.

The second bumper sticker is one I first noticed on a battered pickup truck: "If you don't like my driving, call 1-800-EAT-SHIT." Reading this one is easy in one sense, but a good reading of it requires both information and speculative thought. The information required is intertextual. We need to know a few different things. One is that business telephone numbers often use the formula 1-800, followed by seven letters that spell memorable words, often following the traditional grouping of telephone numbers, so that a three-digit exchange followed by a four-digit individual number turns into a three-letter word followed by a four-letter word. This is possible only because our phones group letters with every number on their buttons save zero and one. In this case, of course, the four-letter word is a four letter word, an obscenity of sorts, rather similar in that respect to the last word of the other bumper sticker. Making the last word a shocker begins to look like a part of the poetic diction of the genre, though our sample is too small to support any generalizations. One is not advised to dial the number, in any case. So far in our reading, the text appears to be a mere insult. I think it is an insult, but not so mere as it first appears to be. If we do a little intertextual digging, we should recall a related formula that appears on the back of larger trucks, inviting people to call an actual number if the driver is not competent or courteous. Presumably, this invitation to get the driver in trouble is not put there by the driver but by his or her employers. It is a kind of advertising, seeking goodwill, and a kind of threat for the driver as well.

Intertextual knowledge of the standard invitation to report bad driving is required for a strong, rich reading of the sign on the pickup truck. To round off the reading, we need only imagine that the driver who owns the pickup truck either also drives a larger vehicle for hire, which displays the invitation to snitch, or simply wants to register solidarity with other truck drivers and assert his or her own independence. Even this very simple and clearly vulgar text, then, invites a skilled, imaginative reading rather than a perfunctory dismissal as beneath both contempt and interpretation. The process of reading involved in both these tiny texts is the same as that required on a grander scale for more ambitious works. And it should be discussed explicitly in classes and demonstrated frequently by students, over a range of textual modes from different times and places.

b. The reading of modern and recent texts can play a major part in whetting the appetite of students for earlier literature. I can imagine a course in which a reading of Keats, starting with his letters, leads to a reading of some of Shakespeare's plays, as Keats was reading them. Keats, of course, was going to the theater, seeing Shakespeare in performance, writing about actors, attending lectures, writing about lecturers. To understand him rightly means understanding his cultural situation, his social situation, the places he lived in, his world. I can also imagine a course in which a reading of Scott Fitzgerald leads to a reading of Keats, for Fitzgerald loved Keats and, in his own letters, urged his daughter to read the poet. One could go on and on.

    c. Students should learn to read a range of texts, from various times and places, in various genres and media, in "high" and "low" forms of textuality. If English teachers have done a good job of teaching reading in the past, they have done it mostly by teaching a reverent approach to masterpieces. Such an approach has its uses, but it is not good training for reading the highly manipulative texts of advertising and propaganda and other persuasive forms. It is not even a complete training in reading literature, because even masterpieces often have a large component of propaganda and manipulation. Good reading involves reading every text sympathetically, trying to get inside it, to understand the intentionality behind its composition. It also involves reading every text unsympathetically, critically—but the sympathetic has to come first or the critical reading is impossible. If we impose our own values on every text, we have nothing to criticize but ourselves. Reading, as I have argued in several other books, involves an attribution of intention, a sympathetic attempt to discern that intention, and a critical distancing and examination of that intention. One might, for instance, utterly reject the sentiments offered in the two bumper stickers discussed above, but the only informed basis for such a rejection depends upon a prior sympathetic reading.

    Reading advertisements, reading films and television shows, reading political speeches, reading poems, plays, essays, stories, and everything else under the sun—this is what we should be teaching. If one were to attempt to "cover" all this, of course, the task would be impossible. No set of teachers or students can possibly do it all. The present curriculum based on coverage, however, is also impossible—we just pretend it isn't by lining up some masterpieces chronologically and calling that literary history. What we need is a greater variety of courses, with a constant and prevailing emphasis on the process of reading, along with whatever constraints on choices that a given faculty thinks appropriate for the best results. Should students know some of the major writers from the early periods of English and American literature? Of course, and departments should set their requirements to make sure this happens. But they should also arrange courses so that all students develop their reading skills as early as possible and continue deepening and enriching them as they progress through the curriculum. That students who graduate in English should be excellent readers, ready to encounter unfamiliar texts, to situate them, interpret them, and criticize them—these are the goals of an English education with respect to the consumption of texts.

PRACTICAL PROBLEMS—AND SOLUTIONS

What I have just described as a discipline of English oriented around the theory, history, production, and consumption of texts will be difficult to achieve because it requires a massive shift in priorities as well as many practical changes in courses and curricula, but it is far from impossible, because people are doing many of these things already, though they may not be consciously perceiving them as stages in a total reorientation of English from a field of study to a discipline. At the present time, however, English departments, especially those in large universities, face an array of practical problems that often seem more urgent than the kind of theoretical reorientation I have been urging. Many of these problems have causes that lie outside the academy, in the national culture or economy, for instance, but they are nonetheless problems that English departments and university administrators must solve at their own level. At this point, with some diffidence, I will try to describe the most pressing of these practical problems and suggest some solutions. Without wishing to argue that the sort of intellectual reconstruction of the discipline that I have been proposing will solve any of these practical problems, I do indeed want to claim that such a reorientation will make it easier to recognize them, to face them, and to make the necessary changes in policy. Some of the problems overlap one another. I will try to take them one at a time and shift focus when the overlap becomes acute.

The first problem I wish to examine is that of graduate study in English, which, as we shall see, overlaps with the problem of the nature of research in the field. The PhD in English, as presently constituted, is a research degree, designed to train graduate students to produce "original research" (which means research worthy of publication) in some part of the field of English. It functions, however, as the necessary qualification for most teaching positions in four-year colleges and universities. The *research* degree as the primary credential for a teaching position is such an established part of higher education that we can scarcely see the oddity of it. I should say at once that I see no problem in requiring mastery of a field or discipline in order to teach it, nor am I a great believer in degrees in "teaching" without such mastery of an academic subject. The problem is not with learning in itself but with research as the only acceptable way of demonstrating mastery—and in particular, with publication as the only acceptable way of demonstrating that research has indeed been done. This is the Germanic model of graduate study, introduced into the United States in the later nineteenth century; moreover, it is this model as influenced by the scientific and quantitative disciplines. In the humanities, this model is no longer working very well. That is part of the problem with graduate studies at the moment, but it is by no means the whole of it.

The other major part of the problem—and especially the problem with the PhD degree—is that every year English departments produce about twice as many graduates with this degree as would be required to fill all the positions that are open in the field. Every year, then, more candidates remain unemployed or in temporary jobs, waiting to compete against the new graduates the following year. This results in a high degree of competitiveness for those scarce positions, which takes the form of demanding more and more in the way of "research" from candidates for positions with their newly minted or recent PhD degrees in hand. The effects of this situation run broad and deep throughout the profession. Morale in graduate programs is disastrous. Students are reluctant to finish their degrees. As a result, they begin to form or join labor unions to protect what seems to be not a transient phase of their educational progress but a permanent way of academic life. Exploitation runs rampant in this situation, making unionization an appropriate response. There are two separate but related problems here. One is with the economic power of the degree in a depressed job market. The other is with the intellectual value of the degree as preparation for actually doing those scarce jobs once they are obtained.

Are graduate students in English learning what they most need to know and getting the experience they really need? Too often, the answer to these questions is that they are not. The pressures of the job market are changing the shape of graduate study for the worse, leading to the production of instant "research" by people who are simply unready to produce it, being thin in their general background and shallow even in their special fields—something I felt personally back in 1959 (see Assignment 1) but now see as more acute and more pervasive. This situation is an aspect of what I discussed in chapter 2 as a loss of truthfulness in academic study—a turning away from any commitment to truth as the proper end of academic study. The idea of academic research as a "contribution to knowledge," the idea of "original research," requires an assumption of progress toward more adequate descriptions of reality. In the sciences, research receives its justification and its support—despite all the lip service to "pure" knowledge—from the exploitable discoveries or patents to which it may lead. In the humanities, research receives its justification—despite all the lip service to the advancement of learning from its applicability to teaching. In fact, I would say that all important research in the humanities is simply teaching by other means than the lecture or the seminar. And conversely, published work in English studies that has no use in teaching or makes no contribution to learning is unimportant—trifling stuff. When Chaucer said of his Oxford Clerk that he would gladly learn and gladly teach, he was implying that the two activities were connected by more than the repeated adverb. Learning and teaching justify one another and support one another. But the pressure for research in English is often in direct conflict with both learning and teaching. And that is a formula for academic disaster—a disaster that is most obvious and most pressing in the situation of graduate studies in English.

The demand for research—and this is widely known—has led to a vast production of articles and books that are published and disappear without a trace. No one even pretends any longer to "keep up" with everything published on even a single major author. There is an eerie hollowness about the enterprise that is one sign of hypocriticism at work. There are indeed some interesting and useful books and articles published every year, and even some of the least significant work shows signs of academic ability and intelligence. But there is a vast effort here, an enormous expenditure of time and energy, that might have been much better spent on matters that bear more directly on the classroom. This situation, as I have said, is widely understood—yet, as with the weather, no one does anything about it. Why is this the case? It is partly because it is not easy to change a system so vast, with so much inertia behind it, but it is also because the testing of ideas in a public exchange with one's peers is a healthy developmental activity. What is wrong with this system is not that it requires intellectual exchange but that intellectual exchange has to masquerade as part of a progress toward the truth—in an academic culture that has largely forgotten truthfulness or consciously rejected it as a possibility.

There are two possible solutions to this dilemma. One is to say that, since truth is out of the question, what we have here is just conversation, with the prizes going to the best conversationalists. This is more or less the Fish/Rorty solution (though there are signs that Fish is changing his position, which I shall discuss before concluding). It has the virtue of ending hypocriticism at the expense of installing cynicism at the heart of the enterprise. Personally, I do not feel this to be much of an improvement. The other alternative is to find a way to reinstate the search for truth, now "disciplined," as Hegel said of Christianity, by the exposure to relativism and cynicism. Personally, I believe that we sometimes arrive at the truth, that some questions are settled and need not be asked anymore. The earth is not a perfect sphere, but we know it is not flat. Still, even if we never complete our journey toward truth, it is important that we travel in the name of truthfulness, for, without this, the journey loses interest, for ourselves and for those we ask to share it with us. What makes Nietzsche interesting to us is the possibility that he may be right about important matters—even if we wish he were wrong. Even more important, his work is interesting because he wants to be right and wants to show that others have been wrong—which means that he needs to know very well what those others have said and meant. What would Derrida be without his struggles with Husserl, with Hegel? Operating under the sign of truthfulness, the desire to get things right, academic discourse can be valuable, even exciting. But this kind of truthfulness requires learning, which is to the humanities what experiment is to the sciences. When academic discourse turns away from truthfulness and embraces fashion, it requires a forgetting or ignorance of its own past, in order to achieve a spurious originality. Such work, even for the forgetful reader, lacks the energy and intensity that comes only from playing with the high stakes of truth and falsehood, getting it right and getting it wrong.

In my discussion of Althusser as a student in Assignment 2, I suggested that it may not be our "truth" that students learn from us, but the way of seeking truth that constitutes our integrity as scholars, the discursive habits by which we reach our conclusions and report on them. This view of a professional ideal may seem distant from the practical problems of developing future teachers in graduate school—but it is not. If we keep in mind the goal of preparing young scholars not just to follow methodological fashions but to master a discipline well enough to teach it and to share their ideas with peers in a common search for truth, we can use this goal to interrogate our present practices and consider alternatives, as I shall attempt to do in the following paragraphs.

The problem of graduate studies in English does not easily admit of unilateral solutions. Any single program that gets out of step with the others risks encountering either even worse results in placing its graduates or losses in prestige (within its own academic base as well as outside) that it would prefer not to endure, because the effects would entail economic as well as other consequences within the present system of academic rewards and punishments. Yet I would like to offer a few suggestions that the boldest and best programs might essay, which, if they work well, should encourage others to follow. I think things are bad enough for the Faustian phrase I used in chapter 2 to apply here. We should not go on living like this. At any rate, as one excessively manacled and pinioned prisoner says to the other in a popular cartoon, "Here's my plan":

No half-measures—a comprehensive rethinking of the PhD program or nothing. To put matters with brutal simplicity, I believe that a strong department could easily admit fewer students, keep them longer, treat them better, and prepare them much more successfully to compete in what is clearly going to remain a very difficult job market. At present, most PhD students are in their programs for a nominal five years, which in practice gets to be six, seven, or even more. Suppose, instead of that, a program that admittedly lasted ten years, but with several of those years consisting of full-time teaching, with a course load comparable to what these teachers would be likely to have in their first full-time jobs. Suppose further that between the years of full-time teaching they would be awarded years of full-time study, fully supported. Planning to support them for ten years instead of five, departments would admit only half as many graduate students as they now do. Such a program could be economically viable for both the schools and the individuals, because graduate students currently carry a teaching load of roughly one-third as many courses as they will teach when working full-time. Sketched crudely, the plan would be something like this: a first year of courses and study, a second year of part-time, supervised teaching and some study, a third year of part-time teaching and study, a fourth year of study, a fifth year of full-time teaching, a sixth year of study, after which instructor status would be awarded, and then four alternate years of instruction and study, with the degree awarded at the end of this time or earlier if all requirements were satisfied. The result would be fewer graduates, who would finish their studies with real teaching experience, and, if their programs were properly designed, real learning as well.

Within such a program there would be much room for variations, but I would myself suggest that the number of official graduate courses and seminars now offered by most programs could be sharply reduced, allowing those senior faculty to teach more undergraduates, and that graduate students should do most of their work as directed study or independent research, in connection with whatever structure of examinations and productive work the faculty might devise. As I indicated above, the years of full-time teaching would make the years of supported study economically feasible for many schools. I have said nothing about dissertations or other forms of research and publication, but I think the kind of structural change I have suggested would accommodate itself to traditional forms of productive study as well as to innovations. I also believe, most firmly, that the alternation of full-time teaching and full-time study would allow teaching and learning to support one another in the happiest and most productive manner. And the ten-year program looks long only when compared to the nominal five-year programs that no longer operate as they are supposed to but often run on and on. Ten years with sufficient support to avoid going deeply into debt, as many graduate students do these days, would also be much better than seven or eight years with a serious debt problem and a degree that is no more than a hunting license for jobs that seem to belong to an endangered species.

Such programs, I am suggesting, would produce extremely attractive graduates, so that the forces of the market itself might lead to emulation, which in turn would result in a serious reduction in the total number of graduates produced each year, giving all such graduates a better chance for a decent academic life. And with senior faculty teaching more undergraduate course [sic], we might begin to find ways to make teaching itself more consequential in the evaluation of faculty, programs, and entire schools. This is a change that seems to be coming these days, but it is being delayed by perceived problems in the evaluation of teaching. Such a qualitative art has not lent itself easily to quantitative evaluation. I believe, however, that truly concerned departments and administrations can find ways of getting better information about how their faculties are doing as teachers, and ways of rewarding faculty on the basis of that information. There are many sources of such information not even being considered now. If an English department, for instance, asked all its graduating seniors to list the three members of that faculty in whose courses they had learned the most, that department would, in several years, have an extremely useful body of information, much more useful than the little surveys taken on the spot at the end of particular courses. I would also suggest—and here administrations will need to play a leading role—that the quality of learning and thinking in lectures, articles, and books be given more weight in evaluations than the quantity. It is, of course, easier to count or measure than to read and evaluate, but this change can be made if the will to make it is present. Too much reliance is now put on perfunctory outside reviews, where internal evaluation might serve better. And far too much stress is placed upon quantity of publication than on the quality of learning and teaching displayed in writing, lectures, course designs, and assignments for student work.

A lot of what I have been talking about is a matter of changes in procedure that might be effected whether or not one reconceives of English as a discipline. And I would hope that some of these suggestions might make sense even to those who reject my larger argument. But these changes have come to my mind as aspects of reconstructing English as a discipline around a core of methods that are essentially pedagogical. That is, once we think of English in terms of what this study will enable students to do with texts, and think of what a teacher needs to learn so that he or she will have something to offer students of textuality, it becomes natural to rethink the production of teachers along the same lines—and by "production of teachers" I mean both what teachers produce and how they are themselves produced. With a shared disciplinary core of knowledge about textuality, we should be able to tolerate a wider range of particular interests among our faculty and offer a more interesting range of courses to our students, always remembering that our justification as teachers lies in what our students accomplish after they leave us. We need to give them the best and most flexible tools for a future that will be more theirs than ours.

One final problem should not be avoided here, and that is the balance of subfields within any given English department. At present, the actual history of English departments, supported by the shaping of the field around the literary history of England and America, has left many such departments with too many faculty in the earlier periods of English literature and not enough in American literature and the emerging subfields of Anglophone literatures, both postcolonial and ethnic American—and with far too many of the courses students actually want being taught by graduate students and part-time faculty. In a sense, to recognize this distribution of fields as a problem is to solve it, but such recognition is resisted by entrenched faculties. As I write, major universities are reporting large decreases in the number of English majors. Tinkering with the old curriculum will not solve these problems. What is needed is a paradigm shift from thinking of English as a field to thinking of it as a discipline. Thomas Kuhn warned us that paradigms are changed not by persuasion of those who hold the old ones but by their dying off and being replaced by people who have embraced the new. What will happen to English studies and the old paradigm of literary history remains to be seen, but the choice seems clear: adapt or dwindle, ending, perhaps, with a whimper.

CLOSING DOWN, OPENING UP

The discipline of English is not a topic on which one should even aspire to say the last word. I have been trying to give a certain focus to a discussion that is already going on about the function of English in American education. Perhaps I can sharpen that focus by comparing my position to that taken by Stanley Fish in his recent book *Professional Correctness*. In this book Fish joins hands with John Crowe Ransom, declaring his agreement "with Ransom's insistence that it is a requirement for the respectability of an enterprise that it be, or at least be able to present itself as, *distinctive*" (Fish, 17, emphasis in original). The enterprise in question, for Ransom, was the one that English departments were (or should be) undertaking. For Fish, the enterprise can be called, quite simply, literary criticism, which he sees as the disciplinary core of English studies. He is insistent that literary criticism or interpretation must be at the center of English studies, because it is the one distinctive thing that such departments have to offer the world. His book, as a whole, is an argument against attempts to politicize the field of English instruction or to move such studies away, in any direction, from the central activity of asking "What is this poem (or novel or drama) saying?" (Fish, 25).

Fish is as insistent as I have been (and as Ransom and Frye were before us) that English studies ought to be a discipline. But in his zeal to protect literary studies from political excesses and false pretensions to cultural influence, he feels obliged to circle the wagons around a very narrow definition of literature that corresponds to a very specialized mode of reading. He also completely ignores the teaching of writing as a potential disciplinary core. In short, he seeks to ratify the domination of rhetoric by literature. What I have been proposing, on the other hand, is a discipline based on rhetoric and the teaching of reading and writing over a broad range of texts. Agreeing with Fish, and with Ransom and Frye, about the need for English to maintain a distinctive disciplinary core, I disagree with him—and the others, as well—in believing that the concept of textuality, which includes literariness but is not limited to it, can best serve that function. I welcome his book, however, as a sign that a professional figure of some consequence, on an important occasion (the Clarendon Lectures, delivered at Oxford in 1993), has shared my concern about the state of the profession and proposed a solution that, however different, should help to open the way to further discussion about the possibilities of English as a discipline. Let the discussion continue.

NOTE

"A Fortunate Fall?" reprinted by permission of copyright owner, Yale University Press. From *The Rise and Fall of English*, 1998, 147–70.

PART 2

*Extending Scholes's Scholarship on
Dispositions and Habits of Mind*

6
FROM ARGUMENT TO INVITATION
Promoting Empathy and Mutual Understanding in the Composition Classroom

Kelsey McNiff

Reflecting upon college students' difficulty understanding and engaging ideas that are fundamentally different from their own, Robert Scholes suggested in "The Transition to College Reading" (2002) that this limitation was symptomatic of a broader cultural disposition in which Americans struggled to "remain open to otherness" (169). Scholes identified two main limitations in student reading—first, when "students simply assimilate the thought and feeling in a text to their own thoughts and feelings," and second, when "students recognize a different position and simply refuse to read or think about it"—remarking with apparent regret that "[t]hese two responses to otherness constitute the American way" (Scholes 2002, 169). To address this problem, Scholes saw a need to critically evaluate the English curriculum as a whole and called upon English educators at the secondary and postsecondary levels to "make some changes both in what we teach and how we teach it" (2002, 167).

To this end, he challenged what he characterized as an "opposition between the aesthetic text and the rhetorical text" (2002, 169), arguing that educators should include in the "literary curriculum" (2002, 170) texts that explicitly make arguments in multiple forms as well as texts that present "conflicting positions" (2002, 168). Beyond simply incorporating persuasive texts into the curriculum, however, Scholes emphasized the need to model and teach how "to put ourselves into a text before taking ourselves out of it" (2002, 169), positioning a genuine effort to understand and empathize with the ideas of others as a critical reading skill crucial to independent thought. As he put it: "The basis of an education for the citizens of a democracy lies in that apparently simple but actually difficult act of reading so as to grasp and evaluate the thoughts and feelings of that mysterious other person: the writer" (Scholes 2002, 171).

Scholes was not alone in his belief that empathy is important to democratic citizenship. Shulman, in his foreword to *Educating for Democracy*, claimed that "one of the supreme tests of political formation is the development of the capacities and dispositions to listen carefully and respectfully to the opinions of others, especially those with whom one disagrees. Such listening is a necessary condition for engaging in the dialogues and debates that are the intellectual backbone of the democratic process" (2007, xi). Similarly, ten Dam and Volman have noted that "democratic citizenship requires not only being able to think critically and politically, it also requires a caring attitude, empathy and commitment" (2004, 371). Like Scholes, many have argued that educators therefore should seek to cultivate students' empathetic imaginations (Von Wright 2002; Fleckenstein 2007; Gerdes et al. 2011; Leake 2016; Damianidou and Phtiaka 2016; English 2016; Tomlinson and Murphy, 2018; Mirra 2018) and that the humanities in particular encourage this habit of mind (Nussbaum 2010; Jurecic 2011, 13–15).

This topic is, however, a contentious one, and some have advocated for a more complex understanding of empathy and its limits. Scholars have demonstrated that empathy through reading does not necessarily lead to action on behalf of others (Keen 2007), that empathy can appropriate or obscure the experiences of others (Shuman 2005; Jurecic 2011, 16–19; Alexander and Rhodes 2014), and that emotional empathy, or the spontaneous mirroring of another person's feelings, can in fact heighten prejudice and cloud moral reasoning (Bloom 2016). Others have highlighted the inequities involved in empathy (Mirra 2018), and some educators have called for pedagogies of critical empathy that are grounded in a consideration of power differentials and social contexts (DeStigter 1999; Damianidou and Phtiaka 2016; Mirra 2018).

While I agree that empathy is not a panacea and that we should maintain awareness that "empathy is always at best an approximation of understanding" (Leake 2016), I see empathy as one of the "deep rules, or habits of citizenship" that Wan (2011) has suggested can be fostered by literacy education (45). As Sullivan (2014) has explained, when we model listening and empathy in our composition classrooms, we model critical reflection, a willingness to embrace uncertainty, and a "dialogical orientation toward the world and others" (3–4). In addition, we model how we can "enact citizenship with others" in such a way that we do not "cast those who disagree as deeply flawed in character" (Clifton 2016, 38), but rather as fellow human beings whose ideas and experiences are worth trying to understand. I define empathy as "a complex imaginative process in which an observer simulates another person's situated psychological states while maintaining a clear self-other differentiation" (Coplan 2011, 5). This definition reminds us that empathy is an act of imagination involving both cognition and emotion (Coplan 2011, 5–6), and that efforts to cultivate empathy should engage students in critical reflection on social contexts and on empathy's limits.

However, while I agree with Scholes that educators should cultivate empathy as a civic virtue, as I read Scholes's essay in the fall of 2017 against the backdrop of our highly polarized political culture, his comments gave me pause. I teach at a small liberal arts college with a student body that is predominantly white (8% minority students), regional (50% from Massachusetts, and 37% from other New England states), and professionally oriented (Endicott College 2019). My reading pedagogy embraces Scholes's suggestion that educators teach persuasive texts presenting multiple perspectives on an issue. Like many composition instructors, I emphasize the importance of being good listeners when we read course texts. My students and I practice playing the "believing game" before the "doubting game" (Elbow 1973). We discuss the need to represent the ideas of others as accurately as we can so that we can respond to them as fairly as we can.

Yet I noticed over the years that students can complete these intellectual exercises without actually relinquishing the authority of their own ideas or fully seeking to explore, inhabit, and reflect upon perspectives and experiences that may differ from their own. As I reflected on this tension in the context of contemporary political speech, in which the acknowledgment of alternate perspectives appears too often merely a nod to fair-mindedness, a new question emerged for me: To what extent might common practices in the composition classroom, and in particular our emphasis on argument and persuasion, imply that we only consider the ideas of others as a means to an end?

Scholes's essay thus prompted me to critically evaluate my own composition instruction and ask what more I could do to model empathy as a civic virtue in my teaching. Although Scholes does not address how we might help students develop "the rhetorical capacity to imagine the other's thought, feeling, and sentiments" (Scholes 2002, 168) not only in how we teach reading but also in the kinds of writing we assign and assess, I took the latter question as my central challenge. This chapter describes how I sought to extend Scholes's reflection by developing an essay assignment that asked students to explore the ideas of others not in service of an argument of their own, but rather in service of an invitation to conversation. Because this was not a research study, in this chapter I do not describe individual student work, nor do I assess individual student learning outcomes. I do, however, share my process of designing, implementing, and revising an assignment sequence aiming to promote listening, empathy, and mutual understanding, and I offer my reflection on how this experience led me to question my near-exclusive focus on argument in my undergraduate composition courses.

TOWARD A PEDAGOGY OF EMPATHY AND MUTUAL UNDERSTANDING

Because my institution has a set curriculum for our required first-year critical reading and writing courses, I decided to design my new essay assignment for a 200-level composition course entitled Argument-Based Writing. As described in the course catalog, students in this class "critically read and respond to challenging academic texts, and compose thoughtful and well-supported argument-based essays and research papers" (Endicott College 2017, 179). The learning objectives focus on developing students' understanding of the elements of academic argument as well as their ability to write logically sound, claim-driven academic essays, conduct college-level research, draft and revise their work, and demonstrate command of standard English grammar.

At first, this course context might seem problematic for an essay assignment focused on empathy, not persuasion. But rather than seeing an emphasis on listening and dialogue as outside the bounds of the course, I saw the habits of mind it would cultivate as relevant to a range of writing contexts, including that of "compos[ing] thoughtful and well-supported argument-based essays." On the one hand, I believed an essay focused on empathy and mutual understanding could challenge students to confront and think critically about their own assumptions, thus helping them develop more sensitive, nuanced, and logically sound positions of their own; and on the other hand I hoped it could enhance students' understanding of the contexts, forms, and conventions of argument-based writing by raising their awareness of alternate forms of rhetoric and when and why we might use them.

I took as my starting point for the assignment Lunsford and Ruszkiewicz's discussion of "Rogerian and Invitational Arguments" in the course text *Everything's an Argument* (2016, 126–29). Here, Lunsford and Ruszkiewicz describe how these forms of argument emerged in response to a dissatisfaction with conventional rhetoric, which can be perceived as "confrontational," and how they instead encourage listening, understanding, and collaboration. With "Rogerian and Invitational Arguments," the text explains, one "begins with careful attention to and respect for the person or the audience you are in conversation with," and "such listening—in effect, walking in the other person's shoes—helps you see that person's points of view more clearly and thoroughly and thus offers a basis for moving together toward new understandings" (2016, 126).

This emphasis on listening and mutual understanding squared with my teaching goals, but I worried that in identifying these modes of communication as "a form of argument" and presenting "invitational strategies" (Lunsford and Ruszkiewicz, 2016, 27) as a means to persuasion, it might lead students to view listening and empathy in transactional terms. For example, Becker and Pike's proposed structure for a "Rogerian argument" included in the textbook encourages students to show openness and respect when framing the issue at stake, and to take time to affirm "the contexts in which alternate positions may be valid," but also describes the audience as "opponents" and suggests the essay culminate in a final section persuading opponents of why it would be in their interest to change their position and accept the rhetors' view (126). In contrast, in the context of his work in psychotherapy, Rogers presented empathetic listening as taking time to fully accompany another individual on and support them in their varied emotional states, and he believed this mindset could help individuals in therapeutic contexts as well as in interpersonal communication, conflict resolution, and compromise (Leake 2016; Encina 2006; Knoblauch 2011, 253).

Invitational rhetoric, as theorized by Foss and Griffin, shares an emphasis on listening and trying to think from the perspective of one's audience but focuses on "offering perspectives" (Foss 2009, 570) and creating the conditions for open, safe conversation between equals, free of the intent to persuade. Foss and Griffin position invitational rhetoric as a feminist rhetoric that functions in opposition to "the patriarchal bias that characterizes much of rhetorical theorizing" (1995, 2), suggesting that "[t]he act of changing others not only establishes the power of the rhetor over others, but also devalues the lives and perspectives of those others" (1995, 3), whereas invitational rhetoric, while it may lead to collaboration or, possibly, change, "asks that rhetors abandon the intent to persuade common in traditional forms of rhetoric in favor of an intent to understand" (Knoblauch 2011, 252). In the context of education, invitational rhetoric has been used professionally to facilitate communication between parents and caregivers (Modesti 2012) or between members of a teaching staff (Modesti 2012; Ryan and Graban 2009) and in the classroom to help students practice expressing "one's perspective in innovative ways not necessarily reliant on argument" (Kirtley 2014, 34; see also Knoblauch 2008).

BUILDING A LEARNER-CENTERED, SCAFFOLDED ASSIGNMENT SEQUENCE

Having identified my theoretical framework, I sought to design an assignment that engaged students in practicing empathetic listening and invitational rhetoric as a way to foreground what Sullivan has referred to as "the discourse of mindfulness" (2014, 56). However, my next challenge was to design an essay prompt and assignment sequence that would engage students in these habits of mind while avoiding the pitfall of transforming these modes of communication into modes of persuasion. As noted previously, I believed that teaching an invitational essay alongside argument-based essays would further model how a range of possibilities exists for engaging audiences, and how our rhetorical choices should reflect our goals, values, and motivation in any given context. For this reason, I decided to incorporate the invitational essay into a sequence of writing assignments in which students would identify a contemporary social problem of concern to them and practice writing about it in a variety of real-world contexts.

Since research in the fields of education and composition shows that student motivation is essential to learning (Pintrich, Marx, and Boyle 1993; Bunn 2013), I hoped that allowing students to choose their own topics would not only heighten their interest and persistence but also would help them see for themselves the value of placing "listening, empathy, and reflection" front and center as they explored them (Sullivan 2014, 56). However, because students' experience of empathizing with alternate viewpoints carries different personal and intellectual stakes depending on the nature of the issue at hand and their relationship to it, before selecting topics we discussed how students would focus on the issue they chose across multiple assignments, including one in which they would seek to understand and empathize with those who disagreed with their perspective, so that students could make informed decisions. While some students focused on social issues addressed in national political debates, such as gun violence, free speech on college campuses, or "right to die" legislation, others identified issues specific to their personal interests or areas of academic study, such as vaccine hesitancy, child beauty pageants, reduced arts funding in public schools, or concussions in youth sports.

When I first taught the assignment sequence during the spring of 2018, students researched the social problem they selected and wrote a proposal essay using Toulmin argument to persuade readers the problem existed and propose a manageable course of action that might be taken to address it. Next, they wrote the invitational essay, in which they sought to engage an audience who disagreed with some aspect of their argument in the proposal essay. Their goal in this assignment was twofold: to demonstrate understanding of and empathy for their audience's perspective and to offer their own perspective in a way that promoted mutual understanding and a safe, open exchange of ideas. Students then wrote letters-to-the-editor in response to a recent news article related to their topic (taking either an invitational or argument-based approach), before finally creating academic posters for their final class presentations.

When we transitioned into the invitational essay unit, we began by considering what is different about our orientation toward our audience when our goal is to engage them in conversation rather than to persuade them of our ideas, and we brainstormed specific personal, professional, and political situations in which one might have these different goals. We read the section on "Rogerian and Invitational Argument" in our textbook, analyzing how this approach compared to classical oration and Toulmin argument. However, we also discussed how our approach in the invitational essay was related to, yet distinct from, the textbook description since our goal in this second essay was not to persuade but to listen, reflect, and "offer" our perspective as a means to facilitating an open exchange of ideas.

DEVELOPING A NEW VOCABULARY

To help my students understand their own acts of writing as having a purpose other than to persuade, I knew they would need a new vocabulary and new models. To this end, we read and discussed Foss's entry on invitational rhetoric in *The Encyclopedia of Communication Theory*, which emphasized "two primary rhetorical forms: (1) offering perspectives and (2) creating external conditions that allow and encourage others to present their perspectives" (2009, 570). According to Foss, when "offering perspectives," the author or speaker simply describes their individual understanding, and when "creating external conditions" crucial to facilitating an open exchange of ideas, the rhetor focuses on three areas: "safety, value, and freedom" (2009, 570).

The first condition, "safety," involves helping the audience feel safe, secure, and respected by the rhetor, and the second, "value," refers to how rhetors can show their audience that they are valued and are not being condescended to (Foss 2009, 570). In exploring these concepts, my students and I discussed how close listening and critical empathy can be linked to the work of creating these "external conditions," as a genuine effort to understand the ideas of others involves humility and "[v]alue is also fostered when the rhetor listens carefully to the perspectives of others and tries to think from those perspectives" (Foss 2009, 570). Foss defines "freedom" as the audience's "power to choose or decide" and explains that this condition can be facilitated through the rhetor's choices, for example in not seeking to control the terms of the conversation, as well as through the rhetor's intent in engaging their audience in the exchange: "Either outcome—acceptance or rejection—is seen as perfectly acceptable by the invitational rhetor" (Foss 2009, 570). After developing our initial understanding of these conditions, my students and I used them as a lens to analyze writing that modeled invitational rhetoric, such as Mustafa Akyol's "Away in the Manger . . . Or Under a Palm Tree?" (2017); in this opinion piece, Akyol's rhetorical choices communicate empathy and respect for his audience as he affirms a multiplicity of viewpoints, and when he offers his understanding, he acknowledges readers will draw their own conclusions, all of which he implies would be equally valid.

PRACTICING AN INVITATIONAL STANCE

To move from a theoretical understanding of invitational rhetoric toward actually writing an essay focused on promoting dialogue and mutual understanding, my students began by exploring the perspectives of people who might disagree with the ideas they advanced in their proposal essays. Rather than guessing at their audience's ideas or presuming to know them in advance, this process required its own body of research. At this juncture, I was also mindful of the challenges of pedagogical empathy, and in particular the question of what views are appropriate to welcome into the classroom environment or to ask students to empathize with. I therefore worked to set the "parameters of discussion" (Mirra 2018, 103) for this assignment as needing to focus on areas of "reasonable disagreement among citizens" (Nussbaum 2010, 10). Students were tasked with using mainstream news outlets, credible blogs, organization or university websites, academic articles, or other relevant and reliable sources that allowed them to hear from their audience not only about their views on the issue, but also about *why* they held the ideas they did. In reading and thinking critically about these sources, in listening closely and attentively, students aimed to understand how people's values, belief systems, individual concerns, personal experiences, communities, or environments may have shaped their views.

After conducting this research, my students completed a creative assignment entitled "Who is your audience?" in which they developed a fictional character who represented the perspective of their audience. To imagine this person in the context of a life experience, I asked students to consider the following: How old are they? What gender are they? Where do they live? Do they have a family? What is their occupation? What has their life been like? What do they believe in? What do they love? What do they fear? How have their values or personal experiences influenced their views? In sum, why do they see the issue in question the way they do? Then students wrote a two-minute monologue written from the perspective of this person, and over two fifty-minute class sessions, students acted out the role of their fictional character, introducing themselves to the class, describing their perspective on the issue at stake, and helping us understand their reasoning and how their life experiences may have informed their views.

Leake (2016) has observed that "perspective-taking" writing prompts help students engage in a "demonstration of empathy," and Scholes has noted that incorporating drama can help students "'get' the author's thoughts, feelings, and sentiments" since "the move to oral interpretation requires no explanation or apology" (2002, 167). This exercise thus aimed to help humanize their audience as well as connect their audience's perspectives to social contexts, "creating space for imagining the world as different than how we may immediately perceive it in everyday life" (English 2016, 1056). In addition, drawing on learning theory that shows transmediation supports reading comprehension (Carraway 2014, 244; Daniels and Zemelman 2004, 32), I incorporated drama to "help learners activate their senses, their imaginations, their emotions, and all their life experiences while interacting with text" (Hoyt 1992, 584) in order to develop a fuller understanding of what they learned from their audience research. Yet the "who is your audience?" assignment led to other, unanticipated learning opportunities as well.

In advance of each monologue, I designated two classmates to be "questioners"; their job was to think of an open-ended, nonevaluative question that would prompt the fictional character to elaborate on some aspect of their reasoning. This task was challenging for students, especially when the monologue presented views with which the students strongly disagreed; most students initially posed their questions in a way that seemed intended to challenge or persuade, for example by beginning with a phrase like, "But don't you think . . ." or "Why aren't you . . ." that transitioned into a statement of their own view, often framing an either/or choice that set up an affirmation or refutation from the speaker. Part way through the exercise, we paused to discuss how this approach to questioning seemed to put the speakers on the defensive, limiting their sense of safety as it implied a right answer. In case students worried that their classmates might be blurring their personal views with those of the fictional character they were enacting, we also reaffirmed that in using their imagination to think from the fictional character's perspective, the student should not be interpreted as necessarily agreeing with or affirming that viewpoint.

We then practiced posing questions that encouraged dialogue, for example by leading with a phrase like "Could you elaborate on your thinking about . . . ," or by beginning with a demonstration of understanding followed by a question seeking clarification or an effort to offer their perspective as an invitation to continued dialogue, such as "It seems like you are really concerned about . . . , and I am curious to hear your thoughts on . . . because one thing I have been worried about is. . . ." This discussion then sparked a reflective conversation about how, while we should not feel barred from expressing our concerns if they differed from the speaker, when our goal was listening and understanding, and when we saw our own perspective as a work in progress, we were more inclined to remain open to new ideas and pose questions in a nonconfrontational way.

DRAFTING AND REVISING THE ESSAY

As participants as well as presenters, then, students needed to put effort into suspending their disbelief and remaining open to new ideas. When it came to drafting the essay, they were confronted with a new challenge: they not only needed to practice thinking from the perspective of their audience, but they also needed to reconceptualize their act of writing itself. In their four-to-five-page invitational essays, students sought to engage an audience who did not share their views on the issue at hand, demonstrate understanding of and empathy for their audience's perspectives, and then offer their own perspective, inviting their audience to join them in a safe and free exchange of ideas about the issue at hand. We thus borrowed the structural framework outlined in *Everything's an Argument* (Lunsford and Ruszkiewicz 2016, 126), but deployed our new vocabulary to clarify our goal of listening and encouraging dialogue.

Writing the draft was not easy, even for students who had demonstrated a good understanding of our theoretical framework and were able to use it as a lens to analyze the Akyol text. For example, when introducing the issue at stake in their introductions, many students framed a debate, often emphasizing its contentiousness or the polarized nature of current discussion about it. Others began their body section with insightful points that demonstrated an understanding of their audience's position, but then quickly moved to refute those points, either within the same paragraph or immediately following it. In terms of voice, students deployed stylistic strategies they commonly used in academic essays, describing issues, evidence, and ideas in somewhat distant, formal, and specialized language. Despite giving more space to their audience's perspectives than they might in an argument-based essay, their drafts still implied a right and wrong position, a way we "should" approach the issue at hand or steps that "need" to be taken to address it.

During our draft workshop of two student essays and my individual draft conferences with students, we discussed how these rhetorical choices, while common in argument-based essays, limited the invitational nature of their discussions. Students described how, while they understood the goal of the assignment, they found themselves unable to figure out *how* to explain or respond to their audience's ideas in other ways. For this reason, they fell back on strategies that had served them well before; they knew how to put other authors' ideas in context by positioning them as part of a debate, and they had learned how to respond to alternate perspectives by imagining the skeptic who was not prepared to accept their claims and whose views should be acknowledged but then refuted. Some students expressed worry that by not refuting their audience's positions, they were contradicting themselves or weakening their own ideas. In other words, my students were doing their best to work within and use the frameworks of knowledge they had, but this experience was the first time they were being asked to write with the aim of generating dialogue, and dialogue alone.

However, when we discussed the kinds of strategies they might use to better create conditions of "safety," "value," and "freedom" in their revisions, students rose to the challenge. I encouraged them to use more conversational language, as they might to engage people who aren't their college professors, but rather their friends or family members. I encouraged them to think of their audience simply as fellow human beings, and to consider how they might spark personal reflection on experiences, feelings, or values. Yes, you can use "I," I told them. Sure, use "we"; I agree that including yourself in this discussion helps emphasize you may have common ground. Rather than setting up a debate and confrontation in your introduction, I asked, how might you frame a shared concern or question worth thinking about together? It appeared that once students felt they had permission to write in a "different" way, to use their imagination, to bring emotion into the picture, and to give space to their audience's perspective without worrying it was undermining their own, they were able to make substantive revisions that affirmed their audience as well as their goal of inviting their audience to join them in conversation.

REVISITING THE ASSIGNMENT SEQUENCE

Generally speaking, I found that students' invitational essays demonstrated more awareness of audience and context in comparison to other essays they wrote in the course. Perhaps because of the difficulty involved in developing a new conception of their purpose for writing and considering the ideas of others, students appeared to engage in more metacognitive reflection about their rhetorical choices and the implications of both what they said and how they said it. As I reflected on the course as a whole, however, I realized that the organization of assignments could better model how seeking to understand the ideas of others might help us develop a more complex understanding of an issue before we draw conclusions about it. When I taught the course a second time, rather than doing a deep dive into alternate perspectives *after* proposing how to address the problem in question, students first presented an argument of fact to establish why they believed the social problem existed, then they wrote the invitational essay, before finally researching and writing the proposal essay, which was the last major assignment of the course.

In tandem with these structural changes, which I hoped would better engage students in a "dialogical orientation" (Sullivan 2014, 4) as they explored and reasoned about the issue, I added a new reflection assignment as part of the transition into the invitational essay unit. This assignment aimed to build students' self-awareness and critical reflection on their own perspectives (Von Wright 2002) as well as on "what they suspect they *do not know*" (Alexander and Rhodes 2014, 475) about people who do not share their views. To this end, the exercise asked students to identify their own assumptions about the issue at stake and reflect on how their preexisting ideas might relate to their own personal and social contexts; it also asked them to identify their assumptions about the views of people who might disagree with them, to explore why they held those assumptions, and to consider what they hoped to learn about their audience through their research.

A research study would be necessary to analyze limitations in their conceptualizations of audience or shifts in their self-awareness and perceptions of the issues at hand, as well as to assess the extent to which these assignments cultivated students' understanding of empathy as a civic virtue. As I have reflected on the experience of teaching the courses, my own attention has focused on the tension between seeking to heighten student motivation by having them choose their own topics and needing to model the critical reading processes at the heart of listening, empathy, and critical reflection. In a further iteration of the course, I would consider limiting the choices for student research topics so that I could more actively participate in the process of curating, reading, and discussing the selection of readings students used to imagine and understand views and experiences that differ from their own. Such a choice might also add depth to the perspective-taking activity, as the imaginative monologues might then yield several distinct characters whose varied experiences and perspectives could facilitate discussion on how this multiplicity of voices enriches, complicates, or otherwise influences our thinking about our own perspectives and the issue at hand (Gallo 1994, 56–59).

CONCLUSIONS

I have described in this chapter how Scholes's work prompted me to reflect on empathy as a civic virtue and develop a new assignment sequence focused on listening, empathy, and mutual understanding. As part of this process, I repeatedly found myself asking why I had always focused almost exclusively on argument in my teaching. To a certain extent, I had assumed that the critical thinking skills developed in a traditional, argument-based curriculum already model a free and open exchange of ideas. In line with this view, Duffy (2017) has suggested that argument as taught in most first-year composition courses can even be seen "as a practice of radical humility, in the sense that to argue is to submit ourselves to the judgment of others, offering up our ideas for scrutiny, criticism, and rejection." I agree that argument is and can be "an invitation to collaborate, to reason together, and, perhaps to find and inhabit common ground" (Duffy 2017), and I also agree that persuasion plays an important role in democracy. Yet Duffy himself has acknowledged that the virtues of "mutual honesty," accountability to evidence, and "intellectual humility" (2017) taught in first-year writing courses "are largely absent from the public square" (Duffy 2014, 211), and I am no longer confident that teaching argument alone enables students to fully understand and enact them.

When we teach alternate forms of rhetoric alongside argument, we model for our students that there are varied contexts for writing and communicating with others, and that in those varied contexts strategies other than persuasion may be better aligned not only to our goals but also to the work of democracy itself. As the political philosopher Sandel (1996, 350) has suggested: "Self-government today [. . .] requires a politics that plays itself out in a multiplicity of settings, from neighborhoods to nations to the world as a whole. Such a politics requires citizens who can think and act as multiply-situated selves. The civic virtue of our time is the capacity to negotiate our way among the sometimes overlapping, sometimes conflicting obligations that claim us, and to live with the tension to which multiple loyalties arise." Just as Sandel argues we must bring our full and complex identities to the public square, resisting the impulse to fundamentalism (1996, 350–51), so we must affirm the humanity and complexity of others, and the complexity of the issues we grapple with as citizens of a democracy. As Knoblauch has claimed, "as we attempt to help students negotiate difference, both within the classroom and in the larger social realm, we do them a disservice" if we are only teaching them the tools of argument (2011, 263). While there is a time and place for persuasion, there is also a time and a place for listening, empathy, and dialogue where mutual understanding, not change, is the goal.

In his 2002 essay, Scholes wrote that "even in these difficult times we must remain open to otherness. If we accept this rhetorical goal as part of our teaching mission, it follows that we must organize a curriculum to support it" (169). This statement continues to resonate today. Carillo (2018) has suggested that an understanding of empathy's role in learning and cognition has particular "relevance in today's divisive climate," and she concluded that as a field we would do well to question the way we "privilege argumentation" (99) and to explore alternative pedagogies that model more holistic ways of knowing. As we work "to connect the development of reading and writing skills to the real world around us" (Scholes 2002, 171), we should continue to ask in what new ways our teaching can "actively nurture the development of more mature cognitive orientations toward the world, toward others, and toward the production of knowledge and meaning" (Sullivan 2014, 37). Indeed, as the federal judge Learned Hand (1944) stated, "The spirit of liberty is the spirit which is not too sure that it is right; the spirit of liberty is the spirit which seeks to understand the mind of other men and women; the spirit of liberty is the spirit which weighs their interests alongside its own without bias." Rather than fearing uncertainty, we should help our students see uncertainty as essential to the "spirit of liberty." In our pursuit of truth, we must be willing to approach the world, and the people we share it with, with the belief that we still have more to learn.

REFERENCES

Akyol, Mustafa. 2017. "Away in the Manger... Or Under a Palm Tree?" *New York Times*, December 21, 2017. https://www.nytimes.com/2017/12/21/opinion/manger-jesus-birthplace-islam.html.
Alexander, Jonathan, and Jacqueline Rhodes. 2014. "Flattening Effects: Composition's Multicultural Imperative and the Problem of Narrative Coherence." *Conference on College Composition* 65 (3): 430–54.
Bloom, Paul. 2016. *Against Empathy: The Case for Rational Compassion*. New York: Ecco.
Bunn, Michael. 2013. "Motivation and Connection: Teaching Reading (and Writing) in the Composition Classroom." *College Composition and Communication* 64 (3): 496–516.
Carillo, Ellen C. 2018. *Teaching Readers in Post-Truth America*. Logan: Utah State University Press.
Carraway, Kimberly. 2014. *Transforming Your Teaching: Practical Classroom Strategies Informed by Cognitive Neuroscience*. New York: Norton.
Clifton, Jennifer. 2016. *Argument as Dialogue Across Difference: Engaging Youth in Public Literacies*. New York: Routledge.
Coplan, Amy. 2011. "Understanding Empathy: Its Features and Effects." In *Empathy: Philosophical and Psychological Perspectives*, edited by Amy Coplan and Peter Goldie, 3–18. Oxford: Oxford University Press.
Damianidou, Eleni, and Helen Phtiaka. 2016. "A Critical Pedagogy of Empathy: Making a Better World Achievable." *Pedagogies: An International Journal* 11 (3): 235–48.
Daniels, Harvey, and Stephen Zemelman. 2004. "How Smart Readers Think." In *Subjects Matter: Every Teacher's Guide to Content-Area Reading*, 21–34. Portsmouth, NH: Heinemann.
DeStigter, Todd. 1999. "Public Displays of Affection: Political Community through Critical Empathy." *Research in the Teaching of English* 33 (3): 235–44.
Duffy, John. 2014. "Ethical Positions: A Discourse for Rhetoric and Composition." *JAC* 34 (1/2): 209–37.
Duffy, John. 2017. "Post-Truth and First-Year Writing." *Inside Higher Ed*, May 8, 2017. https://www.insidehighered.com/views/2017/05/08/first-year-writing-classes-can-teach-students-how-make-fact-based-arguments-essay.
Elbow, Peter. 1973. *Writing without Teachers*. Oxford: Oxford University Press.
Encina, Gregorio Billikopf. 2006. "Empathetic Approach: Listening First Aid." University of California Berkeley, College of Natural Resources. https://nature.berkeley.edu/ucce50/ag-labor/7article/listening_skills.htm.
Endicott College. 2017. *Academic Catalog 2017–18*. Beverly: Endicott College.
Endicott College. 2019. *Facts and Figures*. Beverly: Endicott College.
English, Andrea. 2016. "John Dewey and the Role of the Teacher in a Globalized World: Imagination, Empathy, and 'Third Voice.'" *Educational Philosophy and Theory* 48 (10): 1046–64.
Fleckenstein, Kristie S. 2007. "Once Again with Feeling: Empathy in Deliberative Discourse." *JAC* 27 (3/4): 701–16.
Foss, Sonja. 2009. "Invitational Rhetoric." In *Encyclopedia of Communication Theory*, edited by Stephen W. Littlejohn and Karen A. Foss, 569–71. London: SAGE.
Foss, Sonja K., and Cindy L. Griffin. 1995. "Beyond Persuasion: A Proposal for an Invitational Rhetoric." *Communication Monographs* 62 (1): 2–18.
Gallo, Delores. 1994. "Educating for Empathy, Reason, and Imagination." In *Re-Thinking Reason: New Perspectives in Critical Thinking*, edited by Kerry S. Walters, 43–60. Albany: State University of New York Press.
Gerdes, Karen E., Elizabeth A. Segal, Kelly F. Jackson, and Jennifer L. Mullins. 2011. "Teaching Empathy: A Framework Rooted in Social Cognitive Neuroscience and Social Justice." *Journal of Social Work Education* 47 (1): 109–31.

Hand, Learned. 1944. "The Spirit of History." Digital History. Accessed October 4, 2018. https://www.digitalhistory.uh.edu/disp_textbook.cfm?smtID=3&psid=1199.

Hoyt, Linda. 1992. "Many Ways of Knowing: Using Drama, Oral Interactions, and the Visual Arts to Enhance Reading." *Reading Teacher* 45 (8): 580–84.

Jurecic, Ann. 2011. "Empathy and the Critic." *College English* 74 (1): 10–27.

Keen, Suzanne. 2007. *Empathy and the Novel.* Oxford: Oxford University Press.

Kirtley, Susan. 2014. "Considering the Alternative in Composition Pedagogy: Teaching Invitational Rhetoric with Lynda Barry's What It Is." *Women's Studies in Communication* 37: 339.

Knoblauch, Abby. 2008. "Teaching Toward Understanding: Feminist Rhetorical Theories and Pedagogies in the Composition Classroom." PhD diss., University of New Hampshire.

Knoblauch, Abby. 2011. "A Textbook Argument: Definitions of Argument in Leading Composition Textbooks." *College Composition and Communication* 63 (22): 244–68.

Leake, Eric. 2016. "Writing Pedagogies of Empathy: As Rhetoric and Disposition." *Composition Forum* 35. http://compositionforum.com/issue/34/empathy.php.

Lunsford, Andrea A., and John J. Ruszkiewicz. 2016. *Everything's an Argument.* New York: Bedford/St. Martin's.

Mirra, Nicole. 2018. *Educating for Empathy: Literacy Learning and Civic Engagement.* New York: Teachers College Press.

Modesti, Sonja. 2012. "Invitation Accepted: Integrating Invitational Rhetoric in Educational Contexts." *Current Issues in Education* 15 (1): 1–11.

Nussbaum, Martha. 2010. *Not for Profit: Why Democracy Needs the Humanities.* Princeton, NJ: Princeton University Press.

Pintrich, Paul, Ronald Marx, and Robert Boyle. 1993. "Beyond Cold Conceptual Change: The Role of Motivational Beliefs and Classroom Contextual Factors in the Process of Conceptual Change." *Review of Educational Research* 63 (2): 167–99.

Ryan, Kathleen, and Tarez Samra Graban. 2009. "Theorizing Feminist Pragmatic as Rhetoric as a Communicative Art for the Composition Practicum." *College Composition and Communication* 61 (1): W277–W299.

Sandel, Michael. 1996. *Democracy's Discontent: America in Search of a Public Philosophy.* Cambridge, MA: Belknap Press.

Scholes, Robert. 2002. "The Transition to College Reading." *Pedagogy* 2 (2): 165–72.

Shulman, Lee S. 2007. "Foreword." In *Educating for Democracy: Preparing Undergraduates for Responsible Political Engagement*, by Anne Colby, Elizabeth Beaumont, Thomas Ehrlich, and Josh Corngold, ix–xiii. San Francisco, CA: Jossey-Bass.

Shuman, Amy. 2005. *Other People's Stories: Entitlement Claims and the Critique of Empathy.* Urbana: University of Illinois Press.

Sullivan, Patrick. 2014. *A New Writing Classroom: Listening, Motivation, and Habits of Mind.* Logan: Utah State University Press.

ten Dam, Geert, and Monique Volman. 2004. "Critical Thinking as a Citizenship Competence: Teaching Strategies." *Learning and Instruction* 14: 359–79.

Tomlinson, Carol Ann, and Michael Murphy. 2018. "The Empathetic School." *Educational Leadership* 75 (6): 20–27. http://www.ascd.org/publications/educational-leadership/mar18/vol75/num06/The-Empathetic-School.aspx.

Von Wright, Moira. 2002. "Narrative Imagination and Taking the Perspective of Others." *Studies in Philosophy and Education* 21: 407–16.

Wan, Amy. 2011. "In the Name of Citizenship: The Writing Classroom and the Promise of Citizenship." *College English* 74 (1): 28–49.

7
"EVERYDAY THEORY"
Robert Scholes and the Ethics of Reading

Christian Smith

> *The world resists language as the grain of a tree resists the saw, and saws take the form that they do partly because wood is what it is.*
> —Robert Scholes, *Textual Power*, 112

Every August the Center for Contemplative Mind in Society (CMind) holds a week-long session for professionals in higher education. As the name suggests, CMind's purpose is to further the development and practice of contemplative pedagogies in postsecondary institutions. In 2016 I was fortunate enough to join CMind at Smith College in an attempt to discover methods for integrating contemplative pedagogies into my own teaching practices—specifically, first-year reading and writing courses. While there were many breakout sessions that were helpful in this regard, one in particular made a lasting impact on my teaching practices and the way that I approach reading in the classroom: Rose Sackey-Milligan's session, "Reading Frederick Douglass Contemplatively."

I arrived in one of the many halls inside Smith's Campus Center, where close to thirty participants were sitting in a large open circle as Sackey-Milligan circulated what was to be our shared reading for that afternoon, Frederick Douglass's famous speech to the Rochester Anti-Slavery Sewing Society, "The Meaning of July Fourth for the Negro." After the sheets had been handed out, we were told that we would begin by taking a minute to sit quietly, resisting the urge to begin reading, and only paying attention to our breath and each other. After which, we were instructed that we would each read one paragraph of the text, going from first to last, and then we would take another minute of mindful silence. Then a second round of reading of prechosen paragraphs would be designated to specific readers followed by a third minute of silence. And finally, we would be invited to add a single word response to the text. As a teacher not accustomed to students reading aloud in the classroom and, in the rare instances that we do, it is for the purposes of spurring on discussion rather than resisting discussion or limiting it to a one-word response, I was taken aback by Sackey-Milligan's method of Lectio Divina. In many ways the experience was both novel and familiar. Novel in that the experience of listening to Douglass's words read aloud by all of us gathered there in that room—often through tears, shaky breath, and much hesitation—made it possible to hear Douglass in a way that was inaccessible to me previously when reading the speech silently alone. Because there in that room the words were embodied and given voice in such an unexpected way that the very act of reading itself was defamiliarized from my habitual modes of silent reading. Though, on the other hand, the experience was also familiar in that I was able to frame hearing Douglass speak that day through an article I encountered many years ago, in my first years of teaching: Robert Scholes's "The Transition to College Reading" (2002). In that article, Scholes notes that one of the problems with literacy instruction in contemporary classrooms is that we don't see student reading in the same way that we see student writing, and much is lost with this absence. What we would see if we could witness student reading, Scholes argues, is an inability to engage with otherness and, as a result, a way of reading that reduces difference into something familiar. Much of what I experienced that day in Sackey-Milligan's session reminded me of how contemplative reading practices working with silence and reading aloud can allow us to witness embodied reading in just the way Scholes advocates. In the classroom, such practices may hold potential for both teachers and students to engage other subject positions and a way to work with difference through shared reading. In this way, contemplative reading can be tailored to antioppression pedagogies that, according to Beth Berila (2016), value "critical self-reflection of ideologies, power, and privilege," but can also foster the mindfulness that such pedagogies often lack (3). But how does contemplative reading accomplish this and what is it about reading aloud that defamiliarizes texts in this way?

According to Scholes (2002, 168), "Reading aloud makes the reading process evident to the ear in tone and rhythm and to the eye in bodily posture and facial expression, just as writing makes the composing process evident in written signs." While this elocutionary dimension of reading was fundamental to literacy teachers in previous decades, it has since been abandoned as the emphasis has shifted to undertheorizing reading in favor of theorizing writing. For Scholes, this shift in emphasis did not simply result in worse readers in our classrooms, but readers with an inability to hear the words of others—that is, there is an ethical dimension to reading that was lost and it is this dimension of reading that is indicative of the more pervasive cultural problem of not being very good at "imagining the other" (Scholes 2002, 167). As prescient as Scholes's work was throughout his career, this seems particularly true after the election of Donald Trump in an era when any disagreeable texts can be dismissed as "fake news" and when appeals to small "t" truth are seen as culturally retrograde. As Scholes (2002) argues:

> I want to say that a good person, in our time, needs to have the rhetorical capacity to imagine the other's thought, feeling, and sentiments. That is, though not all rhetoricians are good people, all good citizens must be rhetoricians to the extent that they can imagine themselves in the place of another and understand views different from their own. It is our responsibility as English teachers to help our students develop this form of textual power, in which strength comes, paradoxically, from subordinating one's own thoughts temporarily to the views and values of another person. (168)

Here Scholes is responding specifically to the post-9/11 Islamophobia and, more broadly, to the "American way" of student resistance to otherness as demonstrated in literacy instruction. In contemporary writing classes, students confront texts that run contrary to their own home discourses, chosen ideological positions, or simply against the dominant discourses they have internalized. As a result, literacy instruction needs ways to engage such texts without eliciting immediate responses—responses that, more often than not, are simply reductions of real and painful difference into the comfortably familiar. Citing Katz and Wilner, Scholes (2002) notes that students either "assimilate the thought and feeling in a text to their own thoughts and feelings" or "recognize a different position and simply refuse to read it or think about it" (169). As I was reminded in that session on Smith's campus, and again by rereading Scholes's article, the act of reading a text is always an ethical concern and, to his credit, Scholes never let teachers forget this.

This chapter puts Scholes's work on reading and textuality in conversation with contemporary discussions of contemplative and antioppression pedagogies in composition studies (Wenger 2015, Mathieu 2016) in order to emphasize such ethical questions of literacy instruction in the face of a "post-truth" America (Carillo 2017). This chapter also argues that to contextualize Scholes's ethics of reading in "Transition to College Reading," it is necessary to understand the central concepts in one of his earlier works, *Textual Power* (1985) and specifically the concepts Scholes refers to as the secular and hermetic positions regarding language. The former views language as pure representation, in which signs more or less stand in for empirical objects in the world; the latter is the view that language is essentially nonreferential and self-reflective. For Scholes, the increasing popularity of the hermetic position within English studies at the time of the book's publication was something to be taken seriously because it had such serious consequences pedagogically. In *Textual Power* Scholes not only arrived at the pedagogical hazards of poststructuralism and deconstruction for writing instructors long before other scholars in English studies, but worked to develop an ethics of reading to coincide with teaching for social justice and antioppression pedagogies. In this way, this chapter works to articulate a contemplative literacy that could provide instructors with a way to counteract the above-mentioned student tendencies toward eliding difference and a framework for reading that attempts to foreclose the reinscription of oppressive discourses by prompting students and instructors to identify habitual responses to the shared reading. As such, contemplative reading practices are central to conventional aims of critical information literacy that are so often repeated in faculty meetings and that appear in the Student Learning Outcomes on our syllabi.

The impasse between the secular and hermetic orientations toward language identified by Scholes can also be read in more recent work of Raúl Sánchez (2012), who argues that "the issue today is that composition's modernist and postmodernist legacies together do not offer enough equipment with which to theorize, examine, and teach writing in contemporary contexts" (236). For Sánchez, one possibility is to redefine the negative connotations of "empiricism" in scholarly research as simply "looking at things in a systematic way and then making statements about them" (emphasis in the original, 239). In this way, the divisions between theory and empiricism, much like similar divisions between critical and experiential modes of knowledge production, would be diminished. Similarly, practices of contemplative literacy informed by Scholes's work seek hybrid empirical pedagogies unwilling to decide between invention and discovery, or, said differently, between text and world. Such an orientation looks back toward the "commonsense materiality" of the writer to give an "identifiable object focal point for pedagogy" (Sánchez 2012, 235). With this in mind, literacy instructors could begin to attend to textuality in ways that Robert Scholes discusses in *Textual Power*, particularly his readings of Terry Eagleton and Paul de Man in the fifth chapter, "The Text and the World."

In this chapter, Scholes wants to define textuality in such a way that justifies the practice of putting text in conversation with the world and, thereby, giving teachers a way out of the isolationists' tendencies of theory—theory, I should say, in service of text alone at the expense of the world. The problem of this relationship, between text and world, is not simply another theoretical issue amongst many others, but rather it is "above all others, the problem that makes textual theory necessary" (Scholes 1985, 75). From this relationship, Scholes explores two distinct approaches to addressing the problem: the hermetic and the secular. As Scholes sums up the two positions beautifully, "the secular or worldly critics see texts as historically grounded in public occasions and socially supported codes. The hermetic interpreters see texts as radically self-reflective and nonreferential—and therefore beyond the reach of criticism" (76). Scholes then explicates these positions through the work of Eagleton and de Man—Eagleton's position is identified as secular, while de Man's position serves as a premier example of the hermetic—in order to arrive at a kind of impasse between the two finally noting that the hermetic position ends in a "quietistic acceptance of injustice" as world and text are incommensurable, but with the secular approach, on the other hand, texts are open to interpretation and knowable to the level of subtext and, as such, open to questions of social transformation and justice. Much of Robert Scholes's career was spent attempting to find a productive dialogue between these two positions. In this volume, Kenny Smith's "Truth, Propaganda, and Textual Power" details Scholes's work in this regard and its importance to contemporary literacy instruction, noting that "Scholes is attempting to strike a middle position between poststructuralism, which wants to remove the importance of reference entirely from the text, and more traditional views that see language as a transparent mirror of reality." For Scholes, the stakes of such a middle position weren't simply to add another voice in the already overcrowded debates surrounding theory, but the value of teaching literacy itself.

After the 2016 presidential election, the stakes of the hermetic understanding of texts have been made increasingly clear. The rise of "post-truth" politics and "fake news" have demonstrated that it matters that literacy teachers can reference a world outside of the text and assign relative truth values to specific discourses. Speaking about one such hermetic position, deconstructionism, particularly as it was identified and related to the Yale School of Deconstruction, Scholes notes: "From the perspective of deconstruction, there is nothing upon which we can ground an argument for evolutionary biology as opposed to fundamentalist creationism, since both are discourses, with their blindness and their insights, and neither one can be said to be more or less accurate than the other, there being no pathway open from the text to the world"

(1985, 99). Given this, the hermetic position forecloses not only reading as an ethical encounter with the other, but as a mode of accessing knowledge and language's ability to reference itself. Such a position is the perfect foundation for post-truth politics and Scholes identified it as such. As Bruce McComiskey (2017) reminds us, reading in a climate of post-truth politics is crucial because what it can "accomplish is the reassertion of truth and reality into the epistemological continuum, even if our own and our students' commitments are with reasoned opinions and sound arguments, not truth." Further, McComiskey argues that having truth back "on the epistemological continuum means that the old nemeses of truth (lies, fallacies, and doublespeak) also return to the continuum" (41). Similarly, David Riche (2017) has noted the detrimental influence and circulation of "fake news" in a post-truth climate as "stories that frequently prey on audiences' vulnerabilities both through their outrageous rhetoric and through their subversion of trust in sources" (91). Riche also argues that implementing mindful approaches attuned to how vulnerability operates rhetorically in media—fake news media or otherwise—is necessary in contemporary literacy instruction if we are interested in social justice. Both McComiskey and Riche gesture toward literacy models that accurately reflect Scholes's notion of the secular attitude toward textuality as one that encourages reference to be marked with relative truth value in order to be open to the idea of reading as an ethical practice capable of addressing the questions of social justice while having the goal of being actively antioppressive.

Not long after the publication of *Textual Power*, Lester Faigley (1992) characterized Scholes's work alongside the work of Richard Ohmann and James Berlin as a "cultural studies" approach to literacy instruction as, for Faigley, those scholars all ask students to analyze the subtexts of texts—that is, the ideological positions and role of power that structure texts and call students to be particular kinds of subjects. While Faigley is certainly right to make these connections, particularly given the first four chapters of *Textual Power*, I would argue that typifying Scholes's work as simply advocating a cultural studies approach tells us more about the intellectual climate and fashions of the time than it does about the book. Further, the philosophy of language presented in the latter chapters of *Textual Power* work to nuance Faigley's cultural studies assessment, and it is worth quoting in full:

> The position I take all along, sometimes arguing one side of the case, sometimes the other, is that we neither capture nor create the world with our texts, but interact with it. . . . We divide the world into classes of things: trees, bushes, shrubs, flowers, weeds, and vegetables, for instance, which

need not be divided up in just that way. But neither we as individuals, or our cultural group, nor yet language itself can accomplish this division freely and arbitrarily. The world resists language as the grain of a tree resists the saw, and saws take the form they do partly because wood is what it is. We sense the presence of things through this resistance. But, as with the saw, language differentiates by an act of violence. . . . Human beings become human through the acquisition of language, and this acquisition alienates humans from all those things that language names. (112)

This, for me, is why Scholes's work is as important now as it was when it was first published. With Scholes we get a practical sense of textuality as an ethical challenge to be taken on rather than the play of pure difference that was much more in vogue during the time of *Textual Power*'s publication. Approaching the text, for Scholes, meant initially asking: "What violence is being done here?" (112). Inevitably, the use of language itself entails, for the reader, a kind of epistemological violence alienating the reader from the world they were previously experiencing. But there can be a kind of violence directed toward the writer as well in the refusal to hear and, ultimately, an inability or resistance to read the other present in the text. In many ways such resistances can be approached through contemplative reading practices in the classroom in the ways Scholes argues is necessary to transition to college reading.

There is, of course, precedence for contemplative practices in both eastern and western institutions of learning insofar as the history of contemplative monasticism is tethered to formal education. But what I mean here by contemplative pedagogy in a more contemporary sense is perhaps best defined by Arthur Zajonc (2013) as the "quiet revolution" taking place on college campuses that is defined by "a wide range of educational methods that support the development of student attention, emotional balance, empathetic connection, compassion, and altruistic behavior, while also providing new pedagogical techniques that support creativity and the learning of course content" (83). While there are elements of contemplative practice in higher education, they are too often relegated to outlier status as the dominant models of teaching and learning are objectivist in nature. To quote Parker Palmer's introduction to *Contemplative Practices in Higher Education: Powerful Methods to Transform Teaching and Learning* (Barbezat and Bush 2014), objectivism in education "begins as an epistemology rooted in a false conception of science [and] insists on a wall of separation between the knower and the known" (vii). Palmer's words here are strikingly similar to James Berlin's mapping of the pedagogies and theoretical foundations of composition studies in the 1980s. Specifically, Berlin's discussion (1987) of objective rhetoric is based "on a positivistic epistemology, asserting that the real is located in the material world. From this perspective, only that which is empirically verifiable or which can be grounded in empirically verifiable phenomena is real" (7). Further, for Berlin, such models of education attempt to sidestep questions of ideology by "claiming for itself the transcendent neutrality of science." More recently, arguments for the possibility of a postpositivist pedagogy attempt to close the theoretical gulfs in such discourse. For instance, as Sánchez (2012) argues concerning postpositivist theories of identity, "Identity, according to these theorists, is an indispensable concept because it links the theoretical and the empirical, the conceptual and the historical. Identity is a result of the fact that things happen to people and that people try to make sense of these things" (241). One of the ways people try to make sense of their experience is, of course, through writing and, as such, it is incumbent upon the reader to hear how they are making sense. And as Scholes (2002) argues: "The basis of an education for citizens of a democracy lies in that apparently simple but actually difficult act of reading so as to grasp and evaluate the thoughts and feelings of that mysterious other person: the writer" (171). In many ways this relates to Krista Ratcliffe's (2005) notion of rhetorical listening as it: "also means more than simply listening for our own self-interested intent, which may range from appropriation (employing a text for one's own ends), to Burkean identification (smoothing over differences), to agreement (only affirming one's own view of reality). Instead, understanding means listening to discourse not for intent but with intent—with the intent to understand not just the claims, not just the cultural logics within which the claims function, but the rhetorical negotiations of understanding as well" (205). The reader, employing rhetorical listening, requires a kind of contemplative literacy in that the audience is listening to hear not only the other, but how their own cultural logics, positioning, and home discourses are brought to bear on what they read. Scholes argued that it is a matter of good teaching that literacy instructors must themselves stand back from their immediate responses to texts, tempering their own reactions in measured ways, and allowing space for students to do the same. Given this, we may broaden our definition of argumentative practices to include and acknowledge multiple discourses at play in any literacy event and a necessity to honor those conversations apart from our own positions as readers. In this way, the movement from Scholes's ethics of reading to the arguably larger goals of contemplative pedagogy, typified by Zajonc above, as well as the antioppression pedagogies identified by Berila and others, is an easy one to make.

In the hopes of attending to the literacy practices of our students in such a way that presents reading as an ethical practice, we could offer students opportunities to read contemplatively in order to step back and work toward contextualizing their own discourses, and ideological positioning influences how the text is read. As Scholes notes: "If rhetoric is a schooling in textual virtue as well as in textual power, as I believe it is, this virtue consists largely in our being able to assume another person's point of view before criticizing it and resuming our own" (2002, 169). Literacy instruction, in this way, would be in the direction of social justice from the beginning. Resistance to such assumptions is often typified in antioppression and contemplative scholarship as the result of privilege. As Berila (2016) notes, one of the key features of privilege is the perception that privileged subjects can remain "oblivious" to the "deep entitlement" of privileged identities benefiting from systems of oppression (91). The "privilege of obliviousness" can be counteracted by contemplative reading practices such as Lectio Divina and is, in many ways, the aim of such practice.

At this point, I hope the value Scholes's work holds for contemplative pedagogical practices is clear, including how his work continues to encourage students to further engage the other through rhetorically listening to the voices they encounter in texts and the classroom. As Berila advocates for the use of these practices within the context of antiracist and antioppression classrooms, I would also like to gesture toward Jennifer Trainor's observations locating student racism in habitual and emotive reactions in her study of English classes in an all-white high school, published in *Rethinking Racism: Emotion, Persuasion, and Literacy Education in an All-White High School* (2008). Trainor positions the racism she observed, which often manifested in echoes of prejudices and stereotypes, as articulations of emotionality (4). For these students, emotions were crucial to the generation of meaning in text. Readers make connections between ideas and their own experiences, ideological positions, and preconceived notions about an idea that can be difficult to break. If this is the case, contemplative practices may help us become aware of the role of emotion and habit in the composition classroom as well as encourage us to reroute ways of thinking that might inadvertently support social inequality.

Recently, in a first-year English class, a student of mine was prompted to respond to Ta-Nehisi Coates's *Between the World and Me* (2015). In this initial response written after having been assigned the text, but prior to our class reading aloud with planned silences and limited response, she referenced the circumstances of the death of Michael Brown—the resulting trial and exoneration of Officer Darren Wilson is central to the book and serves as an exigence for Coates's writing a letter to his then-fifteen-year-old son—as somehow justified due to Brown's robbery of a convenience store prior to his murder. To me, as a literacy instructor, the student's reading illustrates the kind of emotionality Trainor describes: it focuses on the immediate reaction from one subject position—in this case an affluent white woman—at the cost of all others. In her response she suggested that because Brown broke the law in robbing a corner store the consequences he encountered were justified. This rigidity in thinking feels more like a knee-jerk reaction than one that recognizes the nuances of the law and the potentials for nonlethal responses to criminality. This response is not hers alone, of course, but echoes much larger cultural discourses and perspectives. What is interesting, however, is that after reading aloud with the text collectively embodied in our own voices, Coates's words had a different impact and the same student responded in ways that sought alternative forms of policing that could lead to nonlethal resolutions.

Contemplative reading practices move us as teachers toward the recognition of such harsh realities and work to articulate just how part of our role as good readers is an ethical engagement with these realities as they are references to lived experiences and not simply "texts." Such practices embody what Scholes meant by rhetoric and his resistance to the uncoupling of rhetoric from ethics, specifically in the context of pedagogy. Contemplative reading practices such as the Lectio Divina method outlined by my experiences with Rose Sackey-Milligan could work in conjunction with other Scholes-inspired pedagogies working toward empathetic literacy instruction such as those outlined by Kelsey McNiff in this volume. In McNiff's detailed assignment sequence, students research the ideas of people who disagreed with them, using "mainstream news outlets, credible blogs, organization websites, academic articles, or other relevant and reliable sources that allowed them to hear from their audience about why they held the ideas they did" in order to "understand how people's values, belief systems, individual concerns, personal experiences, communities, or environments may have shaped their views." As Scholes would argue, this too is part of learning how to read. Reading aloud as a contemplative practice could extend McNiff's invitational aims in productive ways.

Even given this, I realize that contemplative practices—given their history and context—can make many literacy instructors tentative. While notions of "spirituality" may play an enormous role in our personal lives, many of us, perhaps rightly, hold that such practices and beliefs should be kept out of the classroom. Recently, however, thanks to the work of Gesa Kirsch (2009) and Paul Lynch (2018), there are ways to articulate spiritual practice in the classroom that are not aligned with any particular religion or belief. As Lynch notes, "For many, the word spiritual may imply something too religious, too personal, or simply too Oprah. Yet our field's growing interest in mindfulness and meditation, along with our developing understanding of writing as a practice, suggests that a moment has come in which we might see writing as a spiritual exercise" (501). And, as Kirsch notes: "allowing spirituality and contemplation to become a source of creativity, insight, and discovery, we enable students to become more willing to engage with the complex social, cultural, and political issues of our times" (W2). Similarly, Paul T. Corrigan (2013) compares contemplative reading to the more conventional critical and active forms of reading we are used to seeing in the classroom. Corrigan notes that, unlike critical reading, contemplative reading is predicated upon silence and listening. More broadly but in a similar register, Ellen C. Carillo's (2017, vi) *A Writer's Guide to Mindful Reading* encourages students to be aware of their own reading processes as a means of "paying attention not just to the content of the text—what it says—but rather to the process of reading itself by adjusting how you read based on what the piece asks of you." Given our combined disciplinary histories, Scholes's notion of textuality and the distinctions between hermetic and secular orientations toward reading serve as a crucial framework to integrating contemplative reading practices in literacy instruction. As Scholes (2002, 171) has argued, "We need, in short, to connect the development of reading and writing skills to the real world around us and to the virtual world in which that actual world becomes available to us in the form of texts." Contemplative reading practices can serve as one such way to accomplish this.

REFERENCES

Barbezat, Daniel P., and Mirabai Bush. 2014. *Contemplative Practices in Higher Education: Powerful Methods to Transform Teaching and Learning.* San Francisco: Jossey-Bass.

Berila, Beth. 2016. *Integrating Mindfulness into Anti-Oppression Pedagogy: Social Justice in Higher Education.* New York: Routledge.

Berlin, James. 1987. *Rhetoric and Reality: Writing Instruction in American Colleges, 1900–1985.* Carbondale: Southern Illinois University Press.

Carillo, Ellen C. 2017. *A Writer's Guide to Mindful Reading.* Fort Collins: The WAC Clearinghouse and University Press of Colorado.

Coates, Ta-Nehesi. 2015. *Between the World and Me.* New York: Spiegel & Grau.

Corrigan, Paul T. 2013. "Attending to the Act of Reading: Critical Reading, Contemplative Reading, and Active Reading." *Reader* 63: 146–73.

Faigley, Lester. 1992. *Fragments of Rationality: Postmodernity and the Subject of Composition.* Pittsburgh, PA: University of Pittsburgh Press.

Kirsch, Gesa E. 2009. "From Introspection to Action: Connecting Spirituality and Civic Engagement." *College Composition and Communication* 60 (4): W1–W15.

Lynch, Paul. 2018. "Shadow Living: Towards Spiritual Exercises for Teaching." *College English* 80 (6): 499–516.

Mathieu, Paula. 2015. "Being There: Mindfulness as Ethical Classroom Practice." *JAEPL* 21: 14–20.

McComiskey, Bruce. 2017. *Post-Truth Rhetoric and Composition.* Boulder, CO: Utah State University Press.

Ratcliffe, Krista. 2005. *Rhetorical Listening: Identification, Gender, Whiteness.* Carbondale: Southern Illinois University Press.

Riche, David. 2017. "Toward a Theory and Pedagogy of Rhetorical Vulnerability." *Literacy in Compositions Studies* 5 (2): 84–102.

Sánchez, Raúl. 2012. "Outside the Text: Retheorizing Empiricism and Identity." *College English* 74 (3): 234–46.

Scholes, Robert. 1985. *Textual Power: Literacy Theory and the Teaching of English.* New Haven, CT: Yale University Press.

Scholes, Robert. 2002. "The Transition to College Reading." *Pedagogy* 2 (2): 165–72.

Trainor, Jennifer. 2008. *Rethinking Racism: Emotion, Persuasion, and Literacy Education in an All-White High School.* Carbondale: Southern Illinois University Press.

Wegner, Christina I. 2015. *Yoga Minds, Writing Bodies: Contemplative Writing Pedagogy.* Perspectives on Writing. Fort Collins, CO: The WAC Clearinghouse and Parlor Press.

Zajonc, Arthur. 2013. "Contemplative Pedagogy: A Quiet Revolution in Higher Education." *New Directions for Teaching and Learning* 134: 83–94.

8

TRUTH, PROPAGANDA, AND TEXTUAL POWER
A Pedagogy for Combatting Cynicism in the Post-Truth Era

Kenny Smith

In my ten-week introductory academic writing course at the University of California, Santa Barbara, I've experimented with numerous approaches to increase my students' civic literacy. My early efforts were designed to correct misunderstandings in their essays, and, like many instructors, I initially strove to encourage more skepticism. For example, I was frustrated with how students used statistics, almost like they were transparent truths that could be used to squash dissent. To help students become more savvy data consumers, I designed a lesson about basic quantitative literacy focused on how data can be deceptive. Throughout the class, we had fun looking at misleading graphs that I carefully picked from bipartisan sources, studying the impact of truncating the axes or playing around with the scales. While I was initially satisfied with my cleverness, a conversation I heard after class gave me pause. As a group of students were leaving, one of them muttered, "Yeah, that's why I think all statistics are bullshit." Of course, I wanted them to become more critical readers, not to doubt the mathematical foundation of all science. Similarly, I introduced an assignment designed to help students connect research with their everyday lives. Once again, the idea was prompted by issues in student essays, particularly in regard to how they drew upon science—they treated studies as transparent facts, much like they had with statistics. To remedy the situation, I constructed an assignment that asked students to examine the relationship between science and the media. They had to choose a recently published study, look at two media articles that discussed it, and evaluate how well they dealt with the research. By the end of the unit, my students came away with the impression that the media was filled with charlatans looking for clicks. Eventually, I realized the problem wasn't that students were too credulous—in fact, it was the opposite. Because most of their experience was with hyperpartisan rhetoric on social media, they were already predisposed to notice flaws in the news.

This revelation marked the beginning of my journey to revise how I handled the media in my introductory courses. In this chapter, I chronicle my struggle to avoid the moment when skepticism tips over into cynicism, when students move from asking good questions to disregarding the importance of journalistic discourse. Perhaps the media has experienced some growing pains in the digital age, but we still depend on it to keep us informed about contemporary issues. As a longtime fan of news magazines—I'm one of the few people that continues to receive them in print—I want students to not only question the information that appears in their newsfeeds but also to recognize the value of the tremendous reporting being done throughout the country. One of my main inspirations when reshaping my approach to civic literacy was Robert Scholes, who devoted the end of his career to discussing the need to promote "textual power" among students. In our increasingly textual world, he considered it crucial that students have the ability to control texts in a range of discourses, not just those in the academy. While he rarely discussed journalism, he anticipated our current climate in uncanny ways, particularly in regard to how our rancorous discourse would drive us into isolated political bubbles. As a longstanding critic of poststructuralist theory, he also recognized the limitations of its ideas about referentiality, which is necessary for understanding journalism in the post-truth era.

IS THERE A FISH IN MY MEDIA?

Scholes emphasizes throughout his later work the importance of shifting the attention of the English curriculum away from literature and toward textuality. He still recognizes the importance of students developing familiarity with literature, but he argues they need to grow more adept at manipulating a wider range of texts. As he explains, "our culture is organized by the most complex system of textuality the world has ever known," and students need "to be 'literate' across a various and complex network of different kinds of writing and various media of communication" (1998, 130). Of course, while he foresaw the changes coming with technology, he never could have predicted the contemporary media landscape. Not only must we be fluent in several modalities—including images, video, and print—we also must be vigilant because so much of our information comes from social media, where computer algorithms decide what to share in our feeds largely based on what will keep us glued to our screens (O'Neil 2016; Tufecki 2018). Historically, the United States has been able to depend upon a strong national press, so we were unprepared for dealing with such challenges. The dangers became particularly apparent after the 2016 election, when stories began to emerge about the extent the public was influenced by problematic news sources, including everything from Russian propaganda to hyperpartisan ideologues (McComiskey 2017; Scott and Mazzetti 2018; Wilson 2018).

Because of the sheer volume of disinformation in the post-truth era, the first instinct of many teachers is to encourage students to be less credulous. After all, if social media users are gullible enough to share certain kinds of propaganda, the appropriate response seems to be skepticism—perhaps, students just don't know how to ask the right questions, or they haven't looked to see whether the information comes from a trustworthy source. However, as danah boyd (2018) observed in a widely circulated critique of the media literacy movement, the problem is that the public is already "fed up" with the media. We are suffering from what communications scholar Arjun Appadurai (2017) characterizes as "democracy fatigue," a state in which people have lost faith in key democratic institutions. According to a recent report from the Knight Foundation (2018), over 69 percent of the public claim to have lost trust in the media over the past decade, including an astonishing 94 percent of Republicans. These problems are particularly acute among young Americans. In a survey by The Media Insight Project (2018), a majority of adults over thirty saw the news as fairly accurate, while those eighteen to twenty-nine claimed the opposite. According to boyd, the danger is that we might inadvertently reinforce such cynicism, which is often exploited by extremist groups. Once the media is seen as compromised by ulterior motives, it becomes easier to question other truths, such as the norms of democratic governance. Educators in the post-truth era can't afford to subscribe to the idealistic view that the truth will appear once we clear away the debris.

The problem is compounded by the fact that students don't have much experience with journalism. With the rise of digital media, the United States has seen a sharp drop in newspaper circulation, to the extent that no guarantee exists that students have even physically seen one (Barthel 2018). Much like Christopher J. La Casse observes in this volume, students enter college with little awareness of the historical role of periodicals—most of their interaction with journalism happens on social media, where major outlets compete with more problematic sources. In fact, students might not even be able to recognize the difference between journalistic texts and other media—in a recent study examining around 126,000 stories tweeted between 2006 and 2017, falsehoods spread much quicker than the truth, perhaps because of the novelty and emotional resonance of their claims (Vosoughi, Roy, and Aral 2018). Likely because of their lack of exposure to journalism, when I first introduce students to journalistic texts, they are often shocked by how much work goes into their production.

At the same time, we need to be wary about encouraging blind faith in mainstream outlets, as if students will be cured if they just turn to "authoritative" sources. No matter how much effort reporters devote to tracking down sources, they always interpret a story through the lens of their cultural position. All discourses have this problem, but it is particularly dangerous with journalism, partially because the veneer of objectivity hides the ideological work behind the scenes. One notable example is the coverage of the Bush administration's decision to invade Iraq, where reporters uncritically accepted statements of government officials without proper due diligence (Barstow 2008). Many progressive activists have accused journalists of "false equivalence," arguing they provide voice to both sides of an argument even when the evidence overwhelmingly suggests one viewpoint is incorrect (Krugman 2016). While "fake news" is a problem, blind faith isn't the solution—as Scholes (1985, 14) argues, "if wisdom, or some less grandiose notion such as heightened awareness, is to be the end of our endeavors, we shall have to see it not as something transmitted from the text to student but as something developed in the student by questioning the text." The appropriate response to our post-truth culture isn't to construct new idols. Students need to be aware that journalism often hides the truth in its quest to reveal it.

In some ways, we are dealing with the same question that preoccupied Scholes (1985) in the final chapters of *Textual Power*, his treatise on how poststructuralist theory applies to the English classroom—namely, what is the relationship between discourse and truth? Can the truth ever be revealed in a text? Or, as he puts it toward the end of the book: "Is it possible for any text to catch a fish? Is it possible to catch a text?" (129). While the reference to "fish" bundles together numerous allusions, he initially uses it to invoke a pedagogical strategy employed by the nineteenth-century biologist Louis Agassiz, where he offered a student a small fish and asked for a description of it. The student began by regurgitating the details from textbooks, and when disapprovingly asked again for a description, proceeded to write an extensive essay. At that point, Agassiz told the student to simply look at the fish, now a rotting hunk of flesh, and only upon setting aside his preconceptions and genuinely examining the object did he learn something about it.

The problem with Agassiz's perspective is that it is never possible to obtain a neutral view of the fish, unfiltered by our cultural assumptions. As a product of his time, the esteemed nineteenth-century biologist ironically also only had a limited grasp of the fish, in that he was only able to perceive the natural world through the lens of his religious beliefs. Even after the scientific community began to embrace Darwinism, he continued to maintain that all species were "fixed from their creation" and rejected "all fossil evidence for evolution" (Scholes 1985, 143). The only way to "see" a fish is through a discourse, and our responsibility is to increase awareness of that fact:

> The way to see the fish and to write the fish is first to see how one's discourse writes the fish. And the way to see one discourse is to see more than one. To write the fish in many modes is finally to see that one will never catch *the* fish in any one discourse. As teachers of writing we have a special responsibility to help our students gain awareness of discourse structures and the ways in which they both enable and constrain our vision. And the only way to do this is to read and write in a range of discursive modes. (1985, 144)

Scholes is attempting to strike a middle position between poststructuralism, which wants to remove the importance of reference entirely from the text, and more traditional views that see language as a transparent mirror of reality. Although no discourse will entirely capture the fish's essence, each one will provide a tantalizing glimpse, and the job of writing instructors is to illustrate for students how all discourses provide insight while obscuring other possibilities. He later invokes a couplet from an Alexander Pope poem, where the truth is compared to an eel that always eludes our grasp. While language never provides us complete access to the truth, it is always slipping between the cracks of our words, and we can only come nearer to it by attending closely to its movements. To his contemporaries, his conception of truth might have seemed quaint, but he appears prescient given our current historical circumstances—as Christian Smith reminds us in this volume, the post-truth era demands that we reference a world outside of language.

Throughout his pedagogical work, Scholes is continually attempting to tease out the implications of this viewpoint, usually by showing the power of juxtaposing several different discourses within a course. In *Textual Power*, he asks literature instructors to "throw away [their] standard anthologies" and "choose perhaps three collections of short stories by writers whose work will offer good contrast of styles and values" (1985, 25). In *The Rise and Fall of English*, when describing a course he developed with the College Board, he argues that students need to learn the importance of "listening to [America's] voices, understanding how one culture can be made out of many voices, and finding the voices one needs to express oneself and be heard in the midst of this hubbub" (1998, 131). He has students begin with a novel, which he characterizes as a text holding together multiple voices that each reveal something about our culture. Afterwards, students look at voices produced by previous cultures and connect them to contemporary concerns. Then, they look at film, seeing how it brings together music, drama, and speech into a single medium. Finally, they examine how several different stories in the news media discuss the same event, which shows how "even in a single medium, such as print journalism, different newspapers may offer quite different versions" (1998, 141). The reason for putting together discordant discourses is not just to expose students to a wide range of approaches. He believes that the truth is hiding somewhere between discourses, and finding it requires looking from multiple vantage points.

THE TRUTH HIDING IN THE MARGINS

Because of his belief in the limitation of looking at the world through only a single lens, Scholes often emphasizes the importance of empathy, claiming that students need "to have the rhetorical capacity to imagine the other's thought, feeling, and sentiments . . . [and see] themselves in the place of another and understand views different from their own" (2002, 168). However, the process is more complex than just attending to a writer's emotions, for those are also inevitably inscribed within a discourse. When searching for another's perspective in a text, we must start by becoming familiar with the codes underpinning its construction, or we risk seeing nothing but a reflection of ourselves. As he explains about the film unit in his Pacesetter course, the idea "is to help students learn how the medium works from the inside, to become better readers by gaining a deeper understanding of how certain texts are composed" (1998, 139). Particularly when it comes to journalism, the issue is that texts hide the labor behind their production. Due to the rhetoric of objectivity that surrounds the medium, little information is given about the investigative process, which includes everything from corroborating sources to academic research. Every effort is made to hide the writer's presence, to the extent that bylines are a relatively recent invention; historically, they were kept off most stories, a tradition that continues in certain publications (Economist 2013). The result is that we "fill in" the gaps of our understanding of how journalism works from other sources, such as films valorizing reporters as heroes fighting corruption. So long as journalism's labor is invisible, readers will find it difficult to empathize with the writers, making it easier to dismiss them as just advancing an agenda.

In the last iteration of my introductory composition course, my strategy for dealing with this problem was to introduce students to a narrative of a journalist going about his work. Once students got a sense of how reporting works from the inside, they were able to more effectively identify the features of good journalism. We started with a chapter from *Bad Blood*, the recent book by John Carreyrou (2018) chronicling his reporting that brought about the downfall of Silicon Valley medical startup company Theranos. The middle of the book is dedicated to the investigative process, starting with the original tip from a medical blogger and ending with the aftermath of its publication. One advantage to this approach is that it shows the painstaking labor that goes into the production of the news. At the beginning, Carreyrou mentions tracking down Theranos's lab director, who provided him with enough information to know that the company was likely a fraud. Nevertheless, he resists giving into the original rush of excitement, stating that "there was no way the paper would take [the story] with just one anonymous source, however good that source might be" (2018, 228). Even after securing interviews with several witnesses, he headed to Phoenix, Arizona, to gather comments from doctors and patients who had trouble dealing with Theranos's equipment. The book gives insight into the aspects of journalism hidden from the typical article, such as the authors' own views, their changing emotional states, and how they handle resistance to their work, especially when they are confronting powerful figures.

However, the most important observations came when we read the narrative alongside one of the original articles. As Scholes points out, the truth often rests in the margins between discourses, and the conflicting version of events in the two articles helped illustrate the limitations of journalistic discourse. Many students noted its lack of a sensational title—"Theranos's Growing Pains"—which didn't seem appropriate for an article that alleges a company probably committed fraud (Carreyrou 2015). They also claimed the newspaper article was "boring," and many even questioned whether remaining so stubbornly objective was the right approach. Carreyrou never holds back his opinion in the book, at times even suggesting that Elizabeth Holmes—the company's chief executive—might be a sociopath. He questions the youth-worshipping culture that caused venture capitalists to give her millions in resources after she dropped out of Stanford at the young age of nineteen. He explicitly frames the story as indictment of Silicon Valley, portraying Theranos as merely an extreme example of how companies launch with defective products. In the smartphone space, a buggy application only poses limited danger, but recklessness has huge consequences in the medical industry, where people can literally die if treated by faulty equipment. None of these observations, however, are present in the newspaper article. Instead, he focuses on providing a factual account of the company's actions, leaving the audience to read between the lines to discern the larger implications. Given that the majority of readers aren't technology experts, they might miss why the story is important beyond its limited context.

At the same time, the contrast between the two pieces allowed us to tease out the main values of journalistic discourse, such as its corroboration of multiple sources, its lack of sensationalism, and its overall carefulness. We compared a list of journalistic principles we made in class to those outlined by the Society of Professional Journalists (2014) and discussed why Carreyrou might have been cautious even after collecting so much evidence. Disseminating false information can have enormous consequences—with Theranos, not only would he potentially stall its technological progress, but he could permanently damage the company's reputation. To illustrate that point, I showed examples of articles representing a range of different political views. Then, we discussed how well they represented the values of journalistic discourse. One of the articles, which came from the left-leaning outlet *Shareblue*, suggested that Secretary of Transportation Elaine Chao was lazy, solely based on the fact that she had a large number of private appointments on her schedule (Boehlert 2018). While the article might hold a kernel of truth, the lack of cautiousness was evident, including the clickbait title and the not-so-subtle implication that she was "hiding" something from the public. In contrast, we looked at a *Politico* article discussing California representative Duncan Hunter, who was caught illegally using campaign contributions for private expenses (Bresnahan and Bade 2018). The article involved interviews with several sources and direct quotations from the court indictment. It also resisted drawing any firm conclusions, leaving readers to sort through the information and make their own determinations. When dealing with the high-stakes events, students learned that reporters need to engage in more due diligence, even if it means holding back details until they can be corroborated by multiple sources.

Because I didn't want to convey the impression that mainstream outlets were the only sources of trustworthy information, we also examined Reddit's popular "Guide to the News," which was created by the site's users to steer audiences toward quality sources (2017). Like many similar efforts, it ranks each outlet based on its credibility and level of partisanship. During class discussion, students immediately pointed out the impossibility of being completely neutral. The decisions about how to evaluate sources inevitably reflect the creators' biases—*Vox* is rated as the "garbage left," a characterization that many people would dispute, while *Russia Today* is considered of "mixed quality" despite its intimate ties to the Russian government. Even the *New York Times* has been involved in multiple scandals, including one high-profile instance where a reporter repeatedly plagiarized material (Sullivan 2013). No alternative exists to cautiously reading each article and judging it based on its merits. While nothing is wrong with developing a preference for certain media, we need to remain aware that even the best organizations make mistakes.

To help students practice evaluating articles on their own, in the final project of the unit students were asked to pick one of four long-form journalism articles and write an essay responding to its claims. In preparation, students completed a short journal entry where they evaluated the quality of the source, partially through the lens of the journalistic values we discussed earlier in the class. Much like Robert Scholes, my concern was to keep the texts as relevant as possible to their lived experience, so I exclusively picked articles published within the last few years that focused on issues of concern to young college students. I included a wide range of possible options, with the intention of showing them that good journalism employs a variety of methodologies and can be found all over the internet. One of the pieces—Cecilia D'Anastasio's (2018) "Inside the Culture of Sexism at Riot Games"—comes from a games website not necessarily known for its hard-hitting journalism. Despite its origin, the article is a remarkably traditional piece, in that it has an objective tone and attempts to corroborate claims among several sources. In contrast, even though another of the articles came from a traditional print publication, the author inserts themselves directly into the conversation and uses a highly unusual approach, looking at the results of an empathy experiment conducted by the nonprofit group Narrative 4 (Miller 2016). The wide range of options allowed the students considerable freedom, and many discussed how the articles helped give them a new perspective on their own lives.

While the remaining units didn't focus as intensely on journalism, we never left the subject entirely behind, placing the genre alongside the others we examined throughout the term. The second unit focused on academic discourse, with an emphasis on scientific research and how it is presented in academic journals. However, I didn't want to present science as an activity that only takes place within the ivory tower, so we also examined how research is presented in the media, including everything from morning television shows to major news magazines. As I mentioned in the introduction, I wasn't satisfied with my initial version of the unit's main project because it unintentionally presented the media as a bad actor who always sensationalized research. To draw attention to the excellent scientific reporting available in many publications, I asked them to read a long-form article on a scientific issue, locate two studies referenced in the text, and articulate their own perspective. Like many of my assignments throughout the term, the goal was to keep students endlessly moving between mediums, discourse, and voices—in that way, I share Scholes's view that responsible readers are never satisfied with their first interpretation and always look at an issue from multiple angles. Even when information comes from a seemingly authoritative source, we must never stop, for the fish is slippery and hides in the margins. To find it, we must switch browser windows, track down studies, and talk with others, especially when a piece of evidence comfortably confirms our views.

CONCLUSION

Toward the end of his career, Scholes (2002) seemed worried about our culture's direction, particularly in regard to how we were handling the radical voices from the Islamic world. As he argued, "We are not good, as a culture, at imagining the other. After 11 September 2001 we have begun to learn, perhaps, that this deficiency is serious, though I am afraid that much of our response has been to shout our words louder and to try to suppress those that differ from ours" (167). Our culture has unfortunately marched further down that path, with partisan divisions becoming rancorous to the point where it seems like we can no longer come together to solve problems. For educators, his concern was that we weren't preparing students for dealing with an increasingly textual world—that, in our endless debates about what novels to assign students, we were neglecting to place the medium alongside other genres, particularly the ones that had become more important with the rise of visual texts. Now, as traditional journalism is increasingly supplanted by social media, we find ourselves in a similar place, where students are losing touch with a previously dominant genre without an adequate sense of what is lost in the process. Fortunately, research suggests that transparency about journalistic practices helps increase trust in the media (American Press Institute 2018). In addition, an assortment of political organizations and media literacy researchers are working to expand our tools for classifying, understanding, and teaching students how to navigate the twenty-first-century media landscape (Center for News Literacy 2016; Ireton and Posetti 2018; Center for Media and Information Literacy 2021).

Barack Obama has frequently expressed similar concerns about the state of our discourse. Over the first two years of Trump's presidency, he had largely been missing from the national conversation, which prompted *New York* magazine to run a cover asking, in desperation, "Where is Barack Obama?" However, he barnstormed the country throughout the 2018 midterms, offering some thoughts about our political climate. In one speech at the University of Illinois at Urbana-Champaign, he directly responded to his progressive critics, who frequently argued that he was too soft throughout his tenure. He claimed that many urged him to "fight fire with fire" and "do the same things to the Republicans that they do to us," such as "say[ing] whatever works, mak[ing] up stuff about the other side" (2018). He refused to take that path, largely because he saw it as counterproductive—in his mind, "the more cynical people are about government and the angrier and more dispirited they are about the prospects for change, the more likely the powerful are able to maintain their power." The danger of cynicism is that it leads to quietism. Rather than participate in democracy, which is necessary for change, people stay home and try to make the best of their situation. As literacy instructors, we can help combat cynicism in the post-truth era, partially by promoting the reading practices necessary for sustaining democracy.

REFERENCES

American Press Institute. 2018. "Americans and the News Media: What They Do—and Don't—Understand about Each Other: New Research Reveals Miscommunication, Dissatisfaction—and Opportunities." *The Media Insight Project.* https://www.americanpressinstitute.org/wp-content/uploads/2018/06/Americans-and-the-News-Media-2018.pdf.

Appadurai, Arjun. 2017. "Democracy Fatigue." In *The Great Regression*, edited by Heinrich Geiselberger, 1–12. Malden, MA: Polity Press.

Barstow, David. 2008. "Behind TV Analysts, Pentagon's Hidden Hand." *New York Times*, April 20, 2008. https://nyti.ms/2kfCZry.

Barthel, Michael. 2018. "Newspapers Fact Sheet." *Pew Research Center.* http://www.journalism.org/fact-sheet/newspapers/.

Boehlert, Eric. 2018. "Trump Cabinet Secretary Logged 290 Hours of Mysterious 'Private' Time." *Shareblue*, October 1, 2018. https://shareblue.com/elaine-chao-trump-cabinet-secretary-290-hours-private-time/.

boyd, danah. 2018. "You Think You Want Media Literacy . . . Do You?" *Medium: Points*, March 9, 2018. https://points.datasociety.net/you-think-you-want-media-literacy-do-you-7cad6af18ec2.

Bresnahan, John, and Rachael Bade. 2018. *Politico*, August 21, 2018. https://www.politico.com/story/2018/08/21/duncan-hunter-indicted-790861.

Carreyrou, John. 2015. "Theranos's Growing Pains." *Wall Street Journal*, December 28, 2015.

Carreyrou, John. 2018. *Bad Blood: Secrets and Lies in a Silicon Valley Startup.* New York: Alfred A. Knopf.

Center for Media and Information Literacy. 2021. Accessed March 31, 2021. https://centermil.org/.

Center for News Literacy. 2016. Accessed March 31, 2021. https://www.centerfornewsliteracy.org/.

D'Anastasio, Cecilia. 2018. "Inside the Culture of Sexism at Riot Games." *Kotaku*, August 7, 2018. https://kotaku.com/inside-the-culture-of-sexism-at-riot-games-1828165483.

Economist. 2013. "Why Are the Economist's Writers Anonymous?" *Economist*, September 5, 2013. https://www.economist.com/the-economist-explains/2013/09/04/why-are-the-economists-writers-anonymous.

"Fight Fake News." Reddit. 2017. https://www.reddit.com/r/coolguides/comments/5q52tt/fight_fake_news_updated_and_larger_guide_to/.

Ireton, Cherilyn, and Julie Posetti. 2018. *Journalism, Fake News and Disinformation: Handbook for Journalism Education and Training.* Paris: UNESCO.

Knight Foundation. 2018. "Indicators of News Media Trust." https://knightfoundation.org/reports/indicators-of-news-media-trust.

Krugman, Paul. 2016. "The Falsity of False Equivalence." *New York Times*, September 26, 2016. https://krugman.blogs.nytimes.com/2016/09/26/the-falsity-of-false-equivalence/.

McComiskey, Bruce. 2017. *Post-Truth Rhetoric and Composition.* Boulder, CO: Utah State University Press.

Miller, Lisa. 2016. "An Experiment in Empathy." *New York Magazine*, December 26, 2016. http://nymag.com/intelligencer/2016/12/gun-violence-radical-empathy.html.

Obama, Barack. 2018. "Speech at University of Illinois at Urbana-Champaign." Speech, Champaign, IL, October 7, 2018.

O'Neil, Cathy. 2016. *Weapons of Math Destruction: How Big Data Increases Inequality and Threatens Democracy.* New York: Crown.

Scholes, Robert. 1985. *Textual Power: Literary Theory and the Teaching of English.* New Haven, CT: Yale University Press.

Scholes, Robert. 1998. *The Rise and Fall of English: Reconstructing English as a Discipline.* New Haven, CT: Yale University Press.

Scholes, Robert. 2002. "The Transition to College Reading." *Pedagogy: Critical Approaches to Teaching Literature, Language, Composition, and Culture* 2 (2): 165–72.

Shane, Scott, and Mark Mazzetti. 2018. "The Plot to Subvert an Election: Unraveling the Russia Story So Far." *New York Times*, September 20, 2018. https://nyti.ms/2NmUclP.

Society of Professional Journalists. 2014. "SPJ Code of Ethics." Ethics. https://www.spj.org/ethicscode.asp.

Sullivan, Margaret. 2013. "Repairing the Credibility Cracks." *New York Times*, May 4, 2013. https://nyti.ms/Ym8wJS.

Tufekci, Zeynep. 2018. "Facebook's Surveillance Machine." *New York Times*, March 19, 2018. https://nyti.ms/2GIBJJM.

Vosoughi, Soroush, Deb Roy, and Sinan Aral. 2018. "The Spread of True and False News Online." *Science* 359 (6380): 1146–51.

Wilson, Jason. 2018. "Crisis Actors, Deep State, False Flag: The Rise of Conspiracy Theory Code Words." *Guardian*, November 21, 2018. https://www.theguardian.com/us-news/2018/feb/21/crisis-actors-deep-state-false-flag-the-rise-of-conspiracy-theory-code-words.

9
"THE TRANSITION TO COLLEGE READING"

Robert Scholes

I began my work on this assignment, as many students do, by e-mailing an expert for assistance. I wrote to a colleague who has been teaching one of our survey courses at Brown and asked her what she felt were the most important problems or deficiencies in the preparation of first-year students in her literature courses. Her reply, though only a hasty e-mail rather than a considered statement, was so helpful that I quote it here, with her permission:

> I think that the new high school graduates I see (and sophomores with no previous lit classes) most lack close reading skills. Often they have generic concepts and occasionally they have some historical knowledge, though perhaps not as much as they should. I find that they are most inclined to substitute what they generally think a text should be saying for what it actually says, and lack a way to explore the intricacies and interests of the words on the page. Sometimes the historical knowledge and generic concepts actually become problems when students use them as tools for making texts say and do what students think they should, generalizing that all novels do X or poems do Y. Usually the result is that they want to read every text as saying something extremely familiar that they might agree with. I see them struggling the most to read the way texts differ from their views, to find what is specific about the language, address, assumptions etc. (Tamar Katz, pers. com., 17 September 2001)

Her observations confirm my own sense that we have a reading problem of massive dimensions—a problem that goes well beyond any purely literary concerns.

This, in turn, drew my attention to the asymmetry in our topics for this panel, which mirrors the asymmetry in our professional arrangements.[1] Setting aside the institutional differences, which affect everyone, the other two topics were divided into writing and literature. The natural reciprocal of writing—which, of course, is reading—had somehow disappeared, apparently subsumed under the topic of literature. (I have taken the liberty of compensating for this asymmetry in my own title for this piece by replacing the word *literature* with the word *reading*.) But this division of the English project is not just an aberration in the thought of this session's organizer. It is the way that most English departments at college and secondary levels think of their enterprise. This, as I have argued for some time, is an unfortunate error that we need to correct.

Why is it an error? I shall spend the rest of this essay counting the ways. We normally acknowledge, however grudgingly, that writing must be taught and continue to be taught from high school to college and perhaps beyond. We accept it, I believe, because we can see writing, and we know that much of the writing we see is not good enough. But we do not see reading. We see some writing about reading, to be sure, but we do not see reading. I am certain, though, that if we could see it, we would be appalled. My colleague Tamar Katz, like many perceptive teachers, has caught a glimpse of the real problem, which she puts this way: "They want to read every text as saying something extremely familiar that they might agree with." The problem emerges as one of difference, or otherness—a difficulty in moving from the words of the text to some set of intentions that are different from one's own, some values or presuppositions different from one's own and possibly opposed to them.[2] This problem, as I see it, has two closely related parts. One is a failure to focus sharply on the language of the text. The other is a failure to imagine the otherness of the text's author.

One of the great ironies in this situation is that the study of literature, especially as conceived by the New Critics, whose thought still shapes much of our literary education, was supposed to develop the student's ability to focus on the language of texts. If we nonetheless fail to teach close reading—and many of us would agree with Katz and with Arlene Wilner (in this issue) that we do—then the problem may lie not so much in the words themselves as in the otherness of their authors. That is, if the words belong to the reader, they are likely to express the reader's thoughts. What we actually mean by "close" reading may be distant reading—reading as if the words belonged to a person at some distance from ourselves in thought or feeling. Perhaps they must be seen as the words of someone else before they can be seen as words at all—or, more particularly, as words that need to be read with close attention. It is no secret, of course, that the New Critics defined as a fallacy any attempt to read a text for its author's intention. Since then we have had the death of the author, reader-response criticism, the self-deconstructing text, and the symptomatic readings of cultural studies, all of which, in various ways, undermine the notion of authorial intention as a feature of the reading process. And all of them, in various degrees and respects, are right and useful, but only if reading for authorial intention precedes them. The author must live before the author can die. We teachers must help our students bring the author to life.

The reading problems of our students can themselves be read as a symptom of a larger cultural problem. We are not good, as a culture, at imagining the other. After 11 September 2001 we have begun to learn, perhaps, that this deficiency is serious, though I am afraid that much of our response has been to shout our own words louder and to try to suppress those that differ from ours. On the present occasion, however, we must focus on this problem at the level of schooling. I mention the larger picture not to aggrandize the topic but to indicate the depth of the problem, which is as much a matter of ideology as of methodology. English teachers must solve it at the level of the curriculum and the classroom. We must make some changes both in what we teach and in how we teach it, starting in secondary schools.

First, the past. Consider the following advice from a textbook on reading:

> The great object to be accomplished in reading as a rhetorical exercise is to convey to the hearer, fully and clearly, the ideas and feelings of the writer.
>
> In order to do this, it is necessary that a selection should be carefully studied by the pupil before he attempts to read it. In accordance with this view, a preliminary rule of importance is the following:
>
> Rule I.—Before attempting to read a lesson, the learner should make himself fully acquainted with the subject as treated of in that lesson, and endeavor to make the thought, and feeling, and sentiments of the writer his own.

I linger over the word *hearer*, which I have emphasized in this quotation. What has a hearer to do with reading? This unexpected word alerts me to the fact that I am facing a text that I must read carefully, attending to presuppositions different from my own. This advice about the teaching of reading comes immediately after the table of contents in McGuffey's (1879, 9) *Fifth Eclectic Reader*. It applies to what the text calls "reading as a rhetorical exercise," that is, reading aloud—and also reading to express "the thought, and feeling, and sentiments of the writer." That is where the hearer comes in. Odd, isn't it, that attending to "the thought, and feeling, and sentiments of the writer" is exactly what our students now find difficult? The older pedagogy saw it as a problem, too, but had a solution for it. The solution was "elocution," or reading aloud. That is one thing we can learn from our predecessors, for reading aloud makes the reading process evident to the ear in tone and rhythm and to the eye in bodily posture and facial expression, just as writing makes the composing process evident in written signs. In this older dispensation, failure to "get" the author's thought, feeling, and sentiments would emerge during an elocutionary performance. I am not certain how close we can come to the McGuffey method in our classrooms, but I think that we should try to bridge the gap.[3] I know that we can come very close to it in teaching drama, where the move to oral interpretation requires no explanation or apology—which is an argument for getting more drama into our courses.

It should follow that we need to consider including in our courses texts that are difficult for students to read as "saying something extremely familiar that they might agree with"—texts that say things that many students will not, in fact, agree with and that we may not agree with, either. For some years Gerald Graff has urged us to "teach the conflicts." Insofar as our intradepartmental conflicts are concerned, I have never been persuaded that students would care enough about them to make the enterprise worthwhile, but Graff (forthcoming) is clearly broadening his notion of conflicts in *Clueless in Academe*, and I am happy to agree with him about the need to teach texts that express conflicting positions. There has been concern, since Quintilian at least, and probably since the Sophists, about whether a good rhetorician was necessarily a good person. Without rushing in where angels like Richard Lanham have trod warily, I want to say that a good person, in our time, needs to have the rhetorical capacity to imagine the other's thought, feeling, and sentiments. That is, though not all rhetoricians are good people, all good citizens must be rhetoricians to the extent that they can imagine themselves in the place of another and understand views different from their own. It is our responsibility as English teachers to help our students develop this form of textual power, in which strength comes, paradoxically, from subordinating one's own thoughts temporarily to the views and values of another person.

This is one reason that I think it is a bad idea for the Bush administration to tell television networks to censor the words of our enemies in the videos they broadcast. We Americans are seen as arrogant by a large part of the world—and not just the Islamic part—precisely because we do not listen to other points of view, but we have never made it a national policy not to listen to them until now. Nor can our government plead the fact that other parts of the world do not listen to us or understand us as an excuse for refusing to allow us to listen to them. Our form of government and our sort of society depend on the freedom of individuals to interpret texts for themselves. Our roots, as a culture, are deeply embedded in a Protestant tradition of individual interpretation of sacred texts, which rests on access to those texts for all. People died for the right to translate and circulate these crucial texts, taking them out of the hands of a priestly caste. This tradition has also allowed the publication and discussion of profane texts, on the grounds that truth will prevail. It is disheartening, at a time of national crisis, for our government to seek to suppress the words that may enable us to understand our enemies' motives. It is, writ large, the same problem we encounter in students who cannot understand a point of view different from their own.

Katz points out one form of the problem: students simply assimilate the thought and feeling in a text to their own thoughts and feelings. Wilner points out another: students recognize a different position and simply refuse to read it or think about it. These two responses to otherness constitute the American way, I am afraid, and it is a way of responding to texts that we, as teachers, have a duty to counteract. If rhetoric is a schooling in textual virtue as well as in textual power, as I believe it is, this virtue consists largely in our being able to assume another person's point of view before criticizing it and resuming our own. We, and our students, must learn to put ourselves into a text before taking ourselves out of it. Even in these difficult times we must remain open to otherness.

If we accept this rhetorical goal as a part of our teaching mission, it follows that we must organize a curriculum to support it. Our present emphasis on literature, however, is at cross-purposes to this goal because of the way we have defined the term *literature* and because of the methods we employ. In our educational tradition "literature," and its predecessor, "belles lettres," once included powerful speeches and essays along with poems, plays, and stories. But over the past two centuries an opposition between the aesthetic text and the rhetorical text has developed, so that the term *literature* now excludes texts intended to persuade, whether they be essays or orations, advertising or propaganda, in print or in other media. The process through which this has happened is too long and complex for treatment here, but it assuredly did happen, and we are dealing with the results. The insistence that literary texts "should not mean, but be," as Archibald MacLeish put it in his well-known poem "Ars Poetica," contributed mightily. (MacLeish, we should note, was making an argument in a poem that argued against making arguments in poems.) In any case, literature became defined as texts that do not speak to us except with a forked tongue. Paraphrase became a heresy, intentionality a fallacy, the author a mute corpse, and the literary text a self-deconstructing artifact or ideological symptom.

We need to change our definitions as well as our curriculum. First, we need to include more overtly persuasive or argumentative texts in our curricula. We can do it in virtually every kind of course now in the literary curriculum. In the American literature survey, for instance, we can include not only more speeches and documents but texts in traditional literary forms that take strong positions, like Edna St. Vincent Millay's poem "Justice Denied in Massachusetts," about the execution of Sacco and Vanzetti. We can also include critical interpretations of such texts, for example, Allen Tate's attack on Millay's poem in his essay "Tension in Literature" (see Scholes 2001, 17–21, 64–75, for Tate's and Millay's texts).

We can and should do this, in both secondary school and college. The objections to including criticism in literature courses are mainly made on behalf of greater coverage of literature itself, since critical texts must displace some literary texts if they are included. The primary answer to these objections is that, if we are teaching reading, we must give some examples of how it is done, but there is a secondary answer as well. Critical texts, if properly chosen, will differ with one another, so that reading them will lead students to recognize difference itself as they situate their own readings in relation to those of the critics. The purpose of this approach is not to make literary critics more important. They have become too important already. It is to bring criticism out into the open so that every student can be a critical reader. It is to bring criticism back to earth.

Second, newer technologies also offer possibilities for the teaching of reading that we are only beginning to explore. There is a lot of writing on the Web that takes positions and makes arguments, well or badly. There are ongoing arguments, on all sorts of topics, that can be traced through particular threads on Web sites. Part of the problem we face in classrooms, especially in the general-education classrooms of colleges and in the English courses of secondary schools, is that debates about literary interpretation simply do not engage many of our students. These same students, however, may go right from our classrooms to their terminals, where they engage in serious debate about issues that are important to them.

Let me give a trivial example. For my sins, no doubt, I frequently follow discussions on a Web site devoted to the New England Patriots football team. On these pages I have found, and find regularly, debates conducted with a high degree of seriousness and skill over matters related directly to football, including coaching strategies, personnel, media coverage, and training methods. Despite the occasional flame war, these debates typically involve the presentation of evidence (often statistical), the drawing of conclusions, the consideration of opposing views, the eloquent expression of attitudes—in short, all the things that go into persuasive and argumentative writing. One can also find examples of exposition and explanation, such as a clear and cogent description of the differences between one-gap and two-gap defensive line play. There are hundreds if not thousands of comparable sites dealing with everything from motorcycles to religion. We need to see the Web as a constantly replenished source of textual materials for study. We should be asking students to bring back examples from sites of interest to them and to discuss the positions taken, the quality of various presentations, and their own views of the matters at hand.

We need, in short, to connect the development of reading and writing skills to the real world around us and to the virtual world in which that actual world becomes available to us in the form of texts. Without education, as Thomas Jefferson well understood, participatory democracy cannot function. The basis of an education for the citizens of a democracy lies in that apparently simple but actually difficult act of reading so as to grasp and evaluate the thoughts and feelings of that mysterious other person: the writer. The primary pedagogical responsibility of English teachers is to help students develop those skills. We need to give this humble task more attention, and we need to do a better job of it, too. We can start by recognizing it as a crucial object of our discipline—as more fundamental and more important than "covering" any canon of literary works.

NOTES

Robert Scholes, "The Transition to College Reading," in *Pedagogy* 2 (2): 165–72. Copyright, 2002, Duke University Press. All rights reserved. Republished by permission of the copyright holder, Duke University Press. www.dukeupress.edu.

1. This commentary is a revised version of a talk delivered during a session at the National Council of Teachers of English Conference in Baltimore in November 2001. The session, organized by David Laurence, national director of the Association of Departments of English, focused on the transition from high school to college. Each panelist addressed a specific problem: Sandy Stephan, institutional differences; Tom Jehn, college writing; and Robert Scholes, college literature.
2. See Arlene Wilner's discussion of this problem in "Confronting Resistance: Sonny's Blues—and Mine" in this issue.
3. In "'Reading Fiction/Teaching Fiction': A Pedagogical Experiment," Jerome McGann (2001, 147) makes a similar argument for what he calls "recitation": "Over

some years I have observed the (perhaps increasing) disability that students have in negotiating language in an articulate way. This weakness seems to propagate others, most especially an inclination to 'read' texts at relatively high levels of textual abstraction. With diminished skills in perceiving words as such comes, it seems, a weakened ability to notice other close details of language—semantic, grammatical, rhetorical. Recitation—I am talking about oral recitation of the fictional text—forces students to return to elementary levels of linguistic attention. To be effective as a pedagogical tool, however, it must be performed regularly and explicitly discussed and reflected upon. These exercises form the basis for developing higher-level acts of linguistic attention."

REFERENCES

Graff, Gerald. Forthcoming. *Clueless in Academe.* New Haven, CT: Yale University Press.
McGann, Jerome. 2001. "'Reading Fiction/Teaching Fiction': A Pedagogical Experiment." *Pedagogy* 1: 143–65.
McGuffey, William H. 1879. *Fifth Eclectic Reader.* Rev. ed. New York: American Book.
Scholes, Robert. 2001. *The Crafty Reader.* New Haven, CT: Yale University Press.

PART 3

*Thinking about Disciplinary Issues
Alongside Scholes*

10
HOW SCHOLES HELPED ENGLISH DEPARTMENTS CONFRONT THE DEATH OF THE AUTHOR, THE LOSS OF READERS, AND THE EMERGENCE OF INTERTEXTUAL LITERACIES

Thomas P. Miller

There is more than one way not to read, the most radical of which is not to open a book at all.
—Pierre Bayard, *How to Talk about Books You Haven't Read*, 2007

The career of Robert Scholes spanned the changes in literacy that our discipline faced between Barthes's "Death of the Author" in 1967 (reprinted in Barthes 1977) and Bayard's discussion of "nonreading" four decades later. Barthes observed that when we look to authors as authoritative, we foreclose the indeterminacies of writing as "that neutral, composite, oblique space where our subject slips away" (142). Barthes anticipated that the death of the author would lead to the "birth of the reader" as the locus of interpretation. A different future was envisioned in Marshall McLuhan's *Guttenberg Galaxy*, which in 1962 was one of the first sources to discuss the coming of *postliterate* society. The "death of the reader" has become a locus of discussion comparable to Barthes's commentary on the death of the author in the decade since Bayard published *How to Talk about Books You Haven't Read* in 2007 (Abecassis 2010). Bayard defined the literate experience in terms of "the nonreader, who never opens a book and yet talks about them and knows them without hesitation" (3). Bayard's discussion of "the virtues of non-reading" shifts the paragon of literacy from close reading to those who surf around in the "virtual libraries" that we compose as we talk around books we have not actually read. On these and other points, Barthes's and Bayard's standpoints on literacy provide bookends for assessing how Scholes looked to intertextuality as a framework for developing curricular reforms and outreach initiatives aimed at engaging with the interactive networks that were redefining literacy and literacy studies. Scholes's proposals remain important because the historic changes he addressed have contributed to the collapses in majors and jobs that have reached crisis level in the last decade.

The death of the author and the rise of the nonreader provide reference points for reflecting on the generation of English professors who came of age with the research university and were pressed to defend their work within it. At a formative phase in these developments, Scholes pressed English departments to come to terms with their "fall" in standing with the loss of readers. Scholes recognized that literary studies was coming to a position in literate society that had perilous parallels with that which an earlier model of the classics had come to a century earlier. In the 1980s and 1990s English departments began to confront the drops in majors and jobs that have reached historic levels in the last decade. Scholes and contemporaries such as Gerald Graff turned to theory to interpret the broad changes in literacy that were undermining the standing of literature and literary study. Like Graff, Scholes played a leading role in theorizing changes in reader responses to literature, and then in developing pedagogical innovations aimed at coming to terms with those changes. Scholes, Graff, and other professors of literature such as Richard Lanham worked through the turn to theory in the 1980s to write textbooks, propose curricular reforms, and get involved in articulation programs with high schools. Such programs took on new significance in the 1990s as cultural studies helped us understand "articulation" as a critical process through which institutional ideologies circulate through broader social networks (see Grossberg 1986; Clarke 2015). Scholes recognized that the trends that were reshaping the discipline were circulating up from changes in popular literacies, and not down from changes in theoretical discussions in elite universities. Like Graff, Scholes's textbooks and curricular proposals were informed by his research on the history of English departments. That research presented literature not as a "uniquely privileged form of transcendental textuality," but as a socio-institutional construct that evolves in tandem with changes in literate technologies, economies, and epistemologies (Scholes 1998, 151). Parallel lines of inquiry were also advanced in the eighties by compositionists such as James Berlin and Lester Faigley.

Scholes's accounts of the "rise and fall" of English departments set out the fieldwork for his proposal to renew the discipline by reintegrating rhetoric, logic, and linguistics into a renewed trivium that would enable students to acquire "textual power," as Isaacs discusses in her contribution to this section. Scholes built on the close attention to reading and readers that had long been fundamental to "practical criticism" to expand English studies from individual authors and texts to "textual studies" of ideological and social networks. To strengthen the base of the discipline, Scholes developed outreach programs and curricular models that challenged the institutional hierarchies that consigned the teaching of writing and reading to the service wing of English departments. Scholes's model of textual studies was particularly indebted to his studies of semiotics, which had a formative impact on important trends in rhetorical and cultural studies. Soon after arriving at Brown, Scholes established the semiotics program that became the Department of Modern Culture and Media. Ironically, when Scholes wrote about reforming English departments, he did not actually work in one. He recognized the shape of things to come as he moved beyond the confines of English departments and took up the work of building curricula centered on the intertextual workings of media and cultural studies. Now that the hierarchies that have structured English departments are crumbling at their base, we need to review the lessons to be learned from Scholes's efforts to expand curricula, outreach, and interdisciplinary collaborations. The drops in majors, faculty positions, and institutional standing that Scholes addressed have accelerated in most English departments in the decade since the great recession.

ENGLISH DEPARTMENTS AFTER THE FALL

Scholes spent much of his career trying to come to terms with the historic crash in English majors and tenure-track jobs that began in the 1970s and has continued intermittently up to today, leaving our PhD graduates today with about half the tenure-track job openings that were available a half century ago (MLA 2017). While the percentage of baccalaureates in English had been cut in half by the end of the last century, most leaders of our top professional organization have attempted to explain away these declines, even up to the undeniable downturns in the last decade. As late as 2012, one of the more forward-looking presidents of the Modern Language Association (MLA), Michael Bérubé, dismissed concerns about declining enrollments in the humanities by using a shifting set of reference points that failed to confront the fact that two thirds of English departments were facing lower and sharply declining enrollments according to the survey published by the Association of

Departments of English in collaboration with MLA in 2016. Unlike preceding MLA / Association of Departments of English (ADE) surveys, the 2016 survey finally acknowledged that the profession needs to do more than try to defend English departments' traditional emphasis on literary study against vocationalism, new media studies, and the rising popularity of writing courses.

Unlike many MLA reports and leaders, Scholes did not express open disdain for the career aspirations of the broader classes of students who have enrolled in rising numbers in recent decades. As college enrollments rose and the percentages of baccalaureates in English fell, Scholes pressed the discipline to acknowledge its antivocational vocationalism—the professional ethos that Stanley Fish (1985) characterized as "anti-professional professionalism." Scholes's *Rise and Fall of English* argued that English studies had always been a vocational enterprise. English departments were founded to help prepare broader classes of professionals, and with the emergence of the research university, English majors came to mirror the specialized methods and publish-or-perish mindset of other PhD programs. The "anti-professional professionalism" of English departments established literary studies as the pinnacle of disinterested professionalism in the 1970s, but a half century later, this ethos has lost its public standing as disciplinary enclaves of professional expertise have been breached by market forces.

The sharpest drops in the discipline occurred in the 1970s, which saw a 50 percent drop in BAs and PhDs (from 64,000 to 34,000 BAs and from 1,400 to 700 PhDs). As I have discussed in the *Evolution of College English* (193–217), tenure-track jobs for PhDs dropped suddenly and then recovered in an overall downward trend that was repeated in the 1980s and 1990s. Some departments responded to these market drops by expanding their graduate offerings to include creative writing and composition and by opening up undergraduate curricula to include courses in gender, ethnic, and media studies. As Gerald Graff discussed, these reforms tended to be peripheral additions to the curriculum. They centered on a basic reassessment of traditional assumptions despite the efforts of reformers such as Scholes and Graff to get the discipline to reform disciplinary hierarchies. While the percentages of baccalaureates in English were dropping, most departments could depend on steady and even rising enrollments because college enrollments were exploding. Traditionally related disciplines such as speech adapted to changes in communications and saw five-fold increases in enrollments (Miller and Jackson 2007, 683). These diverging trajectories are important to acknowledge because commentators such as Bérubé have sought solace in the relatively constant percentages of baccalaureates in the humanities without acknowledging that those counts have been upheld by rising enrollments in disciplines such as communications, which is counted among the humanities even though they have moved from humanistic to social science frameworks in ways that most English departments have refused to do.

Scholes's analyses of these historical trends are important because he recognized early on that the discipline needed to invest in its basic work with reading, writing, and teaching to rearticulate its public mission. His engagement in that work enabled him to connect his theoretical inquiries with the institutional work that needed to be done to address changes in how students were coming to read literature. Like the rest of his generation, Scholes had learned to attend to the pragmatics of reading from the New Critics. His first books included *Elements of Fiction* (1968) and *Elements of Poetry* (1969), and one of his last was *The Crafty Reader* (2001). His career-long engagements with introductory textbooks built on his scholarly background in practical criticism and his intellectual commitment to using pedagogy to validate theory in practice. This pragmatic perspective was fundamental to his integrated model of literary and literacy studies. That integration is evident in the critical junctures in his career, beginning with his early work on surrealistic "fabulators" such as Joyce and Pynchon who blurred fact and fiction, continuing through his structuralist models of literary genres as social constructs, and concluding with his movement through semiotics to textual studies, which drew all these theoretical movements together in his model of textual power.

Scholes was a leading contributor to our discipline's efforts to understand the forces converging on institutions of the book in the late age of print. From a distance, we can now see that the heady debates over poststructuralism, deconstruction, reader-response theories, and cultural studies in the 1970s and 1980s were an attempt to come to terms with the increasingly unbounded dynamics of literacy that emerged as the culture of the book was confronted with the personal computer and networked literacies. For Scholes, the turn to theory provided a standpoint to renew the discipline's basic work with reading, writing, and teaching. Scholes took "the teaching situation as a theoretical position" concerned with validating inquiry in practice (1985, 166). From this standpoint, Scholes viewed the "apparatus of English" as an intellectual discipline to be tested against its basic institutional mission to teach reading and writing to broader classes of students. Scholes understood that the "arche-institution of English lives in each one of us as a professional unconscious," and he pressed practitioners to reassess their disciplinary priorities against the changes in literacy that were transforming learning and the literate (4). Scholes pointedly critiqued the self-validating binaries that structured the "arche-institution of English": the hierarchy of literature over nonliterature that positioned consumption over production in ways that divorced academic inquiry from the "real world." If we reflect upon how the "professional unconscious" of our discipline developed in the pivotal decades in Scholes's career, we may be able to recognize the continuing relevance of his model of textual studies as a framework that refigured basic work with reading and writing against the networked literacies that have redefined what we study and how we teach it.

FROM THE DEATH OF THE AUTHOR TO THE LOSS OF THE READER

By many accounts, Barthes's "Death of the Author" (1967) and Foucault's "What Is an Author?" (1969) are pivotal accounts of the historic transition from modern to postmodern conceptions of authorship. Modern conceptions of the author were identified with copyright laws (and through them individual property rights), while postmodern models are concerned with how discourse constitutes forms of subjectivity deemed authoritative (Logie 2013). The transition to postmodernism shaped Scholes's model of textual studies, including his concern for intertextuality—a concern that spanned his work with structuralism and poststructuralism. As Barthes and later postmodernists discussed, texts are woven from textualities, for "a text is made of multiple writings, drawn from many cultures and entering into multiple relations of dialogue" (148). Given the interwoven dynamics of textures, "to give a text an Author is to impose a limit on that text," whether the author is configured as an individual or a literary movement or era. Barthes observed that critics claim to speak for the author to establish their own authority: "when the Author has been found, the text is 'explained'—victory to the critic" (147). Barthes called for a switch in interpretive standpoints: "a text's unity lies not in its origins but in its destination" (148). Over the next decades, this shift from authorial intentions to reader and writer subjectivities was instituted by a range of critical schools, including deconstruction, reader-response theories, and related works that attempted to account for the evolving pragmatics of reading such as Steven Mailloux's *Rhetorical Power* (1989).

These schools of criticism were a formative effort to recognize the unbounded dynamics of reading and writing in the decades that gave rise to personal computing and networked literacies. Readers would soon become overwhelmed by too much to read and too little time to read it closely. These trends overwhelmed the close reading strategies at the heart of traditional literary studies. As Scholes discusses, the profession gave rise to mountains of academic publications within sub-specializations that pressed faculty to focus on keeping up with the scholarship rather than to focus on the changing needs of their students (1998, 82–86). Some literature courses responded by expanding their focus of study beyond individual books and their authors to consider cultural studies of processes such as articulation and circulation. Unfortunately, many departments' curricula remained anchored in the close reading of solitary books (Scholes 2011, 33).

In the decades when Scholes pressed the discipline to expand its focus from books to textualities, even highly literate people were feeling increasingly overwhelmed with too much to read and too little time for books. As Bayard (2007) discusses, the literate ceased to be distinguished from the less cultivated by what they read, or even how they read. With the digital explosion, the literate became defined by their ability to find their "bearings" in literate networks: "As cultivated people know (and, to their misfortune, uncultivated people do not), culture is above all a matter of *orientation*. Being cultivated is a matter not of having read any book in particular, but of being able to find your bearings within books as a system, which requires you to know that they form a system and to be able to locate each element in relation to the others, . . . since what counts in a book is the books alongside it" (Bayard 2007, 10–11). According to Bayard, the literate develop their orienteering skills in the "virtual library" by developing integrative modes of lateral reading that treat passages in books as pathways to understanding and composing rather than as ends in themselves: "it is ourselves we should be listening to, not the 'actual' book" because "the writing of self" is the real end to be reached through reading (Bayard 2007, 179). While Bayard can be read as heralding the rise of the click-and-go forms of literacy that have contributed to the attention deficit disorder that besets our culture, he offers many useful insights into the creative potentials of how we have come to read that our discipline needs to consider. Our discipline needs to reinvest in the pragmatics of close reading—the integrative and interactive modes of reading that literate people use to orienteer through literate networks.

In the decades between Barthes's and Bayard's postmortems on authors and readers, our bookish discipline struggled to make sense of the fastest changes in literacy that humanity has ever experienced. Those struggles can be traced back to the theoretical turn in the decade when interactive literacies first emerged at the onset of the digital revolution. Scholes reflects back over those historic decades in the MLA Presidential Address that concludes this volume. He identifies "the critical self-reflection we know as theory" as part of our discipline's efforts to acknowledge its own complicity with the evolution of professionalism and vocationalism. Quoting from John Guillory's *Cultural Capital*, Scholes pointedly notes that "the category of 'literature' names the cultural capital of the old bourgeoisie, a form of capital increasingly marginal to the social function of the present educational system" (Guillory 1993; quoted 726). Scholes pressed his point by arguing that "the failure of theory" to have broader social and institutional impact was part of "the larger failure of the humanities . . . to justify their place in the academy and society" (730). Scholes challenged his audience to acknowledge that literary studies and theories could not and cannot achieve their potential if they are pursued as an end unto themselves. Theory in practice was an abiding concern of Scholes's extraordinarily productive and influential career, and his engagement in basic work with writing and reading remains fundamental to our discipline for the reasons that Isaacs discusses in the following chapter.

WHY TEXTUAL STUDIES WAS NOT ADOPTED BUT REMAINS RELEVANT

In the chapter from *The Rise and Fall of English* included in this collection, Scholes sets out a "discipline of textuality" as a canon of methods rather than a canon of texts: these methods are centered on theory ("the disciplinary core") and include history, composition, and "consumption" (see Corrigan in this volume). Scholes wanted to expand the field to break down the distinction between literature and nonliterature that marginalized the teaching of writing, reading, and other areas of textual studies that he saw as vital to English departments such as political discourse, postcolonial writings, and media and ethnic studies. Scholes's "unified field theory" followed upon his three-book sequence on theory: *Structuralism in Literature* (1974), *Semiotics and Interpretation* (1982), and *Textual Power* (1985). These theoretical works shaped Scholes's popular textbook *Text Book* (1988, 1995, and 2002). The chapter from *Textual Power* that is included in this volume highlights the continuities from Scholes's theoretical writings to his curricular proposals. Those continuities centered on studies of genre and style, with *genre* defined in anthropological terms as domains of action and *style* defined as modalities for articulating such socio-institutional constructions. Scholes's historical and theoretical writings often cite his work with textbooks to ground his analyses in his efforts to help students acquire textual power (see, for example, 2011, 15).

Scholes's overall program of work was focused on shifting English departments from "teaching literature" to "studying texts." While he recognized that the teaching of literature was the traditional center of English departments, he argued that "teaching literature" was actually a misnomer because students were taught literary exegesis and not literary composition. Scholes's co-authored *Text Book: Writing through Literature* presented "writing through literature" as an alternate frame that used textual studies to help students "learn to think as poets think" by mastering the "metaphorical processes that are pervasive in all our forms of textuality" (2002, iv). Scholes's engagement with the creative potentials of work with literacy is critical to understanding the distinction between his pragmatic concern for knowledge in the making and the rather disengaged stance that has often been assumed by cultural studies and literary criticism. Scholes's pragmatic engagement with the creative process of reading to write was fundamental to his efforts to reform the discipline to connect with the interactive literacies that have given rise to the maker movement and the active learning pedagogies that have become a mainstay of curricular reforms in the last decade.

In the decades when literary and rhetorical studies developed uncertain and sometimes hostile relationships, Scholes was one of the few leaders of the largest professional organizations in English studies to see rhetoric as a vital partner in reforming literary studies around the general education mission of English departments. Compositionists have not generally been read by or represented in the leadership of MLA, in part because elite English departments have still not recognized rhetoric and composition as areas of research and undergraduate study. From his position outside English departments, Scholes recognized the vital role played by rhetoric in the liberal arts tradition that was centered on the trivium of the language arts. He recognized that classical rhetoric attended to the intertextual dimensions of genres and style in ways that had been overshadowed by modern conceptions of individual authorship and readership (see Plett 1999). In response to the interactive literacies of our times, Scholes called upon the discipline to adopt a writerly stance on how we read ourselves into and across texts in the ways that Bayard discusses. Scholes's concern for reading as a mode of composition is central to the articulation initiatives and curricular reforms that he uses as proofs of concept in his books on English departments. *The Rise and Fall of English* includes an outline of the capstone high school course that Scholes had articulated in partnership with Educational Testing Service (ETS) and the College Board. This outline and the curriculum overview that concludes *English After the Fall* are easy to gloss over because they briefly encapsulate the models of textual studies that Scholes had elaborated on in the first chapter of *Textual Power.* What makes them important is that they document how Scholes engaged with general education, articulation, and introductory textbooks in ways that helped him make sense of the basic changes in literacy that the discipline had viewed as beneath its concerns. This professional hierarchy is most powerfully apparent in our discipline's failure to invest its intellectual energies in research on reading. As Horning discusses in this volume, the lack of attention to reading in our graduate programs has undercut their ability to prepare successive generations to engage with the transformations in literacy that we have witnessed over the last half century. In our discussions of undergraduate curricula, we have generally tended to focus more on what students are to read rather than on how they read.

Scholes attempted to help English departments address the surging changes in literacy that have washed over them in recent decades. He realized that the forces that were pressing for reforms were rising up through introductory service courses in which faculty struggled to understand how students were coming to read. From his writings for students versed in interactive forms of literacy, Scholes recognized that the teaching of literature had become unmoored from students' literate experiences, and he encouraged his readers to acknowledge that "the business of English departments is to help students improve as readers and writers." This "humble business . . . is the only justification for the existence of these departments in this fallen world" (2011, 34). To renew this "business," Scholes looked to general education as a model for revising our field of study. That was a hard pitch to make. Like most academic disciplines, English departments have a pyramid structure: students progress upward to more specialized courses modeled after the graduate seminars that most of those students will never take. For their part, most of those seminars ignore the lowly work of teaching. Given the scholarly hierarchies that structure our field and the "professional unconsciousness" that sustains them, we should not be surprised that Scholes's proposal to use general education as a model for English majors was not widely adopted. In fact, he admitted that he could not identify a single department that had implemented his proposals (2011, xiv). Ironically, the aspects of Scholes's model that made it most unacceptable are precisely those that make it most useful in considering how English departments can focus on their research on renewing their undergraduate curricula in ways that can help us raise enrollments and strengthen the standing of teaching and teachers.

INTERACTIVE LITERACIES AND INTEGRATIVE LEARNING

> [The loss of readers] will not lead to the death of the imagination. A certain kind of imaginative self-reflection may indeed be going through a death which is a kind of metamorphosis. But imagination dies as the caterpillar, to be reborn with wings.
>
> (Scholes 1979, 210)

Scholes may not have found a lot of takers for his proposals to restructure English departments, but the trends he addressed have proved to be undeniable. In 2002, MLA leaders viewed "the flight of students from English" as a potentially "healthy correction" that would increase the "selectivity" of English majors. In a national survey published by ADE in partnership with MLA, MLA leader David Laurence noted that literary study is characterized by "a specific and valuable sort of uselessness" that needed to be preserved against vocationalism by maintaining a critical distance from such reforms as the rising popularity of writing courses (2003, 4). The trends that have contributed to such reforms can no longer be ignored. The ADE survey published in collaboration with MLA in 2016 reported that ninety percent of departments were revising or had revised their majors to address declines in enrollments (ADE 2018). The report continued to advise departments to uphold the "intrinsic" values of literature through superficial accommodations to popular pressures. For example, English departments were advised to advertise the "instrumental" skills that majors acquire, without worrying too much about how students are to acquire and transfer such writing and reading skills (1). Our discipline's resistance to broader changes in literacy is understandable. The generation of leaders who are now retiring from the profession have seen historic changes that have undermined their standing, most notably declining enrollments, funding, and job prospects for graduate students. And, amidst all of that, they have been pressed to justify their work in terms that many have seen as antithetical to their values. The threats to traditional conceptions of literature have long been clear. As Richard Lanham noted thirty years ago, "Perhaps the real question for literary study now is not whether our students will be reading Great Traditional Books or Relevant Modern ones in the future, but whether they will be reading books at all" (1989, 265). We live in the future Lanham foretold, but our prospects are not as bleak as they may appear. The generation of faculty who came into their own in the 1970s and 1980s was the largest generation in the history of the American professoriate, and their retirement is opening up historic possibilities for reforming English departments. Scholes provided frameworks for undertaking those reforms and strategies for advancing them in broadly engaged ways.

The pieces in this section provide case studies of how to undertake the work to be done, and this whole collection is framed by the broader research programs of the contributors, beginning with our editor, Ellen Carillo, whose research addresses the critical nexus between reading, writing, and teaching in ways that this collection examines. Emily J. Isaacs examines how the academic hierarchies that have divorced literary studies from literacy teaching are being reproduced in writing studies departments. Lynée Lewis Gaillet and Angela Christie provide a framework for examining undergraduate curricula against the needs of graduates, and Robert Lestón calls for considering how English studies prepares students to engage with counterpublics in the interest of expanding access and increasing equity. These concerns take on renewed significance with the renewed emphasis on learning and teaching that has become so visible in higher education. As public institutions have transitioned from steady state funding to a reliance on student tuition, we have all become more concerned with enhancing the student experience and improving retention. This historical transition has also given renewed significance to outreach, including school partnerships of the sort that Scholes advanced. Collaborations with schools, public agencies, and business groups have become increasingly important as our institutions have struggled to overcome cuts to state funding and threats to federal research funding.

These trends have compounded the impact of changes in authorship and readership on English departments. Scholes's model of textual studies speaks to all these trends because it was attentive to the intertextual dynamics of interactive literacies in ways that have become vital to consider. He recognized that in the late age of print, texts were ceasing to be read as autonomous artifacts and were coming to function as nodes in networks. In contrast with the modes of close reading that served as the paragon of literacy in the culture of the book, reading in the "virtual library" has become a process of composing intertextual networks through lateral modes of reading in which readers clicked through interactive texts with interconnected scripts and images. Scholes understood the performative dimensions of reading as an integrative process in which one moved through multimedia texts to compose intertextual networks that incorporated ads and the news of the day alongside snippets of poems and excerpts from books. He pressed English departments to acknowledge that "literary study that cuts itself off from the performing and media arts risks going the way of classics" (1998, 160). Scholes saw creative reading as integral to creative writing, and both as integral to the literary experience. Following in the pragmatic tradition that includes the student-centered pedagogies identified with John Dewey, Scholes defined literature not as an object of study but as a mode of experience. Scholes pointedly challenged the profession to consider whether it wanted to continue to invest its intellectual energies in memorializing the "textual tombs of the great dead" or expand its field of vision to attend to the intertextual networks that were transforming the contemporary literate experience (1998, 145).

The integrated forms of literacy and learning that Scholes helped to articulate have become a vital part of current educational reforms. Reading to write and writing to learn have been integral parts of the student-centered pedagogies that have shaped composition studies since their founding a half century ago. As the chapters in this volume discuss, reading and writing have become interactive processes that integrate data, images, and other media and information. As texts have become unbounded, *literacy* has lost its singularity, and we have engaged in studies of *information literacy*, *media literacy*, *digital literacies*, and *technological literacies*. Scholes's attention to intertextuality was pivotal to these historical transitions, and his articulation efforts provide us with models for how to work with integrative modes of learning and literacy. Integrative learning initiatives include the student engagement programs that many universities are developing to bridge general education and undergraduate majors, as evident for example in the special issue of the Association of American Colleges & Universities' *Peer Review* on "Integrative Learning" in 2005. Service learning, internships, and a range of other experiential learning programs have become mainstays of integrative learning initiatives concerned with helping students apply their formal studies and skills instruction to the pragmatics of situated cognition and collaborative problem-solving (Sandman, Saltmarsh, and O'Meara 2008; Rossing and Lavitt 2016). Many writing programs are involved in such efforts, but English departments are only beginning to apply them to gateway and capstone programs. These integrative-learning reforms are paralleled on the faculty side by the development of more integrated models of research, teaching, and service that have become instituted since Ernest Boyer helped us understand that siloed conceptions of scholarship failed to value the broader work of institutions of public learning, including the vital articulation efforts that Scholes helped to launch (Miller 2012; Jay 2012). Such efforts have taken on transformative potentials with the emergence of the "engaged university" as a historical alternative to traditional research universities. The engaged university emerged as a model when colleges and universities struggled to overcome cuts in state and research funding by forging community and business partnerships to strengthen their public standing (Watson et al. 2011).

As we have become more dependent on student tuition, we have become more attentive to students' experiences and aspirations. If we invest our research in our teaching more fully, we can develop integrated approaches to literary studies, creative writing, and writing at work that can help us increase majors and jobs. Integrative learning and literacy can help us reimagine the roles that close reading and hierarchical reasoning played in the heyday of the culture of the book. That era has passed, and we need to consider works such as Bayard's *How to Talk about Books You Haven't Read* to consider the literacies our students bring to the classroom. Bayard's model has been incisively critiqued by Abecassis for failing to recognize that the "virtual library" is comprised of interconnected hubs that encapsulate the "architecture" of intertextual systems of thought (2010, 966–67). Such interconnected hub texts merit close reading, for as Abecassis discusses, they can help us separate the "noise" from the "signals" to interpret codes. Scholes was attuned to those textualities, and his works can help us engage with the integrated forms of literacy that we need to plug into if we are to make productive use of the historic changes we face. If English departments prove unable to productively engage with those historic changes, then we should consider following Scholes's example and founding our own departments, as Emily Isaacs discusses in her piece in this section and in her important survey of how English departments and writing departments are responding to the changes in literacy that Scholes reviews in *The Rise and Fall of English*. Those changes are transforming what we study and how we teach it. Scholes provides frameworks and programs that can help us engage with the reforms that are needed, and the chapters that follow provide models and principles that can help us work past some of the limitations in his work to undertake those reforms.

REFERENCES

Abecassis, Jack I. 2010. "Pierre Bayard and The Death of the Reader." *Modern Language Notes* 124: 961–79.

ADE Ad Hoc Committee on the English Major. 2018. "A Changing Major: The Report of the 2016–17 ADE Ad Hoc Committee on the English Major." https://www.ade.mla.org/content/download/98513/2276619/A-Changing-Major.pdf.

Barthes, Roland. 1977. "The Death of the Author" (originally published in 1967). In *Image-Music-Text*. Translated by Stephen Heath, 142–48. London: Fontana.

Bayard, Pierre. 2007. *How to Talk about Books You Haven't Read*. Translated by Jeffrey Mehlman. London: Bloomsbury.

Clarke, John. 2015. "Stuart Hall and the Theory and Practice of Articulation." *Discourse: Studies in the Cultural Politics of Education* 36: 275–86. http://dx.doi.org/10.1080/01596306.2015.1013247.

Fish, Stanley. 1985. "Anti-Professionalism." *New Literary History* 17: 89–108.

Grossberg, Lawrence. 1986. "On Postmodernism and Articulation: An Interview with Stuart Hall." *Journal of Communication Inquiry* 10: 245–60. https://doi.org/10.1177/019685998601000204.

Guillory, John. 1993. *Cultural Capital: The Problem of Literary Canon Formation*. Chicago: University of Chicago Press.

"Integrative Learning." 2005. *Peer Review* 7 (3/4). https://www.aacu.org/peerreview/2005/summer-fall.

Jay, Gregory. 2012. "The Engaged Humanities: Principles and Practices for Public Scholarship and Teaching." *Journal of Community Engagement and Scholarship* 3: 51–63. http://jces.ua.edu/the-engaged-humanities-principles-and-practices-for-public-scholarship-and-teaching.

Lanham, Richard A. 1989. "The Electronic Word: Literary Study and the Digital Revolution." *New Literary History* 20: 265–90.

Laurence, David. 2003. "Notes on the English Major." *ADE Bulletin* 133: 3–5.

Logie, John. 2013. "1967: The Birth of 'The Death of the Author.'" *College English* 75: 493–512.

Miller, Thomas P. 2012. "Humanities as a Public Works Project." *Academe* 98: 34–38.

Miller, Thomas P., and Brian Jackson. 2007. "What are English Majors For?" *College Composition and Communication* 58: 682–708.

MLA (Modern Language Association). 2017. "Report on the MLA Job Information List, 2016–17." MLA Office of Research. https://www.mla.org/Resources/Career/Job-Information-List/Reports-on-the-MLA-Job-Information-List.

Plett, Heinrich F. 1999. "Rhetoric and Intertextuality." *Rhetorica* 17: 313–29.

Rossing, Jonathan P., and Melissa R. Lavitt. 2016. "The Neglected Learner: A Call to Support Integrative Learning for Faculty." *Liberal Education* 102 (2). https://www.aacu.org/liberaleducation/2016/spring/rossing.

Sandmann, Lorilee, John Saltmarsh, and KerryAnn O'Meara. 2008. "An Integrated Model for Advancing the Scholarship of Engagement: Creating Academic Homes for the Engaged Scholar." *Journal of Higher Education Outreach and Engagement* 12: 47–64. http://openjournals.libs.uga.edu/index.php/jheoe/article/view/125.

Scholes, Robert. 1979. *Fabulation and Metafiction*. Champaign: University of Illinois Press.

Scholes, Robert. 1985. *Textual Power: Literary Theory and the Teaching of English*. New Haven, CT: Yale University Press.

Scholes, Robert. 1998. *The Rise and Fall of English: Reconstructing English as a Discipline*. New Haven, CT: Yale University Press.

Scholes, Robert. 2011. *English after the Fall: From Literature to Textuality*. Ames: University of Iowa Press.

Scholes, Robert, Nancy R. Comley, and Gregory Ulmer. 2002. *Text Book: Writing through Literature*. 3rd ed. Boston: Bedford/St. Martin's.

Watson, David, Robert Hollister, Susan E. Stroud, and Elizabeth Babcock. 2011. *The Engaged University: International Perspectives on Civic Engagement*. New York: Routledge.

11
WILL WRITING STUDIES ABANDON LITERACY EDUCATION TOO?

Emily J. Isaacs

PART I: WRITING STUDIES WITHOUT LITERATURE

I write from the position of a compositionist who has spent close to three decades residing in English departments while reading the work of compositionists and rhetoricians who advocate separating from English departments and literary scholars (Gaughan 2016; Hairston 1985; Howard 1993; O'Neill, Crow, and Burton 2002; Phelps and Ackerman 2010; Giberson and Moriarty 2010; Shamoon et al. 2000; Estrem 2007). The separatists make compelling arguments, particularly when read immediately after a long department meeting in which you've been insulted or discounted for your choice of discipline or your belief that teaching first-year writing is smart and interesting work, not noble drudgery. Sometimes it *seems* like literary scholars only feel disdain or moral obligation when it comes to the work of literacy education, though I hasten to remind readers that there are many, many English literature professors in English departments across the country who prioritize students' literacy development in their teaching. These professors don't seem to have the megaphone or carry the big sticks, but they exist and teach writing seriously alongside compositionists who are on the same mission. However, despite the kind of big-tent thinking articulated by Robert Scholes, who believed that English departments needed a "major rebuilding" but could flourish with composition and literature united (Scholes 1985, 5), the divide is deep. The bruises and slights, documented and undocumented, have piled up into one great big irreconcilable grievance. Thus, it seems, the majority of compositionists and rhetoricians have turned to writing studies to imagine an academic organizational configuration that provides liberation from the binds of English departments.

I observe that people who advocate for writing independence are much clearer about what they wish to escape—English departments—than what they'd like to become; after twenty years of steady discussion, it's still a moment of possibility. What will we become? Perhaps it's too hard to think from within English. As Louise Wetherbee Phelps writes, "moving from stifling departmental confines . . . frees the imagination" (Phelps 2017). (It is worth noting that Robert Scholes, who clearly thought the work of literacy education belonged to humanities faculty broadly, did have a freed imagination because he worked in media studies and other units as well as within English, a point also made by Thomas P. Miller in this volume.) That the move for independence from English is motivated more by the desire to *leave* English than the desire to *become* writing studies strikes me as both understandable and true to the many narratives I have read. Drawing from a survey of composition and rhetoric faculty in English departments, David Chapman and colleagues cite this anonymous response from a compositionist in an English department that echoes countless unpublished, anguished compositionists speaking at conferences: "Most of the faculty here view English as the study of literature only and believe that writing is a non-, if not anti-, humanistic activity" (1995, 425).

It is the tortured, painful personal experience of the dismissal of one's professional work that places the project of leaving English as the first and sometimes entirely preoccupying priority. But still, what shall we become? With universities increasingly supporting the development of independent writing studies departments, writing studies scholars who come together and draw from traditions in composition, rhetoric, applied linguistics, media studies, technical communications, and creative writing, need to take time to debate what writing studies shall be. At present there is little consensus, with majors and departments in writing studies ranging in their naming practices as much as their academic program foci and methods, reflecting the individuals and existing organizational structural at each college or university that has broken those English bonds, sometimes joining other orphaned faculty or shrinking departments, as universities seek to organize academic units that will invigorate curricula, foster research success, and create new majors that will appeal to the next generation of students, all without increasing expenditures. Each new writing department looks to those that have gone before, but circumstances and contexts are so particular that typically each new entity has had to forge its own path. In this essay I draw on Scholes to implore faculty at new writing studies departments to be very careful: it will be easy to reproduce the characteristics of English departments that Scholes critiqued and to have those with the most status and power make writing studies departments mirror and focus on their own interests and scholarship, which is what led English departments to neglect the crucial work of providing literacy instruction to all students at our universities.

I am at a university with a recently formed Writing Studies Department that has just launched a major in public and professional writing. We are forging one of those paths. Before telling of this department's arrival, let me disclose my own place in the story, and acknowledge that the story of this new department's formation can be told differently by at least a few dozen of us. My version is inflected by my position at the time as an associate dean who had served as the English Department chair, a position that I occupied happily, thinking that we were (finally) all a more-or-less functional family, and one that I took on after twelve years as a writing program administrator. It was when I was out of the English Department and ensconced in the Dean's Office that the long, if low-simmering, English Department composition-literature war erupted, and the Writing Studies Department was created. A new dean, a literature professor with sympathies for composition who was inclined toward taking on bold initiatives, was approached by two tenured writing studies faculty. These writing studies faculty were in conflict with English Department leadership, and especially with the inexperienced English chair, all at a time when the English major was shrinking and first-year composition was challenged by enrollment growth, administrative enthusiasm for general education cost-savings, and reevaluation of the effectiveness of basic writing. Old grievances related to curricula, personnel, and contingent faculty rights, all connected to disciplinary status—and therefore, inevitably, personal and professional status—were easily opened, and an escalating classic composition-literature conflict became an opportunity. Senior administrators, also holders of English PhDs, were likely familiar with composition-literature wars and anxious to enable writing faculty to focus their attention on problems related to retention that first-year composition was seen as both potentially exacerbating and relieving, and thus the last essential domino was in place. A little push, and overnight a department was created.

For the writing faculty who had taken the risk to ask for the break, the decision to create the new Department of Writing Studies couldn't have come fast enough. For me, the most senior of the group and outside of the department during that terrible year, and because I had several close friendships with literature faculty and had thought the department was in a good place in my short stint as English chair, it was too fast. I had thought that a writing track would develop in the English major, improving both the existing literature major and allowing for the composition-literature synergy I believed in. I also believed that the influence and power of English would ensure the long-term health of first-year composition—literacy education—which I strongly felt was some of the most important work that the department did. Many of my literature colleagues agreed on this point. I worried about the heavy weight of first-year composition and creating a department, a major, and, ideally, a graduate program. Who knows if I was overly optimistic. Perhaps. Regardless, as associate dean and member of the discipline, I was happy to assist the writing studies faculty to quickly build a department of twenty-eight non-tenure-track lecturer faculty and two tenured professors that had as assets just two programs: a two-semester first-year composition sequence and a minor in public and professional writing.

That was four years ago, and so the Department of Writing Studies is still in its infancy with a small major and an even smaller cadre of tenure-line faculty. The challenges that the department faces strike me as typical for new writing studies departments. These challenges are addressed repeatedly in Justin Everett and Cristina Hanganu-Bresch's *A Minefield of Dreams: Triumphs and Travails of Independent Writing Programs* (2017), the latest in a series of edited collections that mark two decades of a growing movement toward independence (Giberson and Moriarty 2010; O'Neill, Crow, and Burton 2002; Shamoon et al. 2000). New writing studies departments face both internal and external challenges. Internally, the challenge is to achieve the democratic ideals that are frequently part of the inspiration for independence and that run counter to established university practices, some of which are encoded in labor contracts or university policies; thus, at center are issues of governance, labor, and faculty equality. Will these departments develop mechanisms to make non-tenure-track faculty equal to tenure-track faculty in decision making and lessen, if not abandon, other inequalities (in salary, support for travel, release time, opportunities for teaching, etc.) between faculty types? It'll be very hard to do, especially as external pressures bear down on faculty leadership. It was easy for those of us tenured in English to be sympathetic to our non-tenure-track colleagues when we were in the minority, but what are we willing to give up now that the power to enact democratic practices is in our own hands? How should scholarly expertise in composition and rhetoric, tenure, and rank matter in these new departments? (These questions, with some answers, are well explored in Robert Samuels's *The Politics of Writing Studies*, 2017.)

Complicating these internal challenges are external challenges relating to achieving status within the university hierarchy through established markers: successful program development, enrollments in new programs, support for new lines, advancement for individuals, and access to university resources. These external goals strike me as important: without a department that is recognized as successful by the university's standards—which include, centrally, scholarly productivity and successful degree programs—first-year composition is no more secure than if it were in a nonacademic unit. (Am I right, or is this view just a reflection of old thinking, influenced by my personal investment in scholarship and degree programs?)

Alongside these formation challenges lies the day-to-day consuming work of teaching first-year composition, work I've been preoccupied by throughout my career. How do we get the job done and done well? I have attempted to address this question through a study of 106 state universities that examines a variety of variables relating to writing instruction and administration, finding some significant differences at institutions that have independent writing programs rather than first-year writing programs embedded in English (Isaacs 2018). Relating to administration of first-year composition, institutions that had independent writing departments or programs were more likely to have two research-supported practices in use: directed self-placement (DSP) as a tool for placement, and inclusion of primary research methodologies as part of instruction for writing research papers (154). In addition, institutions that had independent writing programs had more faculty who had presented at the Conference on College Composition and Communication's annual meeting during a two-year period than the average of the rest of the sample (155). However, at the same time, I found that a quarter of the writing departments in my sample did not have any tenure-line faculty teaching first-year composition, as compared with just 8.5 percent of the English and humanities departments. And institutions that had first-year composition located in independent units didn't demonstrate greater success with many key attributes: class size was not smaller and professional development was not more present; there was no evidence of greater engagement with rhetorical methods in first-year composition, and there was just as much focus on remedial, skills-focused instruction. Why are tenure-line faculty in writing departments not teaching first-year composition? Why are markers of success in teaching first-year composition not better met? These empirical nuggets, among others, have made me nervous about the rush to create writing departments. The faculty are happier, but are first-year composition students better served? What is the focus of work in writing studies?

It is from my research perspective and personal context, watching composition and rhetoric grow into writing studies, a movement, a discipline, and occasionally a department, that I read Scholes's valiant but not successful efforts to save English as a cautionary tale for the new writing studies vanguard. Here is the danger: writing studies, focused on disciplinary equality as well as developing and teaching majors and graduate programs, runs the risk of repeating the mistakes of English, forsaking literacy education and the workaday, applied work of teaching writing to first-year students, many of whom dislike writing and don't exhibit much mastery of it. I hope this is simply an anxious person's fears, but my fear is that tenured and tenure-line faculty in writing studies departments, typically the minority in number but holding most of the power, will be drawn toward upper-level and graduate teaching where students are typically stronger or at least more mature, and course subject is closer to their research interest or specialization. In effect, we will walk away from first-year composition even more than we did, or could, when we were in English. Finally, my worry is that in these advanced courses the subject is not so much the students and their struggles and joys with their own writing, but something else, allowing more course time spent on rhetoric, professional writing, or writing studies as a discipline, and much less time spent on student writing, all of which will bleed over into the pedagogy practiced in first-year composition, which is exactly what we suspected happened when our literature colleagues taught composition.

PART II: SCHOLES'S VISION FOR LITERACY EDUCATION

Robert Scholes, a powerful rhetorician and a great humanities professor in the old tradition, had a dream of literary studies and writing studies in harmony under the umbrella of textual study, and he called for composition-literature faculty unity through textual study and tempted us with grand possibilities for literacy education through the humanities:

> We may not be able to make ourselves or those around us better human beings, but we can certainly make ourselves and those who attend to us more literate, more eloquent, and more culturally aware. . . . We have nothing to offer but the sweetness of reason and the light of learning. But if we use them with vigor—and even with rigor—then the humanities may regain their proper place in our schools and in our culture: the place where the heart and the mind meet in language. (Scholes 2005, 733)

Scholes was one of many prolific, prominent literary scholars whose work turned to considerations of English studies, literacy education, and higher education itself. Like others before him (for example, Eagleton 1983; Guillory 1993; Bérubé 1998) and after him (for example, English 2012;

Epstein, Klyukanov, and Emerson 2012), Scholes hoped to save English departments and English studies from fracture, and if not irrelevancy, then reduced relevancy. He recognized and sought to address two problems he saw as intertwined: the loss in status and interest in literature that has resulted in declines in English majors, and the fractious and often contentious division between literature and composition. Risking glibness, in summary, the solution for Scholes was textual studies, an approach, a philosophy, and a big umbrella under which all can stand, safe and sound.

Who would work harmoniously under Scholes's umbrella of textual studies? First, the literature guards dedicated to great literature, included in one canon or another. Second, the literature-as-text crowd born of poststructuralism for whom the advertisement, the one-line screed, and the romance novel are all texts worthy of study. Third, the creative writers who produce text, and Scholes notes, have been treated quite poorly by literary scholars: "[English departments] distinguish between the production and consumption of texts, and, as might be expected in a society like ours, we privilege consumption over production, just as the larger culture privileges the consuming class over the producing class" (Scholes 1985, 5). Fourth, the rhetoricians who are similar to the literature-as-text people, albeit rather than being armed with *literary theory* they are armed with the equally august and long-syllabled *rhetorical theory*, which has the additional advantages of greater age. Fifth, the compositionists who teach students to create texts.

Scholes's vision is theoretically sound: reading and writing, text creation and text analysis, can and ought to sit side by side in the higher educational enterprise. There is no rhyme or reason for English departments to abandon writing and text creation. Scholes's vision for teaching textual studies was put into practice through the textbook he co-authored with Nancy Comley and Gregory Ulmer, *Text Book: An Introduction to Literary Language,* first published in 1988, and reissued twice, finally as *Text Book: Writing through Literature* (2002; 3rd edition). In their opening chapter to students, they write: "[In this book] you will find all kinds of texts: some are usually called 'literary' and some are not. This mixture is essential to our method. We do *not* want to offer you a collection of 'master' works that ask for your passive submission, but a set of texts that you can work and play with, increasing your own understanding of fundamental textual processes and your own ability to use the written word" (xv). Throughout the apparatus of the book, the authors make a compelling case for reading and talking about literature as text.

PART III: TEXTUAL AND CULTURAL STUDIES VERSUS COMPOSITION

Scholes's definition of textual studies and its role in at once saving English and uniting its disparate children is well developed. In *The Rise and Fall of English* and *Textual Power* Scholes puts forth a "modest proposal" for placing textual study at the center of a general education curriculum and, in more advanced form, an English major. I'll attempt to summarize and bring forth a few of Scholes's most salient points: how he comes to decide upon textual studies (drawn principally from his first chapter in *Textual Power*, reprinted in this section), followed by a brief summary of the sketched-out curricula he provides. This sketch should demonstrate how Scholes's articulated theory for integrating reading and writing becomes difficult to imagine enacting for students simply because the conceptual work is so heavy, occupying the core of his attention, while the pedagogical and instructional teaching writing work is glossed briefly.

The case for textual studies is arrived at in the first chapter of *Textual Power* (1985), "The English Apparatus," reprinted in this volume. Scholes pulls from structuralism the organizing principle of codes to understand human experience: "Every meaningful action—wearing a necktie, embracing a friend, cooking a meal—is meaningful only to the extent that it is a sign in some interpretive code" (1). We learn codes by studying like things, and like things are grouped together by their codes in what we call genres (in the arts) and by poststructuralist extension, to institutions. At this point in Scholes's short, elegant leap through theory, he notes that we became necessarily interdisciplinary, and thus, textual study—made expansive by Foucault—is the work that *all of us* in English studies (and really in the humanities) can contribute to and teach, making the big relevant umbrella possible.

Scholes's unifying focus on textual study leads him to recommend that the way for literature faculty to use their skills at decoding texts, literary and otherwise, to regain relevance and value, is to become teachers of decoding, enabling students to become actors and not simply those who are "bombarded with signs" (13). Scholes explains that students need to learn to decode texts so they can "make sense of their worlds, to determine their own interests, both individual and collective, to see through the manipulations of all sorts of texts in all sorts of media, and to express their own views in some appropriate manner" (14). Thus, the next several chapters of *Textual Power* detail how the literary text can be taught as text to facilitate students' understanding of their worlds. The argument is powerful for a way to study literature as cultural artifact embedded in language practices, and it has in various ways been taken up by many contemporary instructors of literature. Scholes's textual analysis pedagogy rests on the same theoretical logic that David Bartholomae draws on in "Inventing the University," published just a year later in 1986, and which is also influenced by Foucault and poststructuralism. Several textbooks have attempted this strategy as well, from Scholes's co-authored *Text Book*, to John Schilb and John Clifford's *Making Literature Matter*, now in its eighth edition, which presents literature as culture-text for decoding.

The issue of teaching writing is addressed to a greater extent in *The Rise and Fall of English* (1998), published thirteen years after *Textual Power*. The pedagogical vision for general education literacy instruction is put forth in chapter 4, "A Flock of Cultures: A Trivial Proposal." To briefly summarize it, Scholes suggests replacing the grand idea of teaching Western Civilization as a general education core in favor of more focused textual study (which is what trivial is meant to suggest). By reinstating an ancient "trivium" of "grammar, dialectic, and rhetoric at the core of college education" (120), Scholes dislodges the "canon of texts" in favor of a "canon of concepts, precepts, and practices" (120). Scholes's development of his vision of how this modern trivium would be enacted is an expansion of the idea of textual study, beginning with grammar understood as "language and human subjectivity" (122) followed by "representation and objectivity" (123). Teaching dialectic is more theoretical, working at a "high level of abstraction and systemization" (124) but intended to teach students "the tradition of clear and systematic thinking" (125). Finally, under rhetoric, Scholes suggests a familiar course of study through the principles of rhetoric, though he notes the appropriateness of the study of poetics too.

The teaching of writing is understood by Scholes as involving reading, listening to lectures, engaging in discussion, and interpreting and coming to understand principal concepts relating to language, text, and the ways in which language and text constitute us and the worlds in which we live or can observe through contextualized analysis. Scholes's ideas are engrossing and appealing, and he does put the nail in the coffin of any idea that general education should be organized around canonical texts. As Robert Lestón in this volume notes, from Scholes's work we find a "logic [that] sees the interplay between production and consumption as co-invested with the charge of the other, rendering the potential for each to be transformed." Similarly, the textbook, *Text Book*, enacts those ideas through the pedagogical scaffolding that asks students to understand literary and nonliterary texts in these ways. However, what seems to be missing from Scholes's work, including *Text Book*, is the scaffolded writing activities and assignments that actually develop students' writing. Thus, he too abandons students' writing. Scholes's pedagogy of textual study is as challenging as it is appealing, raising the question of who will choose the mundane work of teaching students "to express their own views in some appropriate manner" when much more exciting, difficult, class-intensive work in cultural studies analysis lies right there to chew on? Finally, after nearly ten years of decline in all the major disciplines of the humanities makes clear (Schmidt 2018), the dream that textual studies would revitalize and make more relevant English and other humanities departments has not borne out at all.

At the beginning of the third decade of the twenty-first century, as we face declining majors across the humanities and especially in literary studies and as composition and rhetoric faculty are splitting off (to struggle to gain majors) on their own, it is clear that the unifying possibility of textual studies has not been achieved. English departments didn't really embrace textual studies as literacy education, except at the margins (for example, in second-semester first-year composition courses in teaching about literature). While Thomas P. Miller, in this volume, holds out hope that the new generation of English faculty may reform English departments through the pursuit of integrative learning and experiential learning programs that place textual production alongside textual consumption, I am decidedly more skeptical.

At the same time that Scholes advocated for textual studies, he also provided an explanation for why literature faculty would resist it, providing an analysis that is relevant to pioneering faculty in new writing studies departments. He observed about the place of literature and literary study: Whereas throughout the first two-thirds of the twentieth century literature functioned in the university and the culture as "secular scripture," "since the nineteen-sixties we have been losing our congregations, and we are scared to death that our temples will be converted into movie theaters or video parlors and we will end our days doing intellectual janitorial or custodial work" (1985, 13). Thus, for Scholes, many faculty wed to literary studies resist textual studies out of fear of loss of status. To declare oneself a teacher of first-year composition, dedicated to general education, might well be to toss away one's status as it is conferred and maintained in the contemporary university.

PART IV: DISCIPLINARITY VERSUS COMPOSITION: STAY TUNED

I first became worried that advancements in the discipline of writing studies might pull from the pursuit of teaching writing when I participated in a CCCC panel several years ago. Speakers were describing their experiences enacting best practices in first-year composition administration, and one of the speakers described leading first-year composition at a school that had recently built a new department and major. The speaker mentioned the excitement of the new major and department, and while enthusiastic herself, she also observed that there was little departmental energy left for first-year composition, and that faculty with seniority rushed to upper-level courses in the new major.

Today I see several movements within writing studies that seek to establish the discipline as a body of knowledge captured in alphabetic and other textual forms whose fundamental tenets and foundational scholarship needs to be communicated to students, and not as a discipline that is represented primarily by practices—writing practices and teaching practices—as I'd like to argue it should be.

In part III I hoped to convey that Scholes's vision of a big umbrella under which composition studies and literary studies might sit equally (alongside others) was *theoretically* compelling. With a long history of privileging consumption over production in English studies, mirroring the history of art in Western civilization, Scholes well demonstrated the logical folly of the literary scholar superiority complex, insisting that English studies must be rebuilt and "devoted to textual studies, with the consumption and production of texts thoroughly intermingled" (1985, 16). But Scholes didn't provide any evidence that the balance was shifting and becoming equal and that's because it wasn't happening and hasn't happened since then. Consumption (literary analysis) and production (composition) never arrived at equal footing within English departments. So, my question is this: on what grounds would anybody think the new discipline and accompanying academic departments would be different? The conditions are essentially similar. Might it be that the discipline's roots in teaching writing as part of an access vision will make writing studies function differently than English? This is essentially the argument that is made by the editors and many of the authors of *Composition, Rhetoric and Disciplinarity* who declare "we are a discipline that values inclusion and access" (333). Really? I can't imagine that tenured literary scholars in English departments would describe themselves any differently, but given the chance, they took the sweetest morsels—lecturing on and leading discussions about intellectually inspiring and complicated ideas—and I suspect writing studies tenured elites will do the same.

Perhaps I am too cynical, but what will keep that division of consumption—analyzing texts—retaining primacy over production (writing texts) from defining and creating hierarchy in writing studies? At present, as I look to professional conversations, I am skeptical about the discipline of writing studies achieving balance between those faculty involved in teaching consumption (rhetoric and other "content" areas) and those who are involved with teaching production (composition), despite contentions from these scholars that their content focus develops metacognitive awareness that in turn helps students improve their writing.

Over the last thirty years, the field has become increasingly professionalized and achieved disciplinary status, as is asserted persuasively in *Composition, Rhetoric and Disciplinarity* (Malenczyk et al. 2018). As the field has become a discipline, and one that appropriately includes faculty with a wide range of academic preparation and research foci, the rush toward content accelerates. As Sandra Jamieson notes, writing majors are becoming less focused on the "activity of writing" (262) as they turn to having students learn the "body of knowledge" of the discipline (Jamieson 2018). To become a member of the emerging discipline, what knowledge must practitioners gain? In *Naming What We Know: Threshold Concepts of Writing Studies*, edited by Linda Adler-Kassner and Elizabeth Wardle, this question is addressed; readers are presented with thirty-seven "concepts that writing scholars and teachers agree are critical" (2015). According to Adler-Kassner and Wardle, a "modified crowd-sourcing" approach was used to develop these thirty-seven threshold concepts: "underlying, assumed, agreed-upon knowledge critical for participation in a discipline" (2018, 119). The crowd-sourcing method appears to have consisted of the invited contributors raising questions as to how agreed-upon these concepts are. To learn these thirty-seven concepts, this content of the field, how many disciplinary master texts must students read? Who will define these texts? Who will be qualified to teach them? It is not clear, but there is a classroom edition of *Naming What We Know*, putting forth Adler-Kassner and Wardle's proposed content for that which must be read and discussed. *Naming What We Know* is nothing if not an effort to define and root the major in disciplinary knowledge that must be consumed by initiates to the discipline.

Following common academic program development practices, students will need a preview of the discipline of writing studies to attract them to major programs. The new writing studies departments control the most universal of all university requirements: first-year composition. Where once students needed to dive into the literary canon to develop as college writers, in the new writing studies era I worry has arrived, students will need to dive into the composition and rhetoric textual canon, the first iteration of it, *Writing about Writing*, now in its third edition (Wardle and Downs 2017). English attracted majors with literature as content in FYC.

Will writing studies follow the same pattern of introducing a canon of texts and concepts to focus the first-year composition course? To provide relief or escape from the mundane work of drafting, revising, and editing? Robert Samuels describes it thusly: "In proposing a writing-about-writing (WaW) approach to composition with Doug Downs, Wardle seeks to overcome the conflict between content and form by making composition research the content of composition courses" (Samuels 2017, 6).

Despite my critique, I don't know if battling rhetoricians and WaW advocates for control of the foci of first-year composition is any worse than battling literary scholars. And, as with the study of literature, there is value to the proposed content. However, I think writing studies and composition and rhetoric should focus as much on the production of texts—and I am grateful to Scholes for the conceptualization—as on consumption of texts. Who will stick up for the focus on textual production? At a recent department meeting I was delighted to hear several faculty—non-tenure-track colleagues—who teach four courses of first-year composition each semester insist on the value of frequent writing and revision, even though it meant more reading of and commenting on student writing for them. So, a concern for and focus on student production is not yet lost, though it may not be championed so much by those on top of the writing studies food chain. It doesn't seem to be in their interests as defined by past practices, evidenced in the example of English and the failure of Scholes's uniting vision of textual studies, and recent developments and trends I have discussed here. In the end, I predict that status and the maintenance of status will very likely trump all other concerns, though I will welcome looking back in ten years to discover I was wrong in my fearful prediction.

REFERENCES

Adler-Kassner, Linda, and Elizabeth Wardle, eds. 2015. *Naming What We Know: Threshold Concepts of Writing Studies*, edited by Gregory L. Waddoups. Logan: Utah State University Press.

Adler-Kassner, Linda, and Elizabeth Wardle. 2018. "Understanding the Nature of Disciplinarity in Terms of Composition's Values." In *Composition, Rhetoric and Disciplinarity*, edited by Rita Malenczyk, Susan Miller-Cochran, Elizabeth Wardle, and Kathleen Blake Yancey, 111–33. Logan: Utah State University Press.

Bartholomae, David. 1986. "Inventing the University." *Journal of Basic Writing* 5 (1): 4–23.

Bérubé, Michael. 1998. *The Employment of English: Theory, Jobs, and the Future of Literary Studies*. New York: New York University Press.

Chapman, David, Jeanette Harris, and Christine Hult. 1995. "Agents for Change: Undergraduate Writing Programs in Departments of English." *Rhetoric Review* 13 (2): 421–34. doi: 10.2307/465842.

Eagleton, Terry. 1983. *Literary Theory: An Introduction*. Oxford, England: Basil Blackwell.

English, James F. 2012. *The Global Future of English Studies*. New York: Wiley-Blackwell.
Epstein, Mikhail, Igor Klyukanov, and Caryl Emerson. 2012. *The Transformative Humanities: A Manifesto*. New York: Bloomsbury.
Estrem, Heidi. 2007. "Growing Pains: The Writing Major in Composition and Rhetoric." *Composition Studies* 35 (1):11–14.
Everett, Justin, and Cristina Hanganu-Bresch, eds. 2017. *A Minefield of Dreams: Triumphs and Travails of Independent Writing Programs*. Logan: Utah State University Press.
Gaughan, Frank. 2016. "New Department, Familiar Problems: The Composition Requirement as Rationale for Independence." *College Composition and Communication* 68 (1): 200–204.
Giberson, Greg A., and Thomas A. Moriarty, eds. 2010. *What We Are Becoming: Developments in Undergraduate Writing Majors*. Logan: Utah State University Press.
Guillory, John. 1993. *Cultural Capital: The Problem of Literary Canon Formation*. Chicago: University of Chicago Press.
Hairston, Maxine. 1985. "Breaking Our Bonds and Reaffirming Our Connections." *College Composition and Communication* 36: 272–82.
Howard, Rebecca Moore. 1993. "Power Revisited; Or, How We Became a Department." *WPA: Writing Program Administration* 16 (3): 37–49.
Isaacs, Emily J. 2018. *Writing at the State U: Instruction and Administration at 106 Comprehensive Universities*. Logan: Utah State University Press.
Jamieson, Sandra. 2018. "The Major in Composition, Writing and Rhetoric: Tracking Changes in the Evolving Discipline." In *Composition, Rhetoric and Disciplinarity*, edited by Rita Malenczyk, Susan Miller-Cochran, Elizabeth Wardle, and Kathleen Blake Yancey, 243–66. Logan: Utah State University Press.
Malenczyk, Rita, Susan Miller-Cochran, Elizabeth Wardle, and Kathleen Blake Yancey, eds. 2018. *Composition, Rhetoric and Disciplinarity*. Logan: Utah State University Press.
O'Neill, Peggy, Angela Crow, and Larry W. Burton. 2002. *A Field of Dreams: Independent Writing Programs and the Future of Composition Studies*. Logan: Utah State University Press.
Phelps, Louise Wetherbee. 2017. "Between Smoke and Crystal: Accomplishing In(ter)dependent Writing Programs." In *A Minefield of Dreams: Triumphs and Travails of Independent Writing Programs*, edited by Justin Everett and Cristina Hanganu-Bresch, 321–50. Logan: Utah State University Press.
Phelps, Louise Wetherbee, and John M. Ackerman. 2010. "Making the Case for Disciplinarity in Rhetoric, Composition, and Writing Studies: The Visibility Project." *College Composition and Communication* 62 (1): 180–215.
Samuels, Robert. 2017. *The Politics of Writing Studies: Reinventing Our Universities from Below*. Logan: Utah State University Press.
Schilb, John, and John Clifford. 2018. *Making Literature Matter*. 8th ed. Boston: Bedford/St. Martin's.
Schmidt, Benjamin M. 2018. "The History BA since the Great Recession: The 2018 AHA Majors Report." *Perspectives on History* 9: 19–23.
Scholes, Robert. 1985. *Textual Power: Literary Theory and the Teaching of English*. New Haven, CT: Yale University Press.
Scholes, Robert. 1998. *The Rise and Fall of English*. New Haven, CT: Yale University Press.
Scholes, Robert. 2005. "Presidential Address 2004: The Humanities in a Posthumanist World." *PMLA* 120 (3): 724–33.
Scholes, Robert, Nancy R. Comley, and Gregory Ulmer. 2002. *Text Book: Writing through Literature*. 3rd ed. Boston: Bedford/St. Martin's.
Shamoon, Linda K., Rebecca Moore Howard, Sandra Jamieson, and Robert A. Schwegler, eds. 2000. *Coming of Age: The Advanced Writing Curriculum, CrossCurrents*. Portsmouth, NH: Boynton/Cook Publishers.
Wardle, Elizabeth, and Douglas Downs. 2017. *Writing about Writing: A College Reader*. 3rd ed. New York: Macmillan.

12
"NOT A NEAT CONSPIRACY, BUT A MUDDLE"
A College-to-Career Quality Enhancement Plan in the Spirit of Robert Scholes

Lynée Lewis Gaillet and Angela Christie

In 1983, Winifred Bryan Horner edited the groundbreaking *Composition and Literature: Bridging the Gap*, a collection of essays examining the ruptured relationship between reading and writing that included chapters by leading lights such as Richard Lanham, Wayne Booth, Walter Ong, Ed Corbett, J. Hillis Miller, Elaine Maimon—and Nancy Comley and Robert Scholes. Horner handpicked these contributors to the collection because they represented the few who had, at the time, produced scholarship in both literature and composition. By showcasing the work of recognized literary scholars who valued composition, she hoped to increase readers' willingness to collaborate with each other. Horner explains that the collection's authors sought "to uncover fresh and exciting opportunities within our profession" during a period when "the discipline of English and also the humanities in general are being examined and their value questioned" (Horner 1983, 8). Thirty-five years later, the situation has not changed much, demonstrated in declining numbers of English majors, headline articles questioning the value of a humanities degree, and the move to big-data analytics to drive university curriculum design—a move that sidelines traditional humanities courses in reading, writing, and critical thinking. The 2018 Association of the Departments of English (ADE) report, "A Changing Major," sponsored by the Modern Language Association (MLA) succinctly and convincingly reiterates that Scholes's claims and predictions about the future of English studies have indeed come to fruition. In this essay, we take up the mantle left by Scholes, as outlined in his co-authored chapter in Horner's *Composition and Literature* (1983) and explored in depth in *The Rise and Fall of English* (1998). Scholes looks to the past in making radical assertions about the

DOI: 10.7330/9781646421190.c012

future of English, one that muddles through, and ultimately may "risk annoying both traditionalists and avant-gardists by adopting a militant middle position on many of the questions that currently vex English studies" (Scholes 1998, ix). We offer a twenty-first-century illustration of Scholes's vision, one that specifically focuses on preparing English majors for careers and heralds the value of humanities degrees in a time of declination and dismissal.

Horner and Scholes were both troubled by a "fracturing of the language discipline [literature and composition] that is detrimental to work in both areas, as unproductive as it is unwarranted" (Horner 1983, 1), and while other scholars featured in *Composition and Literature* subsequently moved to one side of the argument or the other, Horner and Scholes continued to encourage readers to understand that "the division between composition and literature is truly a matter of attitude and history and that, in joining forces, we can find the strength and the resources to forge new directions for the discipline" (Horner 1983, 8). Horner passed away in 2014 and Scholes in 2016, leaving in their wake legacies of literacy-focused pedagogy. As Scholes explained, the field of English has two choices: "[B]ecome a small, elite field of study devoted to the past, and without responsibilities or general education of the teaching of writing. No 'service course,' no uninterested students fulfilling requirements, just dedicated scholars and students who want to emulate them in pursuit of a humanistic education that is its own reward" (Scholes 1998, 144) or for the field to abandon "a burial ground" of "textual tombs of the great dead" and instead envision itself as a "productive discipline" that reconstructs English studies as an enlivened discipline where texts remain living through a merger with a "canon of methods" (Scholes 1998, 145). According to Scholes, this new method of rapprochement between old and new, literature and composition, aesthetic study for its own sake and skills acquisition lies in successfully addressing two things: how we can "put students in touch with a usable cultural past . . . [and] how we can help students attain an active relationship with their cultural present" (Scholes 1998, 104), brought to fruition by preparing students for careers. As Thomas P. Miller explains in this volume, Scholes's work "remain[s] important because the historic changes he addressed have contributed to the collapses in majors and jobs that have reached crisis proportions in the last decade."

Scholes's 1998 proclamations, predictions, and suggestions are echoed thirty years later in the 2018 ADE "A Changing Major" report, which addresses "the decline in undergraduate English majors across North America that began around 2009" resulting from a "downturn in the United States economy" leading to an increased interest in gaining a higher education degree "for the employment prospects it produced" (1). The report credits the devaluing of the humanities to an elevation of STEM majors with inherent vocational training, a decline in pleasure reading, and a shift in reading practices ushered in by electronic media. "But," Scholes explains, "even in a bad situation, it helps to have a curriculum that both students and teachers can believe in, because they can see that it is aimed at helping students to develop better intellectual equipment for the lives they are actually living and will continue to live" (Scholes 1998, 142). In the final analysis, the ADE report echoes Scholes's thoughts, recommending "that departments and faculty members discuss and identify the big questions motivating literary and writing studies and the intellectual issues that engage scholarship; that bring vigor, dignity, and social purposefulness to English as an academic discipline; and that accommodate a broad range of student interests and perspectives" (Scholes 1998, 24). The quality enhancement plan (QEP) we describe herein attempts to answer this challenge.

Our experiences working at a large urban research university provide an instructive case study, demonstrating how earlier intellectual educational histories ushered in current institutional measures, including contemporary college-to-career vertical curriculum redesigns and QEPs grounded in rhetorical reading and writing. Georgia State University's downtown Atlanta campus recently consolidated with a five-campus community college, resulting in the largest higher education institution in Georgia, fifty-two thousand students. Ranked as the second most innovative university in the nation and second in the country for its commitment to undergraduate teaching in the 2019 "Best Colleges" edition of *U.S. News & World Report*, GSU's first-year writing program and the English Department's participation in freshman learning communities (FLC) have played a major role in new initiatives designed to promote recruitment, retention, and time-to-degree for students; however, other successful retention measures (shifts in central advising, chiefly) contributed to lowered enrollments across humanities disciplines and a reduction in both English majors and minors. As immediate past co-directors of Lower Division Studies at GSU and the current chair of the English Department (Gaillet) and university QEP director (Christie), we are in ideal positions to work toward addressing the shifting needs of our student population and making clear the value of humanistic study, illustrated in the ways in which we are in the process of integrating workplace literacy into the fabric of the institutional strategic mission through the newly adopted College to Career QEP. This QEP dovetails with recent revisions to the university's strategic mission plan, answering challenges put forth by Scholes, offering solutions to literacy problems that he identified over three decades ago and addressing the decline of English majors as described in the ADE report "A Changing Major." As MLA Executive Director Paula Krebs (2018) asserts in the introduction to that document, "In a national climate of declining numbers of students majoring in English, it's time to use the data we have to make real changes in our outreach, in the cases we are making for our majors, and even in our departmental structures and curricula." Scholes prefigured this claim, starkly warning that in addition to revising the English studies curriculum in order to "open a wider world of culture for our students" (Scholes 2010, 232), we must also shift and expand the curriculum to save ourselves: "If we pin our fate to [outmoded literary] texts in too narrow a fashion, our departments will shrink as departments of classical studies have shrunk" (Scholes 2010, 231).

The GSU Reaffirmation Leadership Team designed a comprehensive selection process in adoption of *College to Career: Career Readiness through Everyday Competencies* as the next QEP. Selected in fall 2017, this five-year plan was presented to the Southern Association of Colleges and Schools Commission on Colleges (SACSCOC) On-Site Review Committee in February 2019 and full implementation just began in 2020. As the university explains, "the decision was the culmination of a nearly year-long selection process involving the review of 36 initial topic proposals and then three full proposals that were invited for further consideration." In addition to the final winner, "Global Pathways to Student Success: A Model to Promote Global Learning for All" and "My Experience @ GSU: Experiential Learning across the Curriculum" were the other two final proposals developed and considered. In the official announcement of the winning proposal, the committee explained that "*College to Career* will contribute to the achievement of the university's Strategic Plan, which states that Georgia State will 'facilitate seamless college to career transitions.'" The QEP will affirm this institutional commitment by integrating career preparation into key junctures in the undergraduate experience, starting in the first year and continuing through graduation. The College to Career QEP stipulates that in addition to being career ready, students will also learn to identify, reflect upon, and document their career readiness (GSU "QEP Selection Process," n.d.).

Georgia State University is nationally recognized for its student success initiatives, which grow out of data-driven analytics. These success programs intersect with English because they often involve core courses, including first-year writing classes. The university-level student success initiatives have frequently existed in the margins of our curriculum adjustment plans; however, the QEP prompts us to include student success goals with our student learning outcomes. English students perform well when problem solving and communicating ideas, and our students develop strong writing and editing skills. So, historically, the work of an English major maps organically onto the teaching track profession. However, when we ask students to connect the work of research, documentation, writing, and thinking to broader professional possibilities, they often struggle to articulate how these skills transfer to the workplace. Indeed, students flock to STEM programs because there is a clearer correlation between college training and career paths. National data indicates that students view the college experience as a means/ends equation, and that the value of a degree is determined by its employment marketability (Selingo 2018). Scholes (1998, 145) asks English departments to consider replacing "a canon of text with a canon of methods." The curriculum that we suggest does just that. The shift to student-success outcomes forces a major in the humanities to connect student learning with preparation for postgraduation success in a variety of employment sectors. Instead of designing curriculum that focuses solely on how well a student constructs an argument, in this new plan humanities faculty can also consider how well a student constructs an argument in a digital space (website construction) or how well the argument adjusts to a wide variety of audiences (blog post management). Traditionally the student-learning outcome measures the level at which the argument is constructed. The student success goal, however, measures how well the student uses a career competency skill to demonstrate or produce the well-constructed argument. A curriculum's emphasis on multimodal expression teaches students marketable skills in addition to offering instruction in content, and often the audience shifts from the single classroom teacher to an external audience that may include local community members, stakeholders, or decision makers. These new pedagogical methods answer Scholes's challenge, taking a "turn toward the specific and practical" by making clear ways in which "historical studies themselves should be preceded or accompanied by another core, designed to help students situate themselves in their own culture, and, in particular, designed to make the basic processes of language itself intelligible and fully available for use" (Scholes 1998, 119).

Our institution's last QEP focused on critical thinking through writing (CTW), an initiative now ubiquitous in academic departments across the nation. This QEP resulted in resistant faculty members asking, "Aren't all college curricula an exercise in critical thinking?" Faculty in literary studies and creative writing concentrations at our institution viewed critical thinking and subsequent articulation of pedagogy as too rhetoric-composition in spirit. Those in charge of articulating the CTW programs, training faculty, collecting data, and producing assessment reports found themselves in the uncomfortable position of calibrating presentations and explanations to appease both upper administration and department faculty who held differing disciplinary interests. In the end, the QEP produced, as its name suggests, an enhancement in the quality of instruction—and in the process served to unite faculty in different concentrations. Yes, of course, we always taught critical thinking, but given the nomenclature and auspices of the past QEP, we learned how to more fully discuss this concept, develop assignments with clear outcomes, and present writing as a tool of critical thinking not only to ourselves, but to our students. As Scholes attests, college teachers are ultimately "responsible for helping people to read and interpret critically" (Comley and Scholes 1983, 18).

On the eve of our new QEP, College to Career (CTC), faculty members have similar initial misgivings, but now they possess a confident understanding of how accreditation plans both present opportunities to articulate what students need and want out of a degree in English—and serve to unite reading and writing across the department. The new QEP inspires faculty from all four concentrations housed in our English Department (rhetoric-composition, literature, creative writing, and secondary education) to demonstrate to students and future employers how English courses prepare graduates for a variety of in-demand career paths. This plan also provides a mechanism for illustrating how an English degree provides training more commonly associated with communications, new media, political science, and policy studies departments. The content of our instruction has not changed or altered given the dictates of College to Career; the way we ask our students to encounter, engage, and reflect upon the content has.

This QEP fosters inclusivity and avoids the "fracturing of the language discipline" by relying on the strengths of each concentration, the rich content of diverse courses, and teachers' creative expertise. The plan asks faculty to voluntarily tag existing classes with a career skill—advanced argumentation, communication, advanced research, teaching, or editing and publishing—career aptitudes reflecting employers' stated in-demand skills. Students then choose to earn a training specialization in one of the tagged skills. Regardless of subject matter, classes adopt skills-driven outcomes for course assignments to teach not only course content, but also career readiness. For example, students may reflect on how the use of Tumblr in a fiction-writing workshop facilitates communicating to a mass audience (communications), how writing/producing a short film on deviations in Old English manuscripts aids in understanding digital editing (editing and publishing), or how tracing the change in political values for women in a regional book club relies upon archival research and data mining skills (advanced research).

According to research conducted by the Association of American Colleges and Universities, *Fulfilling the American Dream: Liberal Education and the Future of Work* (Hart 2018), only 13 percent of hiring managers are "very satisfied" with graduates' demonstration and articulation of transferable skills. Most important, those in hiring positions find graduates do not effectively apply what they have learned in their college courses to the workplace in any meaningful or consistent way. The sought-after career skills of communication, critical thinking, and global/intercultural fluency, which are listed as three of the eight career competencies by the *National Association of Colleges and Employers*, are the English degree's mainstays; however, students often do not see the English major as a pathway to success in the employment sector. The decline in English majors since 2009 results from a decline in economic security and the "rising personal cost of (and declining public support for) higher education, which together put pressure on students to value higher education for the employment prospects it produce[s]" (ADE 2018, 1). Students and their parents, who often shoulder college costs, wonder what Shakespeare has to do with board meetings or how to leverage knowledge of trauma narratives during a job interview for a managerial position. Our response to these questions has been an enthusiastic "critical thinking!" and "good writing skills!" In this value-driven economy, students want better answers. Students need faculty to *make* the study of English *valuable*, as Scholes explains in his "Presidential Address 2004: The Humanities in a Posthumanist World," published in this part of the volume: "We must show that what we have to teach will be useful to this society and to the individuals who study with us. And we must also, in our teaching, generate new human standards that reject the fundamentalist leap to absolute truth and the pragmatist denial that such standards are possible" (Scholes 2005, 731). In our plan, English studies can create value for both students and local communities by showing students the ways in which our discipline can become the means to a greater end. Learning how to dramatically recite "Porphyria's Lover," for example, not only teaches a student to appreciate the poem (the meter and rhyme, the conceit, the references to nineteenth-century madhouses) and evoke human compassion, but also how to read a room, sell an idea, gain confidence in front of an audience, speak directly, and interpret and explain language using various modes (i.e., body language and visual cues). The value of composition, for instance, lies in its communication currency. Global policies are made on Twitter; texts relay domestic emergency threats; and many influential people communicate solely through social media accounts—posthumanism is no longer a theoretical future. Our curriculum revision and connections to the broader university QEP initiative illustrate our acceptance of the posthumanist world Scholes spoke of in 2004.

The infusion of career-competency curriculum into the majors and pathways focuses on three QEP student learning outcomes: *awareness, connection,* and *demonstration.* Within the first year, students articulate *awareness* of the career-readiness competencies that are valued by employers. In their undergraduate courses, students make *connections* among specific curricular, co-curricular, and extracurricular activities and the career-readiness competencies that they acquire. Throughout their undergraduate experiences, students *demonstrate* their career-readiness competencies in a variety of interpersonal and digital media frameworks. These learning outcomes grow out of the university's strategic plan: "Become a national model for undergraduate education by demonstrating that students from all backgrounds can achieve academic and *career success.*" In particular, the QEP is responsive to Initiative 3 of the 2016 revision of the strategic plan: "*Establish new pathways that facilitate* **seamless college to career transitions.** "

In anticipation of the QEP implementation phase, faculty in the English Department charted a College to Career curricular map that not only responds to the demands of the QEP, but goes further to present a forward-thinking vertical curriculum. Our department's plan aims to make students aware of the career competencies offered by the major and helps them articulate how the transferable skills they practiced and mastered in their courses reflect the skills most desired by employers. The CTC initiative does not require faculty to change the structure of the classes they teach. Course content remains the same; however, the pedagogical methods adjust to permit practice and mastery of a set of soft skills. For instance, a traditionally taught course in medieval literature asks students to read, discuss, research, and write about the literature they encounter throughout the course of the semester. A CTC-adjusted medieval literature course includes an artifact curation assignment that requires students to choose an artifact referenced in the literature and then practice skills in close reading, digital and archival research, 3D image mapping, artifact replication (using any medium), and digital curation on the course WordPress site. Since the students use soft skills in digital writing, image mapping, and writing for a mass audience, the course can list communication and digital technology as the career-competency focus. As Scholes claims, "A fair number of our students end up working in some aspect of media and practical communications: they work for radio stations, television stations, magazines, and the like. We don't train people in that way." He goes on to explain how English majors actually have an advantage over media studies students in communication jobs: "We are looking to produce a graduate who is effective in communications, but who also knows the theory [of language usage]" (Comley and Scholes 1983, 17). In our new QEP system, faculty interested in adjusting the curriculum to help students articulate their knowledge and skill set can tag their courses in our university's registration system. In the medieval literature example, the course is tagged with *communication* and *digital technology*—two career competencies of eight listed by the National Association of College and Employers (NACE, n.d.). Course tagging alerts students to career curriculum enhancements, and faculty will tag adjusted courses in the major with the full range of eight NACE competencies.

Initial discussions with faculty about the tagging system highlighted the disconnect between the way we speak about the value of our courses (the language of value in the liberal arts) and the way students need to speak about the value of their training and degrees after graduation (the language of employability). Translating the competencies is critical to successful career training curricular enhancements. At first, faculty members had a difficult time connecting the work in the major with things like *leadership*, *career management*, and *global and intercultural fluency*. However, when they were given a set of marketable skills from which to choose and connect to the content and pedagogy of their courses, the value was easy to chart. Our courses train students in advanced argumentation, action plan and implementation, adaptability, data mining and analysis, copy editing, design and layout, podcast production, critical literacy, awareness of global/community issues, and collaborative writing, among other skills. Many of our courses already adopt digital writing and data collection platforms, making tracking of tags easier. Faculty became excited when speaking about their GPS/digital mapping projects and documentary productions. In fact, so many valuable soft skills emerged in our discussions that we had difficulty creating a concise list. Once we narrowed down the skills most exercised in the major courses, we were able to translate them into the QEP's eight career competencies and then to the student learning outcomes that drive QEP actions and assessment. The process of defining common career-readiness skills and emphasizing those for which our curriculum is best at preparing students became an exercise in the image of Scholes's desire to save English departments from fracturing. The process helped our faculty, who teach in four separate concentrations, create the common ground that addresses the two issues on which Scholes deliberates and that Emily J. Isaacs discusses in this volume: "the loss in status and interest in literature that has resulted in declines in English majors, and the fractious and often contentious division between literature and composition." Faculty were able to see, from a skills-building pedagogical perspective, the equal value in each concentration—each of them teach *digital technology*, for example, though they do so by utilizing different content, assignments, and assessment. In the end, students are prepared to demonstrate a proficiency in *digital technology* regardless of the concentration they choose in the English major.

In order to highlight the major's skill-building curriculum, course tagging in the university's registration guide permits competency-specific curriculum pathways to specialization. So, if a student has an interest in digital media, she can take courses applicable to her major that also have a digital media focus. Her degree in literary studies can also include a specialization in digital media writing. The vertical curriculum, then, maintains the spirit of the English major, but infuses it with the applicability and transference most appropriate to the current job market and the postgraduation demands of our students. A degree in creative writing, for instance, is more valuable when students can demonstrate their skills in copy editing, digital design, storytelling and narrative analysis, and communication for a mass audience—skills in demand on the job market. While a degree in creative writing traditionally pigeonholed students into graduate school, teaching, or freelance writing employment tracks, a degree in creative writing with the skill set described above positions the students for a wider range of employment opportunities. Training faculty in how to translate the humanities skills into employment skills is a key factor in developing the vertical curriculum that students need. Faculty members can use the chart below to help translate the most common skills they teach in their classes to the NACE competencies and the student learning and success outcomes developed by the QEP. The process of translation helps faculty develop the more career-specific language that students look for and will use on the job market.

The translation exercise emphasized the marketability of the English major. The adjustment to *how* faculty talk about the major's value puts

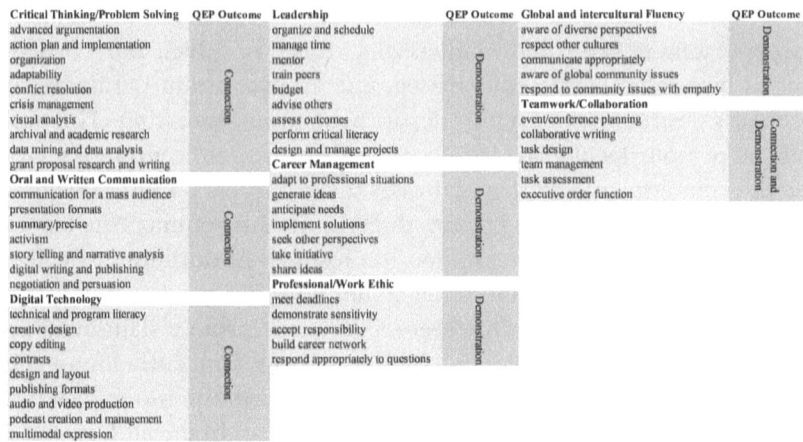

Figure 11.1. Career-Readiness Skills to NACE Competencies Graph with QEP Outcomes

career literacy in conversation with cultural, global, empathetic, and other traditionally humanities-based learning outcomes. English majors are trained in these skills. As Scholes (2005, 731) explains, "We must prepare our students to live and work in this world. And we must justify our existence in the terms offered by this world. But we cannot, and should not, simply accept those terms, for this is not so much a post humanist world as an antihumanist world, and what we have to offer it must be a reasoned critique of its values and practices." The English major curriculum provides a wide range of training applicable to many types of successful and lucrative careers, with web developer, nonprofit executive director, technical writer, and marketing director topping the industry list of high-paying jobs that look for students with English degrees (Monster 2018; Anders 2016). However, when career literacy informs the curriculum and programmatic adjustments, an awareness of these career competencies leads to the continual connection of the humanities to the more pragmatic postgraduation goals. An intentional articulation and focus on pedagogical methods that permit students' demonstration of their proficiency in the major's content through competency-deliberate assignments helps to deconstruct the English major's barriers—those related to student success based on culture, class, and limited employment opportunities. The Georgia State student body is 71 percent African American and 60 percent Pell grant–eligible with over half of students classified as first-generation college students.

Students' educational goals, more often than not, reflect their post-graduation goals. Majors that cannot articulate marketable opportunities beyond teaching and graduate school do not attract these students or their parents, who have a great impact on student decisions about programs of study. In fact, Georgia State University focuses on attracting students from low-income families and is noted as one of the "South's more innovative engines of social mobility" (Fausset 2018). Successful employment postgraduation is a large part of the promise of this social mobility. Students flock to those majors that are intentionally developing career-skills curriculum. Furthermore, the curriculum enhancements that focus on competency development do not have to rely exclusively on a simple addition of a technological component. The transferable-skills curricular adjustments can reflect the needs of students while considering the limitations of the digital divide. Activism, for example, can adopt WordPress as a tool, but it can also sidestep digital dependency altogether. Teaching students how to call for, organize, invite, and document a grassroots rally without using social media or other web-based platforms is useful or, more poignantly, an essential part of our mandate to revalue English studies for our students.

IMPLICATIONS

Scholes reimagines the academic trivium—grammar and language, rhetoric and poetics, reason and logic—renaming it "textuality," in light of "the multicultural and multitextual nature of the world around us" (2005, 732). This reconceptualization of traditional components of English studies resolves conflicts between reading and writing and composition and literature while connecting to job preparation and career readiness. Our students know how to both produce and analyze texts; that is their inherent value to society and employers, in equal measure. We opened this essay with an acknowledgment of the enduring divide between reading and writing within English departments, but Scholes, as echoed in the recent ADE report, points to the folly in this schism. As he explains, "we must see these two aspects of humanistic study as equally important, undoing our present hierarchical structures that relegate writing to a subordinate position below reading" (Scholes 2005, 732). The QEP plan described in this chapter attempts to do just that, to find commonalities across the diverse concentrations of literary studies, creative writing, and rhetoric and composition divisions that share a kind of geopolitical space within an English department. Scholes's 2004 Presidential Address anticipates the 2018 ADE recommendations, foreshadowing the claim that "we teachers of language and literature need to be less narrowly focused on particular periods or genres and broader in our grasp of literary and linguistic history. And also, for good practical reasons, we need to become broader in our grasp of other cultural fields, starting with those closest to us, such as philosophy and the visual arts and media" (Scholes 2005, 733). The tagged skills stipulated within the QEP connect the various concentrations typically housed in English departments, as well as provide interdisciplinary examples of ways in which similar tagging practices could work in other humanities departments, all while documenting marketable skill sets.

While historically the sciences have partnered with industry in the form of grants and cooperative education programs, the new strategic plan encourages the humanities to seek community partners to encourage students to see connections between their training and the workplace and gain valuable training as well, an initiative along the lines of those Thomas P. Miller describes in his chapter in this volume. As a result, Creative Media Industries Institute (CMII) at GSU has formed a partnership with Panasonic to "organize faculty-led teams that put advanced students to work on contracted work"; the Department of Religious Studies has partnered with WellStar Health System to launch the WellStar Religion and Public Life Fellowship to support students interested in nonprofit management and "to provide students with hands-on experience of how religion operates in public life" (GSU "Community and Industry," n.d.); and just this year, the English Department formed a partnership with the hundred-year-old Atlanta Writers Club, which provides an infrastructure and fellowships for faculty and students interested in fiction, nonfiction, memoir, essays, blogs, graphic novels, poetry, screenwriting, playwriting, journalism, and freelance writing to network with publishers, employers, and agents. We predict an uptick in the number of initiatives like these within GSU humanities departments given the college's overt support of community partnerships and the 2017 formation of the GSU Humanities Research Center, created to foster interdisciplinary collaborations.

Commitment to Scholes's theories of learning and suggestions for curricular revision needs to be undergirded by larger initiatives, such as college- and university-sponsored programming and mission statements, particularly within the humanities. These departments should also cooperate with one another in seeking outside funding to implement and facilitate curriculum redesigns that consider alternatives to academic employment opportunities and that, in the process, reinvent course content and pedagogy, broaden venues for disseminating our work, and expand internship opportunities. For example, the English and History Departments at GSU recently collaborated in securing an NEH Next Generation Humanities PhD grant, which addressed "the disparities between graduate student expectations for a career in academia and eventual career outcomes and to promote greater integration of the humanities in the public sphere." This grant allowed two GSU departments to systematically revise existing curricula and assessment that led to a shortened time to degree, to bring in outside employers and alumni who discussed opportunities for working in nonacademic fields, and to expand notions of "what it means to be a humanities scholar" by hosting nationally-recognized humanities experts who discussed new possibilities for both doing and presenting research findings within digital humanities (NEH 2016). One graduate student who participated in the workshops explained that this joint program provided both the encouragement and knowledge to identify what skills he needed for the job market and pathways for obtaining them. We next plan to extend these educational initiatives to undergraduates, asking our graduate students to serve as mentors to undergraduates, through the auspices and organizational structure of a newly acquired Andrew W. Mellon Foundation grant supporting Georgia State undergraduates in progression toward graduate work in a wide range of both academic and professional colleges. As Scholes explains, we need to consider "what [students] need to know and what they need to be able to do, with respect to those things that are in our domain . . ." (Scholes 1998, 65). As we reconsider our curriculum, we must ask, "How will knowing this or doing that strengthen [students] as thinkers, as readers, as communicators?" and how can we "lead students to a position of justified confidence in their own competence as textual consumers and their own eloquence as producers of texts?" (Scholes 1998, 66).

The ADE report rightly asserts that the English degree is "a changing major," and the report authors recommend in their final analysis "that departments and faculty members discuss and identify the big questions motivating literary and writing studies and the intellectual issues that engage scholarship; that bring vigor, dignity, and social purposefulness to English as an academic discipline; and that accommodate a broad range of student interests and perspectives" (ADE 2018, 24). Bipartisan conversation and collaboration across concentrations is essential to bring Scholes's vision for English departments to fruition. We must find common denominators that unite the various areas of traditional study housed in English departments; capture and relay to students, parents, and employers what we already do well; and seek ways to make permeable the liminal spaces that traditionally have divided the academy and local communities. Furthermore, departments and faculty must look to the future, considering the needs of our students, instead of romanticizing the traditional past. Students are the primary stakeholders in this new QEP; we must offer them tools to understand how a "lived curriculum, the temporal and affective experience of how an individual course might fit not only into a student's academic career, but with the lived education they experience as well as the barriers, opportunities, and desires that frame their experiences," as Robert Lestón explains in this volume. Collectively, faculty from literary studies, composition and rhetoric, and creative writing are all writing, composing, researching, and critical-thinking *practitioners* as well as researchers, evidenced in our discipline's commitment to the scholarship of teaching and expressed in our pedagogical *practice*. We would like to give Scholes the final word here; he advises that we need to "stop thinking of ourselves as if we had a subject matter and start thinking of ourselves as having a discipline which we can offer our students as part of the cultural equipment that they are going to need when they leave us" (Scholes 1998, 68).

REFERENCES

ADE Ad Hoc Committee on the English Major. 2018. "A Changing Major: The Report of the 2016–2017 ADE Ad Hoc Committee on the English Major." New York: Associations of Departments of English. https://www.ade.mla.org/content/download/98513/2276619/A-Changing-Major.pdf.

Anders, George. 2016. "14 Jobs for English Majors that Pay at Least $60,000." *Forbes*. https://www.forbes.com/sites/georgeanders/2016/10/03/14-jobs-for-english-majors-that-pay-at-least-60000/#98ad324f1def7.

Comley, Nancy, and Robert Scholes. 1983. "Literature, Composition, and the Structure of English." In *Composition and Literature: Bridging the Gap*, edited by Winifred Horner, 96–109. Chicago: University of Chicago Press.

Fausset, Richard. 2018. "Georgia State, Leading U.S. in Black Graduates, Is Engine of Social Mobility." *New York Times*, May 15, 2015. https://www.nytimes.com/2018/05/15/us/georgia-state-african-americans.html.

Georgia State University (GSU). n.d. "Community and Industry Partnerships." Accessed March 27, 2021. https://cas.gsu.edu/faculty-and-staff/faculty-affairs/community-industry-partnerships/.

Georgia State University (GSU). n.d. "QEP Selection Process." Accessed February 3, 2020. https://sacscoc.gsu.edu/quality-enhancement-plan/qep-selection-process-update/.

Hart Research Associates. 2018. "Fulfilling the American Dream: Liberal Education and the Future of Work." Association of American Colleges and Universities. https://www.aacu.org/sites/default/files/files/LEAP/2018EmployerResearchReport.pdf.

Horner, Winifred, ed. 1983. *Composition and Literature: Bridging the Gap*. Chicago: University of Chicago Press.

Monster, Christine Laue. 2018. "Here Are the Highest Paying Jobs for English Majors." *Business Insider*, February 6, 2018. https://www.businessinsider.com/the-highest-paying-jobs-for-english-majors-2018-2.

National Association of Colleges and Employers (NACE). n.d. "Career Readiness Defined." Accessed February 3, 2020. http://www.naceweb.org/career-readiness/competencies/career-readiness-defined/.

NEH Staff. 2016. "Next Generation PhD Humanities Grants." National Endowment for the Humanities. https://www.neh.gov/divisions/challenge/featured-project/next-generation-humanities-phd.

Scholes, Robert. 1983. "An Interview with Robert Scholes." *Iowa Journal of Literacy Studies* 4 (2): 13–20.

Scholes, Robert. 1998. *The Rise and Fall of English*. New Haven, CT: Yale University Press.

Scholes, Robert. 2005. "Presidential Address 2004: The Humanities in a Posthumanist World." *PMLA* 120 (3): 724–33.

Scholes, Robert. 2010. "The English Curriculum after the Fall." *Pedagogy* 10 (1): 229–40.

Selingo, Jeffrey J. 2018. "College Students Say They Want a Degree for a Job. Are They Getting What They Want?" *The Washington Post*, September 1, 2018. https://www.washingtonpost.com/news/grade-point/wp/2018/09/01/college-students-say-they-want-a-degree-for-a-job-are-they-getting-what-they-want/?noredirect=on&utm_term=.a3185e9fdf88.

U.S. News and World Report. n.d. "2019 Most Innovative Schools." *U.S. News and World Report*. Accessed February 3, 2020. https://www.usnews.com/best-colleges/rankings/national-universities/innovative.

13
ATTENDING TO THE TACTICAL
Robert Scholes and the Legacy of White Language Supremacy

Robert Lestón

Robert Scholes was most influential at a time when the role of the literary critic, figures such as Cleanth Brooks, Lionel Trilling, and even Harold Bloom, had fallen out of vogue, and it appeared that the long-standing, white-male tradition of Literary Criticism of the twentieth century was gasping for breath. French poststructuralist and postmodernist theories flooded into the humanities. Issues of canonicity fueled academic debates. References to "dead white males" wafted through taverns at literature conferences. Postcolonial critics emerged. The Arnoldian spirit that the role of criticism was to propagate "the best that is known and thought in the world" was on the brink of radical rethinking. English programs scrambled to gain new footing. It was during this angst of the oncoming new millennium that Scholes entered the fray and put forth two significant contributions: (1) that the most important work English professors do is teach, and (2) that teaching should be based on a rhetorically based curriculum. "Scholes was one of the few leaders," writes Thomas P. Miller in this volume, "to see rhetoric as a vital partner in reforming literary studies around the general education mission of English departments" (chapter 19). The change in the air offered an opening to seriously reconsider what English departments should be doing in the first place, and Scholes filled that hole by arguing for the importance of using rhetorical strategies to give students the "justified confidence in their own competence as textual consumers and their own eloquence as producers of texts" (1998, 66).

Scholes pushed English departments to seriously reconsider their approaches to curriculum design, but implicit within his rhetorically oriented approach was that students would become consumers and producers of texts that would mirror the institutional construct of Standard American English that continues to be defined by a long and troubled history of white supremacy and colonization. In 1974, the

DOI: 10.7330/9781646421190.c013

Conference on College Composition and Communication adopted "The Students' Rights to Their Own Language" which stated, in part, that the supremacy of "a standard American dialect" was a "myth" and requiring students to adapt to such a version amounted to one social group attempting to exert its dominance over another. Twenty-two years later, in 1996, when Scholes was drafting *The Rise and Fall of English*, the Oakland School Board published their decision to recognize AAVE as its own language, an event that thrust the boundaries of language use into the national spotlight. Despite these decisions and the movements they reflected, the form of literacy for which Scholes openly advocated was inextricable from white, middle-class language use.

I'll hedge a bet that it comes as little surprise that Scholes advocated for the language use that is the expected norm in schools and in business. Without doubt, the epistemic colonization of Standard American English over the popular and scholarly imagination is itself mirrored by the colonial heteropatriarchy of higher education that through colonial and economic conquest has come to dominate the globe. I bring up language use because, as the rise of decolonial and translingual rhetorics can attest, a much larger number of literacy workers today are ready to call into question the exclusionary practices of the academy. Students from underrepresented groups who don't fit neatly into the academic language paradigm can no longer be ignored. These literacy workers recognize that marginalized communities have ways of knowing, doing, and being that have the potential to refigure and pluralize how knowledge is made and spoken in academic contexts. Scholes took a positive step in that direction, moving from passive canon-worship toward actively scrutinizing how the education machine works. Scholes's intent in designing curriculum was to emphasize the moves and tropes—that is, to emphasize the *strategies* of the dominant discourse. Scholes did not go so far as to challenge what that discourse was, but he was willing to ask how it functioned. In this chapter, I draw upon the language of the strategic but, borrowing from Michel de Certeau's *The Practice of Everyday Life* (1984), I also seek to draw our attention to a corollary, the *tactical*. Strategies are the ways by which institutions maintain power, and Scholes's intention was to teach students those rhetorical moves, but *tactics*, on the other hand, are the ways excluded groups creatively adapt to the institutions and environments designed to keep them out or keep them down.

This essay opens with some brief discussions of how the tactical has been used by media activists and service-learning scholars, then turns to the question of the tactical as it relates to students transitioning into academia. Here, Scholes offers an insightful anecdote about how

Louis Althusser strategically used the academic system to have a brilliant academic career, and I go on to contrast this case with one of the more famous cases of nonassimilation in composition studies, the case of Quentin Pierce. Quentin Pierce's story was introduced to composition studies by David Bartholomae in 1993, in an essay that has been bounced around by composition scholars for decades as they have struggled to figure out how to attend to its raw, emotional power, a perfect example of a student turning to the tactical as a survival strategy. We'll meet some interesting figures along the way, figures such as Asao Inoue, Jean-Paul Sartre, and Malcolm X, who will help us make sense of the relationship between tactics and strategies or at least show us that the relationship is more complex than we might think. Scholes approached rhetorical instruction from the position of providing students with a variety of tools to help them assimilate into the dominant discourse; I find it necessary to open spaces within institutions to provide room for the increasing diversity of thought and people found in today's educational institutions. I see the difference as one primarily founded on a particular disposition of listening, and I hope to suggest the critical need for tactical spaces within institutions through the story of Quentin Pierce.

WHAT IS THE TACTICAL, ANYWAY?

What I am calling tactical is what Nancy Fraser introduced as "subaltern counterpublics" in order to counter the continued social production of the liberal bourgeois subject outlined by Jürgen Habermas in the controversial *The Structural Transformation of the Public Sphere* (1992), a liberal bourgeois subject, by the way, that Robert Scholes himself problematically targets as the primary aim of his curriculum (discussed below). Fraser's subaltern counterpublics are the formation of discourses that function as homemade tactical alternatives that historically disenfranchised groups have developed to reframe their own social positionality. "Members of subordinated social groups," writes Fraser, "women, workers, peoples of color, and gays and lesbians—have repeatedly found it advantageous to constitute alternative publics." Subaltern counterpublics "invent and circulate counterdiscourses, which in turn permit them to formulate oppositional interpretations of their identities, interests, and needs" (1990, 67). Because the institution is a site of power, faculty, particularly those who have become aware of their own white privilege, have a key role to play in the facilitation and circulation of counterdiscourses to accommodate the struggles students experience as they attempt to assimilate. It must be stated *explicitly* that students of color and students from historically disenfranchised groups have the most to lose if a sense of the tactical is not taken up, whether or not the lexicon of the tactical is specifically deployed.

In activist circles, the tactical is popularly associated with "tactical media," a term forwarded by media activists such as the Critical Art Ensemble (CAE), the Electronic Disturbance Theater (EDT) and other similar groups from the mid-1990s who repurposed Malcolm X's slogan "By Any Means Necessary" into "By Any Media Necessary." Tactical media has been closely associated with guerrilla tactics intended to be temporary interventions that disrupt the dominant political and economic system through mediatized civil disobedience. One well-known exemplar is the development of the EDT's FloodNet program that crashed former Mexican President Ernesto Zedillo's website twice a month for all of 1998 as a response to the Acteal Massacre that occurred in 1997. *Las Abejas* (The Bees), a pacifist indigenous community who live in Acteal, were sympathetic to the Zapatista uprising in the mid-1990s and were slaughtered because of their pro-Zapatista sentiments. Paramilitary troops arrived in Acteal on a Sunday just before Christmas in 1997, and fifty churchgoers were slaughtered, including children and pregnant women (Dominguez 2002, 387). The FloodNet project was a collaborative effort organized by the EDT's Ricardo Dominguez that would simulate a continuous refresh on web browsers when directed to a specific web address, causing the site to crash (known as a Distributed Denial of Service attack). Dominguez and fifteen thousand of his friends and affiliates staged digital sit-ins of Mexican President Zedillo's website throughout all of 1998 as a response to the massacre. The goal for tactical media practitioners was to combine the power of imaginative critique with emerging network technologies to engage in highly visible art performances that spoke to global injustice. Since the 1990s, there have been thousands of related performances, including such recent examples as the "99 percent bat signal" during the Occupy protests, "pepper spray cop" memes from the UC Davis sit-in, the "die-ins" of the Black Lives Matter movement, and many more.

Shifting to writing studies, the language of the tactical is best known through the public sphere and the service-learning community, beginning primarily with Paula Mathieu's *Tactics of Hope: The Public Turn in English Composition* (2005). Borrowing from de Certeau's tactics, Mathieu sought to reverse the central emphasis of university-community partnerships so that the needs of the community (rather than those of the institution) would become the primary rather than the secondary or tertiary concern. Consequently, this discourse community has undergone considerable debate concerning what role service learning and community partnering should take (Spray 2007; Parks 2009; Feigenbaum 2015). Critics attempted to reframe the tactical/strategic binary by suggesting that the relationship between the two poles is less a binary and more like a yin-yang symbol, so that the two are always interconnected and part of the other (Feigenbaum 2015, 129). The power imbalance between wealthy institutions and the poverty in surrounding areas points to the structural difficulty of service-learning projects, and the language of the tactical and the strategic has productively helped to navigate these contested spaces. Where strategies are the methods by which institutions of power maintain and expand their influence, tactics look for opportunities to attach themselves to the strategies of institutions in order to expose weaknesses in systems that could then be exploited and disrupted. A helpful way to avoid separating strategies and tactics into an oppositional binary pair is to seek opportunities for resistance and refiguration in ordinariness of everyday life.

TACTICS AS READING

By focusing on the consumer, de Certeau hopes to extract acts of production *within* consumption, echoes that appear in Scholes's *Textual Power* (1985) and *Protocols of Reading* (1991). For de Certeau, everyday practices such as reading, writing, and walking have the potential to transform an unjust order through infinitesimal everyday actions. To appreciate how the everyday can form acts of refiguration, however, requires a heightened mode of listening or attunement to the everyday, what Asao Inoue calls "a deep and mindful attending" (2019). Scholes can be read as a prototactician to the extent that he attuned himself to the everyday, in-between spaces of reading. Without explicitly deploying the language of the tactical, Scholes recognized that reading was a site where tactics and strategies were invested with the interplay between pleasure and power. Scholes argued that "an important part of the teacher's function" is to "show students how to move from reading the text to interpreting and criticizing the codes that sustain the text's implications" (1985, 61). Scholes wanted students to be strategic or "crafty" in their readings by taking a strategically critical stance rather than accept the truth of any text simply because it was presented before them by their instructor. But as Paul Corrigan and Alice Horning in this volume remind us, Scholes—like de Certeau—also argued that readers were foremost consumers, and as consumers, their primary endeavor was to attain pleasure from their textual encounters. De Certeau chooses the term *poaching* to indicate those moments in reading when little bits of pleasure are sought for, even when reading the most mundane of texts. As such, everyday acts of reading reveal an interplay between strategic reading (reading for information, codes, comprehension) and tactical reading (reading for pleasure, personal use, sharing). From a student's perspective, how the instructors are attuned to this back and forth makes all the difference in how they measure the success of their students' reading experiences. Helping to know what students are experiencing as they read amounts to, as Ellen Carillo has argued, making their reading—like their writing—visible. By using methods that help disclose their everyday reading encounters, teachers can discover how students experience and *poach* for pleasure even while they mine for critical codes and implications (see Carillo 2017, 60).

Making meaning from codes/implications may be part of how texts produce pleasure, but pleasure can be found anywhere in a text. That pleasure can be so powerful and is so important that Scholes argued that the "exchange between pleasure and power" was an essential factor in distinguishing English studies from the other disciplines (1987, 71). In fact, by the time he gets to *The Rise and Fall of English* a decade later, Scholes is convinced that the pleasure of reading is intimately connected to the whole reason English studies exists in the first place and the whole reason why those of us who pursue its study have made it our vocation. The tactical pleasure of reading changes lives. It changed ours. It can change the lives of our students.

> We do stand for something, do we not, we who love English, who have come to consciousness and culture through this language, who have found in it not merely a medium of expression but a vocation, a calling, the professional center and public justification of our lives? We stand, I believe, for something far deeper than our particular curricular or institutional settings. We stand for whatever dignity this language can afford the human beings who find expression in and through it. We stand, above all, for sharing the powers and pleasures of this language with one another and with all those who seek our guidance in attaining those powers and pleasures. That is what I believe we stand for. (1998, 71–72)

Such a logic sees the interplay between production and consumption as co-invested with the charge of the other, rendering the potential for each to be transformed. If strategies seem static and tactics seem subversive, an increased attunement of the kind Scholes, Inoue, and de Certeau call for reveals that the two are not simply a struggle between power and powerlessness but often function together to change operational logics and cultural practices over time.

SCHOLES MEETS QUENTIN PIERCE

Perhaps the section above helps us to see Scholes as a prototactician of reading, but one helpful aspect of thinking about tactics is that they are scalable for thinking about power differentials in different environments, and so I now turn to the institutional level. To make a long story short, I turn to Althusser to set up a contrast to David Bartholomae's introduction of Quentin Pierce in order to draw the distinction between two students attempting to assimilate into the university. Scholes explains that Althusser learned to succeed in his secondary studies by mimicking his teachers so that he learned to identify with them completely; he imitated their phrases, tastes, and judgments. He copied their voices, inflections, and intonations, doing exactly as they had instructed him to do. Eventually, a professor saw through his artifice, finding his attempts unsuitable for an academic career. Althusser responded by studying the writing of this new professor and learned to better emulate the dominant discourse. This time round, Althusser did more than win the praise of his professor. He learned a second set of "tricks," of manipulating the people who mattered, including the "entire French university system" and went on to "have a brilliant academic career" (1998, 64).

Scholes's story is a success story, of the student figuring out how to "play" or "game" the university, perhaps, even, how to "invent" it. Althusser learned how to flatter his professors, and when they became more demanding, he relearned how to give back exactly what the professor valued. Scholes explains:

> We have a word for the artifices that Althusser employed in his youthful attempts at academic success. The word is rhetoric. He had bad teachers who allowed him to get by with learning a rhetoric that had no textual power beyond the domains of their own classrooms. And he had a good teacher who taught him a rhetoric that stood by him throughout his career as student, teacher, and political philosopher. . . . What we can attempt to offer our students are the artifices that work, a rhetoric that will enable them to gain the respectful attention of those around them for their feelings, thoughts, and values. (1998, 64–65)

Scholes calls it "artifice." Our students have another name for it, and so do we when we're not writing academic papers. It suggests that there are different levels of artifice; we just need to teach the students the kind of BS that will get the attention of the people that matter. If you're a student from one of the subaltern publics that Fraser talks about, it sounds like a familiar story of your needing to learn a particular language that's been set up by people who never took your needs, your culture, your socioeconomic status into consideration when they were erecting the barriers for entry into civic and professional life. Once again, it calls to my mind Asao Inoue (2019) who's fed up with making the college education experience one that is exclusively dominated by a colonizer's language:

> I'm saying, we must change the way power moves through White racial biases, through standards of English that make White language supremacy. We must stop justifying White standards of writing as a necessary evil. Evil in any form is never necessary. We must stop saying that we have to teach this dominant English because it's what students need to succeed tomorrow. They only need it because we keep teaching it! (2019)

As suggested when this essay opened, much has changed since the 1990s, and the issues concerning the configuration of English studies were and, in some areas, continue to remain important. But even if Scholes advocated moving from an Arnoldian-inspired English curriculum toward a rhetorically oriented one, even if Scholes's rhetorically oriented curriculum continues to address the needs students face in particular contexts, and even if we read Scholes as a proto-tactician, the fact of the matter remains that Scholes does not go nearly far enough for the current environment. Take what Scholes says just a few pages after the Althusser anecdote: "We teachers of language and literature are mostly bourgeois subjects, engaged in trying to replicate ourselves in the service of government and corporate interests. Our job, as I see it, largely comes down to developing better bourgeois subjects—better than ourselves, that is, as well as better than they might be without our teaching" (1998, 67). The tactically oriented approach I'm advocating for is not one where we see the job of the profession to develop "better bourgeois subjects," but to find ways to allow those students who will never be bourgeois to transform it into something more accommodating.

One of the more well-known figures in composition studies in the 1990s, the days when composition and rhetoric was experiencing explosive growth toward professionalization in the academy, David Bartholomae introduced the field to Quentin Pierce in 1993 in an essay in the *Journal of Basic Writing* that he called "The Tidy House: Basic Writing in the American Curriculum." Bartholomae gives an account that this student work was in response to the reading of existentialism and Sartre in a basic writing class. After he received this paper, Bartholomae explains that he confessed to the department chair that he should never like to teach developmental writing again, that he never wanted to be put in a situation where he knew that so many of his students were going to fail. Eventually, Bartholomae would actually run a developmental writing program, but he never dropped Sartre from his curriculum. In fact, Bartholomae upped the strategic ante that Scholes was shooting for, requiring difficult texts in the name of learning the discourse of the academy. "I wanted to imagine a course," he writes, "where students worked with the materials valued in the college curriculum. I did not want to take those materials away from them. I wanted, rather, to think about ways of preparing unprepared students to work with the kinds of materials that I (and the profession) would say were ours, not theirs, materials that were inappropriate, too advanced" (1993, 7). And so, this line of thinking, of working with materials that were "inappropriate and too advanced" would develop into works such as the canonical "Inventing the University" and the widely adopted anthology, *Ways of Reading*.

Every time I read it, I'm struck by Quentin Pierce's power. The paper ends like this:

> I don't care.
> I don't care.
> about man and good and evil I don't care about this shit fuck this shit, trash
>   and should be put in the trash can with this shit
> Thank you very much
> I lose again.

Bartholomae held on to Quentin's paper for eighteen years before discussing it. Quentin Pierce's piece was written in 1973, during the Watergate scandal, the Vietnam War, the rise of countercultural revolution, and, among other movements, the Black Panther Party. The text can be read in numerous ways, the struggle of a basic writer being the most prominent, but the influence that Quentin's performance has had on composition studies has sent ripples throughout the entire community since its publication (Carter 2010; Harrington 1999; Rickert 2007; Phillips and Leahy 2017; Sirc 2002). As Mina Shaughnessy told us, changing the institution is about changing how the profession talks about those students who don't fit (1977; Bartholomae 1993, 21). Without a doubt, Quentin Pierce is doing just that.

Almost all of the commentators echo a similar, compelling call. Writing instructors need to find ways to receive these . . . well, what do we call them? Texts? Submissions? Works? Acts of desperation? Phillips and Leahy coalesce many of the voices by making a practical suggestion concerning assessment: a student who produces a work that does not meet the particular requirements of an assignment but otherwise produces work that is "arresting or successful" would not only find room to explore their ideas but would be assessed according to "how well they fulfilled the new expectations they had a hand in creating," expectations that the instructor could not have anticipated (2017, 125). That's helpful, but aside from how we might cope with similar instances, the fact that Quentin Pierce's piece has led so many composition scholars to return to it again and again emphasizes its *existential* force.

I choose the term "existential" deliberately, to remind our readers that the assignment Quentin Pierce was responding to was spurred by reading Sartre, an author who Bartholomae associated with the language of the institution. Bartholomae believed that providing students with Sartre would eventually empower them, much in the same way that Scholes felt that students would gain entrance into the academy by learning its discourse.

Perhaps we wish that Bartholomae taught his course by another means. After giving his students an essay on Sartre and a prompt that read "If existence precedes essence, what is man?" Bartholomae explains that he "knew from the first week that I was going to fail them; in fact, I knew that I was going to preside over a curriculum that spent 14 weeks demonstrating their failures" (1993, 5). I can imagine myself and many of my colleagues, firmly rooted in the twenty-first century, hollering backwards across the decades to Bartholomae in 1973, "Don't do it! If you know you're going to fail them then you're doing something wrong!" Would it have mattered? He wanted the students to learn *our* language. Sartre for Bartholomae, like Althusser for Scholes, represents the language of the university. So, in the terms we've been using, it was a *strategic* choice, a strategy of the powerful of which those who are not in power must contend with in order to survive.

I can't help but ask, who do we benefit when we uphold the institution and attempt to give students the strategies to participate in it? De Certeau suggests that it is a myth that the primary goal of the institution is to educate students. The primary goal of the institution is to continue its own survival. These two goals sometimes work in unison, but they are not the same thing. De Certeau indicates four predominant objectives an institution must establish in order to guarantee its survival. First, the institution must have a place where it exists. Second, it must manage its relationship with those allies and threats that exist on the outside. Third, it must extend its control of place over time so that it can manage variables that will allow its continued existence. Last, and this concerns us teachers most of all, the power of the institution is what produces its knowledge (1984, 36). The stories that it tells about itself become its truth, but that knowledge can only be produced because it had already established presence and identity. The power at my institution and one of the knowledges it has been complicit in producing—that there is a Standard American English all students should master—extends beyond my own institution into your institution through nationalized standards and accrediting agencies that expand the power, scope, and production of these knowledges. It should not come as a surprise, then, that many decolonial thinkers from Frantz Fanon and beyond have recognized that western higher education has not only become globally ubiquitous but has also failed to account for other ways of making knowledge. When knowledge is produced by the power of an institution, that knowledge reinforces itself to continue its survival and reproduction. Consequently, it asks students to reproduce that knowledge.

But Quentin Pierce did something different. He wasn't going to play a game he couldn't win. He didn't write a bad essay that failed to live up to the expectations of the professor. He hadn't learned to imitate his professors as had Althusser. He didn't have any tricks, artifices, or stored rhetorics that might work in this situation. Rather, he became tactical, creating an alternative discourse that changed the rules of the game, making it obvious that a professor can inflict harm upon his students.[1]

In our story so far, Sartre represents the institutional strategy that effectively blocked Quentin Pierce's entrance to the club. But let's rotate the camera on Sartre and see the picture from a different angle while we also move the setting from Bartholomae's classroom to Malcolm X's library. When listened to with a particular attunement, perhaps Sartre, a strategic figure for Bartholomae but a tactical one for Malcolm X, might be liberated from Quentin's trash can. In his own library, Malcolm X had two of Sartre's books that he studied.

One of the books he had was Sartre's *Black Orpheus* (1948), a book sensitive to the plight of African descendants that continues to generate interest in the tension between Sartre and Fanon. It was thoroughly annotated by Malcolm X, and contained a railway ticket inside as a bookmark. Another was *Dirty Hands* (1948), the play about an assassin that contains the line "Lies . . . were created in a society divided by class. It is not by refusing to lie that we will abolish lies: it is by eradicating class *by any means necessary.*" In the hands of Malcom X, the figure of Sartre starts to morph into something different, a figure among Fanon and other influences that would help Malcolm X find the language to demand that Black men and women needed to be liberated "by any means necessary." By the time the transformation is complete, no longer is Sartre a tool of white supremacy that crushes students; he becomes an agent toward the *eradication* of white supremacy. Though he never wanted violence, Malcolm X recognized that the larger dominant culture had no qualms enslaving, imprisoning, and systematically wiping out nonwhites. "That's our motto," he said. "We will have freedom by any means necessary."

Inspired by the Black Nationalism for which Malcolm X advocated, Huey Newton and Bobby Seale formed The Black Panther Party in 1966. During the time that Quentin was writing his paper, the Black Panther movement was militant and strong. Quentin Pierce likely saw and heard about the telegenic Panthers, who uniformly wore black leather jackets, berets, sunglasses, and, of course, carried shotguns in the open. And so, to draw the connection to a close, in the academy Sartre stands as a strategic figure blocking entrance to the prosperity that comes from getting a higher degree; but in the street, Sartre stands alongside tactical agents demanding equality for those who, like Quentin Pierce, have been excluded. Although Quentin wanted to throw Sartre and "good and evil" into the "trash can with this shit," Quentin Pierce and Sartre are coupled through the tactical "by any means necessary." What all of this brings to mind is that like a yin-yang symbol, the tactical and the strategic take part in the other, and what is essential, I would argue, is how we listen and attend to these spaces.

The question that remains is whether there is a larger failure going on here in terms of the project that Scholes laid out. The reason that Scholes wants students to learn "the artifices that work," the reason Bartholomae wants students to learn the language of the institution, and the reason we want to as well is not so they can go on and have brilliant careers and become productive members of society. The reason is simpler than that. The reason is that we are in the position to decide what students should learn, and some of us have decided. And yet, this is not a foregone conclusion. What would Scholes have said to Quentin Pierce, I wonder. We'll never know, but Scholes recognized many of the tensions we've been discussing, and I'd like to think it would have been something along the following lines:

> In this country, schooling must prepare us for manipulation—and I trust you detect the ambiguity in that expression. In a certain sense it is inevitable that school should prepare us to be manipulated. To learn at all we must be docile. But if docility should be the end of learning, our society would be doomed, because all new thinking emerges from resistance to what is accepted. Creativity in art, in science, in business, and in public affairs depends upon the ability to reject dogma and go beyond the status quo. A citizen in a manipulative democracy must be prepared to resist manipulation. . . . The future of the republic depends upon the people's ability to resist being fooled completely all of the time. (Scholes 1987, 74)

So, what are we to do? I would suggest that the existential angst expressed by Quentin's piece discloses that there are numerous different experiences our students are going through at any one time, and the curriculum we teach in our class is only one curriculum of at least two others to which we should be listening and attending. Those of us who read and look for guidance in figures like Robert Scholes consider it our jobs to pay attention to the *delivered curriculum*, that is, the one of our own classroom designs. But if we focus merely on this curriculum, we are likely to get trapped by the discourses and expectations of the institution. Another perspective asks us to step back and consider how what students may be attempting to learn in our class fits into their *experienced curriculum*, a perspective that asks us to remember the days when we ourselves were students and had to juggle the demands of different kinds of materials, books, demands, personalities, and schedules each semester. Last, Quentin Pierce's story also invites us to attend to the *lived curriculum*, the temporal and affective experience of how an individual course might fit not only into a student's academic career, but with the lived education they experience as well as the barriers, opportunities, and desires that frame their experiences (see Yancey 2009, 15–16).

The tactical, whether it be through everyday experiences of reading, doing digital sit-ins, or writing disruptive papers that challenge institutional norms, needs to be cultivated whenever possible. Tactical spaces should be opened and brought specifically into the curriculum, and I would argue the best ones would begin by taking the time to listen deeply to the words of students, so that they feel like they have been adequately heard and understood. For Quentin Pierce, who would be in his sixties if he made it out alive, a tactical space within the institution might have allowed him to express his existential angst about Sartre, or to discuss or disrupt a bothersome force. It might have given the institution an opportunity to be changed by one more passionate writer.

NOTE

1. To his credit, Bartholomae made Quentin Pierce's paper a primary reading in his future classes. (1993, 8).

REFERENCES

Bartholomae, David. 1993. "The Tidy House: Basic Writing in the American Curriculum." *Journal of Basic Writing* 12 (1): 4–21.

Carillo, Ellen C. 2017. *A Writer's Guide to Mindful Reading*. Fort Collins, CO: WAC Clearinghouse.

Carter, Geoffrey V. 2010. "Everything Is in Everything: Why Writers Block Still Matters." *Pre/Text* 20 (1–4): 45–73.

de Certeau, Michel. 1984. *The Practice of Everyday Life*, translated by Steven Randall. Berkeley: University of California Press.

Dominguez, Ricardo. 2002. "Electronic Disturbance: An Interview." In *Cultural Resistance Reader*, edited by Stephen Duncombe, 379–96. London: Verso.
Feigenbaum, Paul. 2015. *Collaborative Imagination: Earning Activism though Literary Education*. Carbondale: Southern Illinois University Press.
Fraser, Nancy. 1990. "Rethinking the Public Sphere: A Contribution to the Critique of Actually Existing Democracy." *Social Text* 25/26: 56–80.
Habermas, Jurgen. 1992. *The Structural Transformation of the Public Sphere*. Oxford, England: Polity Press.
Harrington, Susanmarie. 1999. "The Representation of Basic Writers in Basic Writing Scholarship, Or Who Is Quentin Pierce?" *Journal of Basic Writing* 18 (2): 91–107.
Inoue, Asao B. 2019. #4C19 Chair's Address. YouTube video, 46:23. "National Council of Teachers of English," April 4, 2019. https://www.youtube.com/watch?v=brPGTewcDYY.
Mathieu, Paula. 2005. *Tactics of Hope: The Public Turn in English Composition*. Portsmouth, NH: Boynton/Cook.
Parks, Stephen J. 2009. "Strategic Speculations on the Question of Value: The Role of Community Publishing in English Studies." *College English* 71 (5): 506–27.
Phillips, Stephanie, and Mark Leahy. 2017. "Anticipating the Unknown: Postpedagogy and Accessibility." *Peitho Journal* 20 (1): 122–43.
Rickert, Thomas J. 2007. *Acts of Enjoyment: Rhetoric Žižek and the Return of the Subject*. Pittsburgh, PA: University of Pittsburgh Press.
Scholes, Robert. 1985. *Textual Power*. New Haven, CT: Yale University Press.
Scholes, Robert. 1987. "Textuality: Power and Pleasure." *English Education* 19 (2): 69–82.
Scholes, Robert. 1991. *Protocols of Reading*. New Haven, CT: Yale University Press.
Scholes, Robert. 1998. *The Rise and Fall of English*. New Haven, CT: Yale University Press.
Shaughnessy, Mina. 1977. *Errors and Expectations*. New York: Oxford University Press.
Sirc, Geoffrey. 2002. *English Composition as a Happening*. Minneapolis: University of Minnesota Press.
Spray, Roxanne. 2007. "Asking, Listening, Learning, and Reflecting: Tactical Approaches to Community-University Partnerships." *Pedagogy: Critical Approaches to Teaching Literature, Language, Composition, and Culture* 7 (2): 285–94.
Yancey, Kathleen Blake. 2009. "Reflection and Electronic Portfolios: Inventing the Self and Reinventing the University." In *Electronic Portfolios 2.0: Emergent Research on Implementation and Impact*, edited by Darren Cambridge, Barbara Cambridge, and Kathleen Blake Yancey, 5–16. Sterling, VA: Stylus.

14
"THE ENGLISH APPARATUS"

Robert Scholes

> *By imagining that they have got hold of an apparatus which has in fact got hold of them they are supporting an apparatus which is out of their control, which is no longer (as they believe) a means of furthering output but has become an obstacle to output and specifically to their own output as soon as it follows a new and original course which the apparatus finds awkward or opposed to its own aims.*
> —Bertolt Brecht, *Brecht on Theatre*

> *We must also describe the institutional sites from which the doctor makes his discourse.*
> —Michel Foucault, *The Archaeology of Knowledge*

As individual speech acts are to the language in which they are spoken, so are many other individual actions to the codes of the cultures in which they occur. This is the most fundamental and durable insight of structuralism, the insight upon which all later semiotic studies have been founded. Every meaningful action—wearing a necktie, embracing a friend, cooking a meal—is meaningful only to the extent that it is a sign in some interpretive code. Human beings are aware of this and often resent it. Various kinds of joking and wit have been developed precisely to challenge orthodoxy, to trouble the codes, to force the orthodox out of their codified grooves of thought. Orthodoxy replies by codifying unorthodox behavior, setting aside times and places for approved Saturnalias, designating certain attire as the jester's special clothing, and telling poets they have a "license" to be odd. This dialectic between codification and play is an enduring feature of human existence.

In literary or textual studies the great structuralist insight takes the form of noting that a text is to its genre as the speech act is to its language. The genre is a network of codes that can be inferred from a set

DOI: 10.7330/9781646421190.c014

of related texts. A genre is as real as a language and exerts similar pressures through its network of codes, meeting similar instances of stolid conformity and playful challenge. No one who has ever studied seriously the history of any art can doubt the importance of precedent, schema, presupposition, convention—all those things that in literary study we call genre and style—in the actual production of texts. The more one knows about a given historical situation the more one realizes the struggle behind even the smallest innovations in any art or craft, a struggle first to master and then to transcend a given generic or stylistic practice.

These two terms—*genre* and *style*—are often loosely used, and perhaps they are not susceptible to any complete clarification, but for our purposes it will be useful to make at least a rudimentary distinction between them. *Genre* refers to things regularly done and *style* to a regular *way* of doing things. In painting, landscape is a genre and impressionism is a style. Genres are social and durable; they persist through changes of style. A style is more local, often personal, as when we speak of Shakespearean comedy as opposed to Jonsonian comedy or Monet's impressionism as opposed to Renoir's. Both genres and styles, however, manifest themselves in recurrent patterns or codes that can be constructed by analyzing a set of individual texts.

Certain poststructuralists—Michel Foucault in particular—have begun studying the ways in which institutions are comparable to genres. Using this kind of approach one may consider "the prison" or "the hospital" as a generic institution, arising at a particular time and moving through history like any other systemic network of possibilities. Individual prisons may thus be seen as texts enabled and constrained by the generic possibilities of penology at a given time, just as a given literary text may be seen as an utterance based on the historically available possibilities of a literary genre. Concepts like genre and style are useful because they give us access to the invisible forces that shape textual production, just as the concept of "language" gives us access to the forces that shape our speech. In all these cases we have a material thing: this utterance, this particular text, that particular hospital or prison, seen in relation to an immaterial thing: the English language, the picaresque novel, the institutions of penology or medicine. These notions of institution, genre, and language—immaterial things with material and behavioral effects—are powerful tools of thought, whose interrelatedness has only recently become apparent. This new perception of the ways in which languages, genres, and institutions are related is leading many scholars to reconsider the dimensions of their academic disciplines, as they rediscover the very objects of their study. Anthropological analysis, as Clifford Geertz has shown in *The Interpretation of Cultures*, has come to resemble literary criticism,[1] and literary criticism now leads back toward the cultural and institutional coding of human behavior. This is happening, whether we want it to or not. The question is how we should adjust to it—"we" being members of an academic institution which is itself the invisible source of the power that controls as it enables our professional lives.

Using the strategies that have been developed in recent literary theory, I propose that we consider "English" as a generic concept, an epistemic institution or apparatus that limits and enables the specific manifestations of "English" as a discipline or field of study, including its political embodiment in this or that English department, each of which can be seen as a political and economic instance of a generic arche-department. I am not proposing a full-scale social or historical study here, but I think readers familiar with English departments will *recognize* a certain descriptive truth in the following sketch of crucial aspects of the arche-department of English that presently authorizes our professional behavior.

To sketch this invisible apparatus (as Brecht would call it) we can proceed in what is now a classic structuralist/deconstructive mode of analysis. First we will locate the binary oppositions which organize the flow of value and power in our institution; then we will proceed to criticize or undo the invidious structure of those oppositions. Though there is much in structuralism and even more in deconstruction that I find misleading or unfruitful, this combined strategy of interpretation through the laying bare of basic oppositions followed by the deconstructive critique of those oppositions seems to me immensely rich in its critical potential. It is becoming a basic part of the critic's repertory, likely to endure even the excesses of its current vogue.

The arche-institution of English lives in each one of us as a professional unconscious, revealing itself in actions and aversions that we experience in our roles as institutional beings, often under the impression that either "reality" or "our own free will" is responsible for situations and events that can be shown to have an institutionalized character. This is by no means entirely a bad thing, any more than other personal accommodations to cultural pressures are bad things, but they may become bad when new information or new events require adaptation and adjustment. When the political or economic course of a whole society seems dangerous or dubious, an uneasy awareness of this sends ripples of institutional self-doubt through all the professions that are, in their various ways, in complicity with that society, bringing aspects of professional life that were invisible, or seemed inevitable, into the light of critical scrutiny. Such doubts, which are strictly analogous to crises in Kuhnian scientific paradigms, open fissures that enable us to perceive the initial gestures of appropriation and marginalization which have organized the institution itself. These organizing gestures can then become the basis for our analysis and critique.

The field of English is organized by two primary gestures of differentiation, dividing and redividing the field by binary opposition. First of all, we divide the field into two categories: literature and nonliterature. This is, of course, an invidious distinction, for we mark those texts labeled literature as good or important and dismiss those nonliterary texts as beneath our notice. This division is traversed and supported by another, which is just as important, though somewhat less visible. We distinguish between the production and the consumption of texts, and, as might be expected in a society like ours, we privilege consumption over production, just as the larger culture privileges the consuming class over the producing class (as noted, for example, by Paula Johnson in "Writing Programs and the English Department").[2]

One further distinction and our basic structure will be complete. This is the least obvious, the most problematic, and, therefore, perhaps the most important. We distinguish between what is "real" and what is "academic" to our own disadvantage. At some level we accept the myth of the ivory tower and secretly despise our own activities as trivial unless we can link them to a "reality" outside academic life. Thus we may consume "literature," which comes from outside our classrooms, but we cannot produce literature in classes, nor can we teach its production. Instead, we teach something called "creative writing"—the production of pseudo-literary texts.

The proper consumption of literature we call "interpretation," and the teaching of this skill, like the displaying of it in academic papers, articles, and books, is our greatest glory. The production of literature is regarded as beyond us, to the point where even those writers who are hired by academies to teach creative writing are felt to dwindle into academics themselves, and we suspect that their work may only be creative writing, too. How often are the works of the faculty of the Iowa Writers Workshop studied in the classrooms of the Iowa English department?

The consumption of non-literature can be taught. It is called "reading," and most college and university English departments are content to hope that it has been dealt with in secondary school—a hope that seems less and less well founded as we go on. But actual non-literature is perceived as grounded in the realities of existence, where it is produced in response to personal or socio-economic imperatives and therefore justifies itself functionally. By its very usefulness, its non-literariness, it eludes our grasp. It can be read but not interpreted, because it supposedly lacks those secret-hidden-deeper meanings so dear to our pedagogic hearts. Nor can it be produced when cut off from exigencies of its real situations. What *can* be produced within the academy is an unreal version of it, "pseudo-non-literature," which is indeed produced in an appalling volume. We call the production of this stuff "composition."

The structure of English as a field can then be pictured in the accompanying simple diagram, which operates for most of us as a semiconscious mental construct, manifesting itself concretely in our departmental behavior, including curriculum design, teaching assignments, and economic rewards. Both an ideology and a hierarchy are captured in this scheme. The greatest value is placed upon the things in the top categories, and the least upon the things at the bottom. In many English departments we can find sexual and economic structures mapped upon this value system with higher paid, predominantly male faculty members at the top and lower paid, predominantly female colleagues at the bottom. What to do?

For many teachers, the proper response to this situation is simply inversion of the hierarchy. Since composition is in demand, let the "law" of supply and demand work until composition replaces interpretation at the top of the heap. Fortunately or unfortunately, things don't work this way. The demand for more composition courses operates *within* a larger economic system that privileges literature and its interpreters. As long as the prestige system is in place, the social and economic structures of English departments will align themselves with it. Even if it were a good idea, the hierarchy could not be inverted. But it is not a good idea.

The proper remedy for our troubles must begin with the deconstruction of our basic system of binary oppositions itself. The whole purpose of laying bare a structure such as this is achieved only when we can complete its verbal deconstruction by practical action. This is the very point at which most "deconstructive" critics would recoil with horror from contamination by praxis. They are only too aware that praxis requires gestures of appropriation, usurpation, marginalization. One cannot act in any collective way without becoming vulnerable to later deconstruction and ultimately to critical rejection. This knowledge leads to the widespread phenomenon of deconstructive paralysis, a permanent state of equivocation before the bridge that leads from thought and writing to consequential action. The foreknowledge of guilt leads to an abdication

Production	Texts	Consumption
✕	literature	interpretation
creative writing	pseudo-literature	✕
✕	non-literature	reading
composition	pseudo-non-literature	✕

Figure 14.1.

of responsibility. This is why deconstruction is itself a *pharmakon*, a healing medicine and a dangerous drug, depending upon the amount of it that we imbibe and what other agents we mix with it.

The literature/composition opposition must not only be deconstructed in critical writing, it must be broken down in our institutional practice as well. We can begin, however, by rethinking the mental structure of smaller binary oppositions that support the great one. From this kind of rethinking a new practice can emerge.

1. *Literature/Non-Literature.* Under pressure from structuralists and poststructuralists, this distinction has already been seriously called into question. Without developing each point, let us list some of the cogent critiques of this binary opposition. First, any fragment of any text may be brought within the body of an avowedly literary text: the most banal speech or writing may appear in a novel as an aspect of characterization or setting, to great literary effect. Second, all texts have secret-hiddendeeper meanings, and none more so than the supposedly obvious and straightforward productions of journalists, historians, and philosophers. Finally, we all know that many texts that are formally literary (i.e., look like poems, plays, or stories) are of less interest than many other texts that are cast in an explanatory, meditative, or expository form. The "great books" are not all belletristic, and if belletrism falls, then any text may be studied in an English course. And who is to say that Locke or Gibbon is less valuable than Dryden or Gray? The literature/non-literature distinction cannot survive a critique that succeeds in separating literariness from value, yet that is precisely what all the formal and structural studies of the past decades have enabled us to do.

2. *Production/Consumption.* Taken in the form in which they present themselves to us, these terms are equivalent to writing and reading. The way out of our dilemma here is first to perceive reading not simply as

consumption but as a productive activity, the making of meaning, in which one is guided by the text one reads, of course, but not simply manipulated by it; and, second, to perceive writing as an activity that is also guided and sustained by prior texts. The writer is always reading and the reader is always writing. The student who reads the "world" and writes about it is also sustained by other texts while producing her interpretation of whatever things or states of affairs are being considered. Some written readings are more productive than others, or more creative, but this is *never* simply a matter of the form taken by the produced text.

3. *Real World/Academy*. This is the subtlest and most pernicious distinction, rising again and again to challenge us. Schools have been functioning as a preparation for something that "commences" as schooling ends, but this state of affairs is not given to us as a part of the nature of things. We have drifted into thinking of our lives as marked by stages that are deeply divided from one another. This has not always been so in our tradition. Men as well as boys walked alongside the peripatetic philosophers. There are signs, now, that these rigid chronological distinctions may be losing force. Even Yale University has finally decided that adults may actually be educable.

It can be argued that study and work may be performed by the same person at the same stage of life but that they are still not the same thing; and this is true, up to a point. But one who studies in order to publish new discoveries and receive financial rewards for them is in the "real" world, is she not?

Or is her world real only if she seeks to minimize the effort and maximize the profit? And what of one who studies in order to improve her own mind? This improved mind becomes the goal and product of the labor, and any actual texts produced are then evidences of this other, invisible product. Is an improved mind real? Is it marketable?

I think we must answer these last questions affirmatively. Something real is going on inside academies, but the method of this real production has much artifice in it. Students as a class may be defined by their involvement in what Erving Goffman has called "practicings":

> In our society, and probably in all others, capacity to bring off an activity as one wants to—ordinarily defined as the possession of skills—is very often developed through a kind of utilitarian make-believe. The purpose of this practicing is to give the neophyte experience in performing under conditions in which (it is felt) no actual engagement with the world is allowed, events here having been "decoupled" from their usual embedment in consequentiality. Presumably muffing or failure can occur both economically and instructively. What one has here are dry runs, trial sessions, run-throughs—in short, "practicings." (*Frame Analysis*, p. 59)[3]

There is a difference between practice and earnest, which we must acknowledge. We err only when we make the gesture of erecting this difference into two "worlds," one of which is held to be all practice, the other all earnest. The neophyte drill press operator must practice, too, before being given real projects. More important for our purposes, however, is the fact that all who write, whether in an ivy-covered study or a crowded office, are involved in a process that moves from practice to earnest, beginning with dry runs, trial sessions, rough drafts, scratchings out, and crumpled sheets in the wastebasket. There is, then, something inescapably academic about all writing, whether in school or out of it, and many a text begun in school has finished in the world. The "real" and the "academic" deeply interpenetrate one another.

We have been considering the system of oppositions that organizes our activities within the grip of the English apparatus. Certainly, seeing these oppositions as problems to be resolved, rather than as unassailable assumptions, is a step in the direction of a new practice. But it must be followed by other, more drastic steps. In such situations there are always those who cry out for the most drastic solutions: "Destroy the apparatus!" they advise us, and they mock all attempts at more gradual amelioration as mere tinkering with a pernicious and doomed institution. In this, as in many other questions, I find myself looking for a middle ground between reform and revolution. The most radical talk often produces the least action or generates an overwhelming reaction, thus becoming literally counterproductive. On the other hand, situations sometimes arise within institutions that require changes too great for any tinkering to achieve them.

In my judgment the English apparatus needs a major rebuilding, and I offer that mechanical metaphor as a way of moving beyond the revolution/reform opposition. We cannot replace this apparatus because we are implicated in it. We cannot shut it down because it sustains our professional lives. We must keep it running while we rebuild it extensively. This will not be easy. Our analysis up to this point has revealed a hierarchical structure in which the consumption of literature is at the top and the production of pseudo-non-literature at the bottom. Another way to map this structure would be to see the teaching of literary consumption at the center of our apparatus and all our other activities positioned around it, with composition at the outer-most margin. Rebuilding this apparatus is going to mean rearranging the hierarchy: repositioning or redefining literary study, because literary study is the dominant activity in this institution; it is the focus of power that holds everything else in place. We must begin our efforts at rebuilding by asking what we mean when we proclaim ourselves teachers of literature. We must mount a critique of what we do when marching under our traditional banner with the strange device that says, "Teaching Literature." The device of course does not seem strange to those who march under it. No device does. Those who march are "insiders," as Frank Kermode would say (see *Genesis of Secrecy*, passim).[4] And they usually march happily, without questioning their situation as marchers. To step outside the line of march, to scrutinize the device and see it as strange for the first time—defamiliarized, as the formalists put it—is to become, perforce, a theoretician. This scrutiny may lead to such questions as Where is the march heading? Why? For whose benefit? And what does that device mean, anyway? In recent years more and more of our marchers have stepped outside and started asking questions. We need to consider why they have done this. Something has been troubling the march itself. Somehow the fit between our practice and the world in which we practice has grown uncomfortable. Some of us can ignore the discomfort, fix our eyes on the ground, and keep marching. Others want to hoist a new banner along with the old—one that says, "Bring back the world of our comfort." But nothing comes back as it was. That is the most fundamental lesson of history.

Stepping outside the metaphor of the march, we can begin our critique of practice by scrutinizing this sign under which we have served for so long. What does it mean to "teach literature"? It does not mean that we give lessons in how to do or make literature, for that we explicitly exempt from our claims. We may indeed teach the making of pseudo-literature, or "creative writing" in some part of our establishment, but that is emphatically not what we mean by "teaching literature." In an art department the faculty is normally divided into two categories: artists and art historians. You cannot do that with an English department. The division is there, but the terminology is not. Teachers of literature would feel diminished to be called "literary historians." And the language simply has no word for the maker of literature. We cannot call our colleague in creative writing "literators" or "literatists." When William Faulkner was a colleague at the University of Virginia, the most honorific thing we could do about his designation was simply to call him a writer. The word "creative" in his case would have been too perceivable as the insult it is.

The word "literature," then, has a much higher standing in our language and culture than the word "art." The sign of this status is that empty place in our lexicon where we might expect to find the word that is to "literature" as "artist" is to "art." The prestige of literature is so great that we have a taboo against naming the one who creates it. In our culture literature has been positioned in much the same place as scripture. We have a canon; we have exegetes who produce commentary; and, above all, we have believed that these texts contain treasures of wisdom and truth that justify the processes of canonization and exegesis. When we say we "teach literature," instead of saying we teach reading, or interpretation, or criticism, we are saying that we expound the wisdom and truth of our texts, that we are in fact priests and priestesses in the service of a secular scripture: "the best that has been thought and said"—provided that it has been said indirectly, through an aesthetic medium. We will not teach Hume or Gibbon, however powerfully they think, however elegantly they write, because they are too expository or referential for us. We will bestow the name of literature only upon those texts that displace their intention sufficiently to require exegesis. We priests do love our mysteries, and the consubstantiality of beauty and truth is one of them.

This notion of literature as a secular scripture extends roughly from Matthew Arnold to Northrop Frye in Anglo-American academic life. It is linked with the rise of the study of modern literatures to a central place in the liberal arts curriculum. And it is the dissolution of this particular consensus that has been troubling us of late. Since the nineteen-sixties we have been losing our congregations, and we are scared to death that our temples will be converted into movie theaters or video parlors and we will end our days doing intellectual janitorial or custodial work.

Is there a way to avoid this fate? There is indeed, but we shall have to theorize to find it. First, we must consider what went wrong; then, we can think about making the best compromise between our dignity and the actual needs of our constituents. What went wrong with the idea of literature as secular scripture can be described simply as the loss of faith in the universality of human nature and a corresponding loss of faith in the universal wisdom of the authors of literary texts. If human nature is always and everywhere the same, then it follows that every literary text may express aspects of that great universal truth. But if human beings are constituted differently in different cultural situations, then the varieties of literature must be seen as temporal rather than eternal. If literature is not scripture, then it cannot be outside of human time.

If the text were a vehicle for eternal truth, then the teacher's function would be to guide the student toward the correct interpretation of the text, so that the truth might stand revealed. But if the text is understood as necessarily partial, its truth value various in relation to historical changes in human situations, then this sort of interpretation—what Paul Ricoeur calls "the restoration of meaning"—will not suffice. We will need a "negative hermeneutic" as well (see Ricoeur's *Freud and Philosophy*, p. 27, and Fredric Jameson's commentary on this in *The Political Unconscious*, pp. 284–85);[5] that is, we will have to restore the judgmental dimension to criticism, not in the trivial sense (discredited by Frye and others) of ranking literary texts, but in the most serious sense of questioning the values proffered by the texts we study. If wisdom, or some less grandiose notion such as heightened awareness, is to be the end of our endeavors, we shall have to see it not as something transmitted from the text to the student, but as something developed in the student by questioning the text.

This question of the relationship between criticism and interpretation is a large subject that will require much fuller consideration, but at the moment we must continue to pursue our investigation of what went wrong with the tradition of literature as secular scripture. I have been suggesting that part of what went wrong was a loss of faith in the universality of human nature, and I should like to qualify this statement before moving on. Certainly, one of the reasons that those texts we call "great" persist over long periods of time is that they induce in us reflections that can be assimilated to our own situations. We feel that Milton's devils, figures like Mammon, Belial, and Moloch, are not simply collections of words but representations of human types that one may encounter today in the halls of Congress and even in our departmental meetings. Experiencing this, we are inclined to say that Milton has an insight into universal truths; but it seems to me better to understand that Milton's power with these figures, which is achieved, after all, in the rhetoric of their discourses to the assembled demons, is a result not of some disembodied genius, but of Milton's developed verbal skills plus his awareness of parliamentary debates that in fact resemble our own deliberative arguments, for good historical reasons. Where Spenser's Mammon, for instance, is a miser of a type no longer actively present in our culture, Milton's Mammon not too long ago materialized as our Secretary of the Interior.

I have been using the notion of truth in characterization as a shorthand notation for the larger concept of truth in literature. My point is finally that the strengthening of our sense of history and of cultural variety has made the notion of literary truth more of a problem, requiring a more critical response, in which what is truth-for-us may be sorted out from other textual matter. Something similar must be done with respect to authorship. Scripture itself was once held to be the work of God, who was the author and guarantor of all its meanings. Hence, interpretation was the recovery of those meanings, and criticism was heresy. Now, one may be a pious Christian and still speak of the Pentateuch not as the work of God, or of Moses, but of the Yahvist, the Elohist, and various translators and redactors. Similarly, the deepest research into the lives of authors of secular literature reveals only rifts and discontinuities of personality, enacted in behavior that is often vastly different from the wisdom we have been wont to find in their literary texts. Where the texts are ambiguous, often the lives are, too. Arriving at the character of an author is now inescapably a historical, a critical, and a fictional act.

This loss of faith in the scriptural status of literature has coincided with drastic changes in the needs of our constituents. The students who come to us now exist in the most manipulative culture human beings have ever experienced. They are bombarded with signs, with rhetoric, from their daily awakenings until their troubled sleep, especially with signs transmitted by the audio-visual media. And, for a variety of reasons, they are relatively deprived of experience in the thoughtful reading and writing of verbal texts. They are also sadly deficient in certain kinds of historical knowledge that might give them some perspective on the manipulation that they currently encounter.

What students need from us—and this is true of students in our great universities, our small colleges, and our urban and community colleges—what they need from us now is the kind of knowledge and skill that will enable them to make sense of their worlds to determine their own interests, both individual and collective, to see through the manipulations of all sorts of texts in all sorts of media, and to express their own views in some appropriate manner. That they need both knowledge and skill is perhaps a matter worth pausing to consider. We have sometimes behaved as if certain skills, such as composition and even the close reading of poems, could be developed apart from knowledge, especially apart from historical knowledge. We are paying the price for that error now. One does not have to be a Marxist to endorse Fredric Jameson's battle cry, "Always historicize!" (the first words of *The Political Unconscious*).

At any rate, the needs of our students are clear enough, and it should also be clear that our traditional role as exegetes of the sacred text of literature will not answer to these needs, but perhaps this point can stand some elaboration. In an age of manipulation, when our students are in dire need of critical strength to resist the continuing assaults of all the media, the worst thing we can do is to foster in them an attitude of reverence before texts. The reverential attitude, a legacy of romantic aestheticism, is the one most natural in literary interpretation as we have practiced it. It is the attitude of the exegete before the sacred text;

whereas, what is needed is a judicious attitude: scrupulous to understand, alert to probe for blind spots and hidden agendas, and, finally, critical, questioning, skeptical.

This rickety, demanding English apparatus has important work to do in our society, but it will do this work well only if we can rebuild it. The essential change—the one that will enable all the others—must be a change in the way that we define our task. To put it as directly, and perhaps as brutally, as possible, we must stop "teaching literature" and start "studying texts." Our rebuilt apparatus must be devoted to textual studies, with the consumption and production of texts thoroughly intermingled. Our favorite works of literature need not be lost in this new enterprise, but the exclusivity of literature as a category must be discarded. All kinds of texts, visual as well as verbal, polemical as well as seductive, must be taken as the occasions for further textuality. And textual studies must be pushed beyond the discrete boundaries of the page and the book into the institutional practices and social structures that can themselves be usefully studied as codes and texts. This is what a *re*constructed English apparatus ought to do. It is, of course, also what has been attempted in these very pages.

NOTES

"The English Apparatus." Reprinted by permission of copyright owner, Yale University Press. From *Textual Power*, 1986, 1–17.

1. Clifford Geertz, *The Interpretation of Cultures* (New York: Basic Books, 1973).
2. Paula Johnson, "Writing Programs and the English Department," *Profession* 1980: 15 (1980).
3. Erving Goffman, *Frame Analysis: An Essay on the Organization of Experience* (New York: Harper and Row, 1974).
4. Frank Kermode, *The Genesis of Secrecy: On the Interpretation of Narrative* (Cambridge, MA: Harvard University Press, 1979).
5. Paul Ricoeur, *Freud and Philosophy: An Essay on Interpretation*, trans. Denis Savage (New Haven, CT: Yale University Press, 1970); Fredric Jameson, *The Political Unconscious: Narrative as a Socially Symbolic Act* (Ithaca, NY: Cornell University Press, 1981).

15
PRESIDENTIAL ADDRESS 2004
The Humanities in a Posthumanist World

Robert Scholes

Are we in a posthumanist world? Who knows? Clever thinkers from Nietzsche and Henry Adams to Foucault and Lyotard have been giving us this message. And if we are in such a world, how can there be a place for the humanities in it? Plodding along behind those brilliant minds, I shall try to puzzle out the situation of the humanities at a practical or pedagogical level, by looking at what some humanists have been saying about the humanities recently and then considering briefly the history of humanism and humanistic education. After that, I shall make some modest proposals about what is to be done.

For perspectives on our present situation, I have chosen words from some of our contemporaries who have given this matter serious thought. My first exemplar is George Steiner, whose commitment to the humanities over the past decades cannot be questioned. In May 2000, Steiner gave a lecture in the Netherlands called "The Muses' Farewell." (It later appeared in *Salmagundi*.) He began by pointing out that a crisis in the situation of literature is a regular topos in literary texts, taking Milton's phrase "Nymphs and Shepherds dance no more" as his prime example. Milton wrote those words around 1630, when the metaphysical poets were flourishing, when Dryden had just been born, and when the glories of Milton's own epic achievement were all in the future. Musing on this text and its situation, Steiner suggested that the Muses were actually in pretty good shape in 1630, and then he asked whether our own sense of loss is just another instance of this recurring theme—or if it indicates some decisive defeat of humanism, from which we may not recover.

After chronicling the staggering offenses of the twentieth century against humanity, he asked, presciently, "Today, what news of mass-murder, of judicial torture, of programmatic ideological venom and falsehood, would surprise us?" Thinking of the European Holocaust in particular, though recognizing that there were other horrors as well, he posed the question, "where were the Muses?" and then gave this response:

> European humanism proved powerless in the face of bestiality. This bestiality sprang from within the very heartland of high culture. Goethe's beloved tree shadowed Buchenwald; Gieseking's lustrous cycle of Debussy's piano music took place within hearing of the trains bound for Dachau. In numerous individuals, in the personal lives of the butchers and torturers, a cultivated literacy, a taste for music and the arts can be documented. One can play and sing Schubert in the evening and torture in the morning.

And he concluded, wryly, after contemplating various literary and philosophical figures, "The Muses knew how to goose-step" (150). Looking deeper into the question, he then approached the matter that is our concern today:

> Central to European civilization from the Renaissance onward, has been the *credo* that the spread of education, the cultivation of sense and sensibility through literature and the arts, the dissemination of the exemplary values manifest in the classics, would gradually attenuate, indeed efface the atavistic ferocities of the "human animal." This *credo* is as crucial to Pico della Mirandola and Condorcet as it is to Schiller, Auguste Comte, and Matthew Arnold.

Reviewing this situation, Steiner asked, poignantly, "What went wrong?" (151). And he tried, tentatively, as he said, to provide an answer. The answer he proposed, which he found "close to suicidal," is that "it may be . . . that the humanities *do not* humanize in any deep sense, that, given the immunities of mandarin and high bourgeois culture, they can *dehumanize*" (151–52). From this point, he reached the further conclusion that the humanities are now debilitated by an unwillingness to confront this situation. His list of symptoms of a humanistic malaise was not startling. He mentioned things like "the mushrooming of spurious disciplines" and the "inanities of political correctness." And then he compared the situation of the humanities with that of "the exact and applied sciences and technology," which he found to be thriving, with the gap between them and the humanities widening rapidly. "This is so in regard to intellectual and social prestige, to material support and reward, to manifest consequence," and, "above all, to the enlistment of human talent" (152). In the sciences, he observed, truth-values are tested and "the sum of knowledge is cumulative." In the humanities, on the contrary, "[a]nyone can say anything" (153). At this point, his argument would seem to demand that he indicate what the humanities might offer that could balance the powerful truth claims of the sciences, but he never quite managed to do that. So let us leave him there, lamenting, and look at a second perspective.

My colleague on the MLA Executive Council John Guillory has given our issue serious thought in his book *Cultural Capital*, though that is by no means the only object of his investigation. Let us look at things from his angle and see how this view meshes with Steiner's, beginning with some words from Guillory's preface. There he notes that "the category of literature has come to seem institutionally dysfunctional, a circumstance which I will relate to the emergence of a technically trained 'New Class,' or 'professional managerial class.'" He continues, "To put this thesis in its briefest form, the category of 'literature' names the cultural capital of the old bourgeoisie, a form of capital increasingly marginal to the social function of the present educational system" (x). Guillory then provides a pithy summary of how and when the category of literature as we know it developed—a matter on which I shall offer my own perspective before concluding—and then moves on to discuss the rise of literary theory as a symptom of the larger problem. He sees the development of a new canon of theory as a response to "new institutional conditions of intellectual work," and he goes on to define intellectual work, and he goes on to define these conditions as follows:

> These conditions, the transformation of the professional literary critic's intellectual labor by the technobureaucratic restructuring of the university, ultimately account for the dual form of the syllabus in the graduate schools, the two canons of literature and theory. The syllabus of theory has the oblique purpose of signifying a rapprochement with the technobureaucratic constraints upon intellectual labor, symptomatically registered as a fetishization of "rigor." (xii)

To the words of Guillory I would like to add a more recent view of the matter by Terry Eagleton, who sees the rise of theory in a related though significantly different way. In his book *After Theory*, he argues that theory emerged from a growing awareness in the 1960s that higher education was becoming "locked ever deeper into structures of military violence and industrial exploitation." And he continues, "The humanities had lost their innocence: they could no longer pretend to be untainted by power. If they wanted to stay in business, it was now vital that they paused to reflect on their own purposes and assumptions. It is this critical self-reflection which we know as theory" (27). For Guillory theory was an attempt to bring the humanities into alignment with an increasingly technobureaucratic culture. For Eagleton, on the other hand, theory was an attempt by the humanities to think their way out of a co-option by military and industrial structures that had already taken place.

At this point I must sum up, however crudely, what I believe these signposts tell us about the situation of the humanities today. The perspectives of these three critics are different, and their conclusions are comparably different in their details, but there is a broad general agreement among them about the situation of the humanities. To put it simply, they see it as dire. For Steiner the humanities not only fail to humanize, they may actually dehumanize, by putting a concern for texts in the place where concern for other human beings ought to be found. For Guillory the problem is that the texts most valued by humanists—call them literature—are losing their value in the cultural marketplace, because they are not considered useful by a new dominant class of professional managers. For Eagleton the humanities, thoroughly implicated in an oppressive capitalist culture, have tried to theorize their way out of that implication and left the job unfinished.

Steiner noted a significant gap between the humanities and the sciences, science being the domain of testable truths and the humanities the domain of unverifiable opinions. For him humanistic learning is now of a lower order than scientific learning—and it may have a bad effect on you if you acquire it. For Guillory the change need not be grounded in such an absolute difference in the relation of these fields of study to truth, but it is traceable to a power shift in society, in which the "old bourgeoisie" yields place to a new "professional-managerial class" that he calls "technobureaucratic." For Eagleton theory itself went wrong by abandoning the claims of humanistic truth in a welter of relativism and perspectivism. All three speak of a renunciation of responsibility leading to a loss of authority and respect. Contemplating this situation, we need to ask what—if anything—we can do to alter it. I shall try to answer that question before concluding. But first, being a humanist, I want to search the past for a perspective on our present situation. I fear this perspective must be cruelly foreshortened, like that in Andrea Mantegna's painting of the dead Christ, simply to be presented in the frame of this discourse, but I shall try, like that great master, to keep the proportions proper as I go.

The notion of "the humanities" as a subset of academic disciplines is relatively recent, but behind this collective plural lies the concept of humanism, which we associate with the Renaissance and which gave us such things as the painting by Mantegna to which I alluded. That painting, which I have gone to the Brera Museum in Milan to see—sent there by some words of Ernest Hemingway, who admired Mantegna and that work in particular—that painting itself embodies humanism, for it is a painting of a dead man rather than of a sleeping God. And what humanism signifies, for us, is a shift from a view of the world organized around a concept of God to one organized around a concept of humanity. The notion of art as concerned with the making of beautiful objects rather than icons pointing to essences or divinities is a humanist notion. So, too, is the understanding of literature as a set of beautiful texts, though this view is not fully developed until, roughly, the time of Immanuel Kant, at the end of the eighteenth century. The concept of literature that we have today is derived from the Enlightenment notion of *belles lettres*, which is itself derived from the original Renaissance notion of *literae humaniores*.

Starting from that point, we should notice that the Latin word *humaniores* is a comparative, meaning not just "humane" but "more humane" letters or learning. And it was an invidious comparison. There was a less humane learning on hand at that time, in the form of the nascent sciences, starting with the more practical parts of Aristotle's work. The "more humane" studies were those proper to a courtier or gentleman, with conduct books like Baldassare Castiglione's *Il libro del cortigiano*, hovering in the background, if not directly overhead. The notion of "more humane" letters thus divided the intellectual world into poetry and rhetoric, on one side, and other kinds of less humane learning, on the other. A further distinction emerged in the Enlightenment, within the "more humane" kinds of study, separating oratory from *belles lettres*, thus relegating rhetoric and, ultimately, composition to the less humane side of this invidious distinction, and this distinction was made more powerful by the development of a new concept of "taste."

We can find this concept deployed in a passage in Lord Kames's *Elements of Criticism*, a work that represents the situation of English studies just before the Romantic revolution. A great ideological change in the function of such studies was signaled by the publication of David Hume's 1757 essay "On the Standard of Taste" and Kames's adaptation of Hume's views in his three volumes of lectures on the elements of criticism in 1762. Kames took up the question of taste in the introduction to this course of lectures and returned to it in the final lecture. Arguing in the introduction that "the God of nature" has constructed the world so that human beings can pass from "corporeal pleasures to the more refined pleasures of sense; and not less so, from these to the exalted pleasures of morality and religion" (5–6), he continued in this vein:

> We stand therefore engaged in honour, as well as interest, to second the purposes of nature, by cultivating the pleasures of the eye and ear, those especially that require extraordinary culture, such as are inspired by poetry, painting, sculpture, music, gardening, and architecture. *This chiefly*

> is the duty of the opulent, who have leisure to improve their minds and their feelings. . . . [A] taste in the fine arts goes hand in hand with the moral sense, to which indeed it is nearly allied. Both of them discover what is right and wrong. . . . [T]hey are rooted in human nature. (6–7; emphasis added)

It is painfully clear how powerfully the social and economic are commingled with the aesthetic and moral in this formulation. Human nature reaches its peak among the opulent, who have the leisure to cultivate their taste. And good taste is closely connected to good behavior, making the rich not just richer but better than their inferiors in opulence. And we may note in passing that Adam Smith, who lectured on rhetoric in Glasgow before turning his attention to *The Wealth of Nations*, was a friend of Hume's and Kames's. The weak point in the Kamesian formulation was in that phrase "nearly allied," used by Kames to describe the connection of taste to virtue. Hume taught us to be skeptical of moving from association to causality, but humanists from Castiglione to Steiner have wanted to believe that taste entailed virtue, and many find it hard to abandon that belief, even now.

On the heels of Kames, of course, came Romanticism and the elevation of imagination and especially imaginative literature to a position of cultural eminence theretofore unknown. Samuel Taylor Coleridge, in particular, codified the notion of the primary imagination as that of God the creator and the secondary imagination as that of poets, who were also creators—thus giving literature a quasi-scriptural dimension. And after the Romantics came Matthew Arnold, who in his youth knew William Wordsworth and was a powerful interpreter and critic of Romantic poetry. Arnold, who understood very well the Enlightenment notion of taste and the Romantic notion of imagination, dismantled them both and combined them with virtue in his new definition of culture as "a study of perfection" (473). Dismissing the notion of taste as a mere social attainment in the opening pages of *Culture and Anarchy*, Arnold went on to define culture as the achievement of inward perfection, a secular state of grace, to be attained by studying those "master-work[s]" (238) or "classic[s]" (304) in which the student would find (as he says in "The Function of Criticism") "*the best that is known and thought in the world*" (265).

Pretending to have abandoned the notion of taste, Arnold simply assumed a human desire for perfection and further assumed that this desire would lead people to connect beauty and virtue, thus finessing what Kames had made explicit and therefore vulnerable to criticism. The assumption that human beings are driven by a desire for perfection is a charming notion, and Arnold's apparent belief in it makes him an attractive human being. But, having read his contemporary Nietzsche on the will to power, I do not think we can follow Arnold's assumption or build an educational system on such a shaky foundation. Renaissance humanism, as transmuted by Enlightenment and Romantic values, will no longer sustain us. To that extent, we are indeed in a posthumanist culture. As Steiner reminded us, the humanist credo survived from Pico della Mirandola through Condorcet, Schiller, and Auguste Comte, down to Arnold. But we did not need the Holocaust to expose its weaknesses. That had been done eloquently, just before Arnold published *Culture and Anarchy*.

I am referring to John Henry Newman's lectures *The Scope and Nature of University Education*, later incorporated into the work we know as *The Idea of a University*. Newman had many interesting things to say about what he called "liberal education," but I concentrate on just one aspect of Newman's thought. To begin with, he defined liberal education as "a gentleman's knowledge" (91), which chimes nicely with Guillory's argument that the humanities were the cultural capital of the old bourgeoisie and seems to echo Castiglione and Kames as well. But Newman parted company with this tradition, making a devastating argument against the notion that liberal education promotes the virtue of those who possess it. This is the point at which his argument intersects with the lament of Steiner that I quoted earlier. But listen to Newman on Steiner's topic:

> In a word, from the time that Athens was the University of the world, what has taught men, but to promise without practising, and to aspire without attaining? What has the deep and lofty thought of its disciples ended in but eloquent words? Nay, what has its teaching ever meditated, when it was boldest in its remedies for human ill, beyond charming us to sleep by its lessons, that we might feel nothing at all? (95)

If George Steiner had remembered Newman, he might not have been so shocked at the ability of the Muses to goose-step or at the gap between promising and practicing in the humanities. But, as Newman pointed out so cogently, we professors of humanities have regularly deceived ourselves, claiming—falsely—to be especially virtuous ourselves and to be the teachers of virtue to others. And he admitted this, with terrifying eloquence, in the course of *defending* liberal education! What Newman called "useful knowledge," scientific and technical knowledge, had in his view "done its work," but, as he asserted, "liberal knowledge as certainly has *not* done its work—supposing, that is, as the objectors assume, its direct end, like religious knowledge, is to make men better" (99; emphasis added). But Newman did not suppose this for a minute.

For Newman the end of liberal education was "not to steel the soul against temptation, or to console it in affliction, any more than to set the loom in motion, or to direct the steam carriage . . . ; it as little mends our hearts as it improves our temporal circumstances." The virtues of a cultivated intellect, Newman told us, "may attach to the man of the world, to the profligate, to the heartless," and he went on to argue that the exaggerated claims made on their behalf by "their professors and their admirers" have opened them to charges of "pretence and hypocrisy" (99–101). What we call the humanities will never, according to Newman, make those who acquire them virtuous. Such acquisitions can improve the minds—but not the morals—of those who make the effort of acquiring them. The easy path from taste to virtue, first blazed in the Renaissance and then mapped in the Enlightenment, was concealed by Arnold, who offered the pursuit of perfection in its place, but had already been exposed and totally rejected by Newman, for whom perfection was not a proper goal for human beings. Newman was making a case for an education in the humanities, but it was not a case based on spiritual improvement. He argued that a mind enhanced by liberal education is a good thing in itself for the one who possesses it. But he had another source in mind for the teaching of moral virtue—namely, Christian dogma—and he was lecturing to some Irish gentlemen as the rector-elect of a university in Dublin, where theology and Christian ethics would most certainly be part of the curriculum, as it was when James Joyce came to study there half a century later (and we all know how virtuous Joyce became).

Mathew [sic] Arnold did not share Newman's faith. And, as an inspector of schools, he knew that education had to extend beyond the class of "gentlemen," though some of his followers in the United States—the New Humanists, in particular—never abandoned that notion. However, as a distinctly secular thinker about these matters, Arnold could not assume that morals would be dealt with by instruction in Christian dogma. And neither can most of us, I am afraid. We know all too well that one can teach the catechism and even perform the miracle of the Eucharist on Sunday but still bugger the altar boys on Friday. And we know that our students will either join the professional-managerial class or serve that class in some way. We can see Cardinal Newman, now, as a kind of intellectual Pre-Raphaelite, arguing a prehumanist theory of education, in which what we call the humanities would have a place in a culture once again oriented toward the divine. We can learn from him—but we cannot, I think, follow him there. How, then, can we discover where we must go and what we must do to preserve the studies to which we have devoted our lives?

If we assume that Guillory and Eagleton are right in seeing the rise of theory as occasioned by a new awareness on the part of humanists of a need to explain and justify their activities in a culture dominated by technobureaucrats, we shall also have to admit, as they both suggest in their different ways, that theory failed to achieve its ends in this respect. That is, theory never succeeded in explaining to the dominant class just how the humanities could contribute to the world this class was making, while humanistic attention to theory opened the humanities to the charge that they were neglecting their traditional duty—which was to inculcate virtue in the young by means of the Great Books. We were thus charged with not doing what we were never able to do but had claimed, for centuries, to be doing.

I am tempted to call this poetic justice, but the situation calls for a response better than irony. The failure of theory, it seems to me, represents the larger failure of the humanities, as a whole, to justify their place in the academic world and the larger world as well. In the academic world, theory was an effort to solve what I will refer to as the Steiner problem. What John Guillory stigmatized as the deconstructive "fetishization of 'rigor'" was partly a response to the situation Steiner described in the words "[a]*nyone can say anything* about literature or art or music." The insistence on rigor, however, was also an attempt to convince the larger world that the humanities might offer useful training to people hoping to become successful technobureaucrats. The problem with this strategy, as a reading of Eagleton suggests, is that it accepts the worldview of the technobureaucracy, which is a version of pragmatism.

Yet, in the domain of theory, the main opposition to deconstruction took the form of a pragmatic opposition to theory itself. The most effective opponents of theory asserted that anyone can indeed say anything—and not just about literature but about politics or human values as well—and that this should be no cause for alarm. We live in communities of interpretation, and there are no grounds shared by different communities that would allow them to settle their differences reasonably. One problem with this pragmatic position is that when translated to geopolitics, it means that war is the only way to resolve differences. In the great world, pragmatic philosophy supports technobureaucratic attempts to bring other nations into one nation's interpretive community—by force. But the great world is a complicated place. It is a world of weapons, to be sure, but not all the weapons take the form of bombs, guns, or other engines of physical destruction. Some of the weapons are rhetorical, taking the form of mythmaking and media domination. However, this is a world in which pragmatic technobureaucracy is not the only kind of authority.

The other great source of ethical authority and political power in this world is fundamentalism—which is in many respects the polar opposite of pragmatism. For the pragmatist, there is no absolute truth; there are no universal values. For the fundamentalist, there is only one truth, and nothing but universal values. And this is the case whether we are talking about Christian fundamentalism, Islamic fundamentalism, Marxist fundamentalism, or any other kind of fundamentalism. For the fundamentalist, there is a single source from which the truth flows, and it flows directly to its chosen interpreter, often from a sacred text. What pragmatism and fundamentalism share is a rejection of what was once called dialectic: an attempt to reach the truth with the aid of reason. In their different ways, then, they presuppose a world in which disputes cannot be settled diplomatically. There is one other difference, however, between these two types of belief. A conquered pragmatist will presumably say, "Oh, I'm in a new interpretive community. I'd better believe what the others believe"; whereas a conquered fundamentalist is likely to become a terrorist—regardless of what kind of fundamentalist he or she may happen to be.

We also face, in these United States at the present time, an eerie alliance between pragmatism and fundamentalism. And we have a Constitutionalist fundamentalism as well as a Christian fundamentalism, which combine to make an Americanist fundamentalism that draws strength from its opposition to Islamic or Arabist fundamentalism. The good technobureaucrat will function perfectly inside this interpretive community, too. And that, my friends, is the world in which our schools must function, the world in which we study and teach, the world our students will enter when they leave us. We must prepare our students to live and work in this world. And we must justify our existence in the terms offered by this world. But we cannot, and should not, simply accept those terms, for this is not so much a posthumanist world as an anti-humanist world, and what we have to offer it must be a reasoned critique of its values and practices. In this connection, as in so many others, I am reminded of the words of a poet.

> The blood-dimmed tide is loosed, and everywhere
> The ceremony of innocence is drowned;
> The best lack all conviction, while the worst
> Are full of passionate intensity.

But our case is even more dire. In our world, those who lack all conviction have joined forces with those who are full of passionate intensity. Those words of William Butler Yeats come to me because I am a humanist, and poetry is one of the tools that the humanities have given me for coping with the world. I draw strength and insight from those words and from the other texts that are part of my cultural equipment. I would like to pass this heritage along to future generations, because I think it is needed—now more than ever. But we humanists cannot simply embrace the past and say we stand for that. We must show how our heritage and our disciplines can help our society through the difficult present and into the unfathomable future.

This means, I believe, that we cannot simply prepare students to serve the technobureaucratic culture as cheerful pragmatists or to enter the ranks of the solemn fundamentalists. That is, we cannot serve this culture by acquiescing in its aims and values. We must resist the temptations of both pragmatism and fundamentalism—and we must do so without rejecting the practical virtues that are a part of pragmatism or the moral virtues that are part of religious faith. With people of faith who are not fundamentalists, we have no quarrel. With practical people who do not reject the idea of generally applicable standards of ethics and truthfulness, we have no quarrel. But we have a difficult task ahead of us. We must show that what we have to teach will be useful to this society and to the individuals who study with us. And we must also, in our teaching, generate new human standards that reject the fundamentalist leap to absolute truth and the pragmatist denial that such standards are possible.

We cannot make ourselves or anyone else virtuous, but we can illuminate the question of what virtue is. We cannot, as Stephen Dedalus found out so painfully, create a conscience for our society. But we can raise the consciousness of those around us—and ourselves—about the humane values on which conscience is based. We cannot interpret the crucial texts of our culture with fundamentalist certainty. But we can help those who study with us learn to read and interpret our foundational texts in ways that are careful, sensitive, and rational. This means that we must read and discuss the important religious and political texts in our classes. If the humanities retreat into belletrism, they are doomed. But we must also provide a new justification for studying those texts that come to us from literature and the arts. We must show that the works we value are not beautiful objects from some lost past but tools for thinking and feeling, ways of understanding the world and its people. We should, however, resist the temptation to turn the works we love into sacred texts. Our lesson must be that there are no sacred texts that are beyond interpretation—for interpretation is at the heart of the humanistic enterprise.

Which brings me back to the question of theory. As I have indicated, the turn to theory was necessary. To the extent that theory failed, it failed because it became too self-absorbed and lost sight of the main object of theoretical inquiry, which is how language and other modes of representation function in the world. That is what we have to learn and what we have to teach. But theory has not really failed. It appears to have failed because it took a wrong turn and ended in a cul-de-sac. Still, the humanities need theory. I almost want to say that the humanities *are* theory. All the works I have cited here, from Castiglione to Eagleton, are theory.

When you get in a cul-de-sac, the only thing to do is to go back until you find the right way and continue from there. For the humanities, this means going back to the kind of thinking that connects to the roots of our enterprise, roots that were in place before the Renaissance bent them to its own ends—roots in the theories called grammar, rhetoric, and dialectic. Over the years, I have found students eager to learn how language works, how texts work, and how culture itself works. These are the matters that we have to study and teach. We have a precious gift to give those who study with us: the gift of an understanding of textuality and ideology in a world in which people are bombarded with ideologically loaded texts from morning to night. The question, then, becomes a simple one. How can we best offer this gift to those who need it?

As I have argued elsewhere (in *The Rise and Fall of English*), I believe we need to start over again, from the old prehumanistic or protohumanistic trivium. In the old trivium, grammar had an honorable place. For us this means emphasizing the "language" in Modern Language Association. We offer the gift of better use of language, and I think we all believe that knowing another language gives people better command of their own. We also need to know, as Gayatri Spivak recently reminded us in *Death of a Discipline*, how other people think and how they see us, which, as a Scottish poet told us long ago, is a precious gift. To see ourselves as others see us, we need to learn how their languages represent the world. We can begin there—with language. And along with language itself we must teach those disciplines that Aristotle first codified—adding poetics to the rhetoric of the trivium—those disciplines concerned with the ways language can be used to awaken and direct the emotions. Yeats (him again) said that he made rhetoric from his quarrels with others and poetry from his quarrels with himself. I think there are problems with this formulation, but it is a place to start. How language is used externally and internally in those texts that still speak powerfully to us—that should be a central part of humanistic studies. And, finally, what the old trivium called logic or dialectic—the use of language under the aegis of reason, which has been a part of our studies since Plato—this too must be an important part of our teaching. Given the multicultural and multitextual nature of the world around us, I would give this revived trivium a new name—call it "textuality"—and I would situate it at the base or center of our enterprise.

In closing—and I am as happy as you are to hear those blessed words—I want to urge a serious reconsideration of our enterprise as a neohumanism, in which we think of ourselves as humanists first and members of this or that administrative unit second. We should seek to broaden the range of our studies instead of allowing that range to shrink to a specialization. We must also admit that writing and reading—composing and interpreting texts—are at the core of humanistic studies. And we must see these two aspects of humanistic study as equally important, undoing our present hierarchical structures that relegate writing to a subordinate position below reading. Beyond that, we teachers of language and literature need to be less narrowly focused on particular periods or genres and broader in our grasp of literary and linguistic history. And also, for good practical reasons, we need to become broader in our grasp of other cultural fields, starting with those closest to us, such as philosophy and the visual arts and media. This means, among other things, that we need to restructure graduate studies, so as to encourage breadth of learning in those who will become the neohumanists of the future. And, finally, we need to contest the dogmas of fundamentalism and pragmatic technobureaucracy in the academy and in public discourse about rights and values.

We need to show that our learning is worth something by the uses to which we put it in broadening the minds of our students and helping our fellow citizens to more-thoughtful interpretations of the crucial texts that shape our culture. We may not be able to make ourselves or those around us better human beings, but we can certainly make ourselves and those who attend to us more literate, more eloquent, and more culturally aware. In the struggle against antihumanism, we cannot use the methods of our opponents, either mental or physical. We have nothing to offer but the sweetness of reason and the light of learning. But if we use them with vigor—and even rigor—then the humanities may regain their proper place in our schools and in our culture: the place where the heart and the mind meet in language.

NOTE

Reprinted by permission of copyright owner, the Modern Language Association of America, from "Presidential Address 2004: The Humanities in a Posthumanist World," PMLA Vol. 120, No. 3 (2005): 724–33.

REFERENCES

Arnold, Matthew. 1949. *The Portable Matthew Arnold.* New York: Viking.
Eagleton, Terry. 2003. *After Theory.* New York: Basic.
Guillory, John. 1993. *Cultural Capital.* Chicago: University of Chicago Press.
Kames, Henry Home. 1970. *Elements of Criticism.* Vol. 1. New York: Johnson Rpt.
Newman, John Henry. 1955. *The Scope and Nature of University Education.* London: Dent.
Spivak, Gayatri Chakravorty. 2003. *Death of a Discipline.* New York: Columbia University Press.
Steiner, George. 2002. "The Muses' Farewell." *Salmagundi* 135–36: 148–56.
Yeats, William Butler. 1959. "The Second Coming." *Collected Poems.* New York: Macmillan, 184–85.

AFTERWORD

Douglas D. Hesse

The group at dinner at Boudro's on the San Antonio Riverwalk was Robert Scholes, then president of MLA; Bob's wife, JoAnn; Gunther Kress, noted semiotician and leader of The London Group, whose work on multimodality was receiving wide interest; Gail Hawisher, friend and former colleague who had done pioneering work on computers and writing, most often with Cynthia Selfe; David Laurence, MLA director of English Programs and ADE; and me, their host. As program chair for the 2004 Conference on College Composition and Communication, I'd invited Scholes and Kress to be featured speakers for the convention, which drew about three thousand people for three days. Since both had come at some inconvenience, Kress from London and Scholes from the endless road trips of a renowned scholar and association leader, I'd wanted to be hospitable. But I'll confess a selfish interest in hearing the conversation of two men who were intellectual luminaries. They'd never met, but they knew one another's work, and they talked with friendly animation, Scholes at the head of a rectangular table, Kress to his right, his voice still inflected by German after decades as an expatriate. If I reported the conversation, I'd be making things up, as I made no notes afterwards, and time has worn all but the visual memory.

I start with this anecdote, first, because reading the chapters in this book made me think of many times I'd encountered Robert Scholes in person and through his written language, and second, because the chapters made me recognize how much my convention program that year—as well as my thinking since then—was shaped by Scholes's ideas. Consider some of the other invited speakers: Wayne Booth, Sandra Cisneros, Deb Brandt, Harvey Graff, and Min Zhan Liu, among others. Rhetoric, composition, and pedagogy were central, of course, but so were literature, linguistics, and the politics of language, in a mix faintly echoing the kind of thing imagined in so much of his work. The theme I'd chosen was "Making Composition Matter," with two intentionally ambiguous terms. There was "Matter" as in "importance," having stakes, versus "matter" as in "material," having substance to be analyzed and accounted for. There was also "Composition" as in the school subject versus the act of arranging and together, with the additional sense of selecting the elements to be arranged, as in a chemical assay. How might composition be best composed? Of what matter? My sense was that it included rhetoric and language, writing and reading, with any manner of texts produced and studied—literary, practical, aesthetic, deliberative, alphabetic, visual.

That March weekend, San Antonio was hosting the movie premiere of a bad remake of *The Alamo*. A parade featuring longhorn cattle and the film's stars, Dennis Quaid and Billy Bob Thornton, was considerably less well attended than the Cesar Chavez March for Justice the next day. Another invited speaker was NPR education reporter Claudio Sanchez, and late Saturday morning after his talk, we were walking past the Alamo. I asked Sanchez what he thought about the idea of yet another movie. "What the hell do you think I think?" he replied. I can only imagine what Scholes made of the city that weekend; Scholes the exquisite reader, writer, rhetorician, and semiotician, who'd called for "shifting our concerns as English teachers from a curriculum oriented to a literary canon toward a curriculum in textual studies" (Scholes 1985, xi).

I'd first met his ideas as a sophomore in a writing class at the University of Iowa. It was 1975, and the professor was Carl Klaus, with whom he'd collaborated since they'd been colleagues in the 1960s. Two of the texts were Walker Gibson's *Persona* and *Tough, Sweet, and Stuffy*. The third was Scholes's and Klaus's *Elements of Writing*, a short book (137 pages), intentionally so because "reading about writing is one of the least rewarding activities known to civilized man," ranking "right around watching a bowling match on television" (1972, 1). The book focused heavily on sentence types, a kind of practice they likened to Czerny's finger exercises for pianists, exercises "analytic and synthetic; or seen in another way, creative and critical" (101). When I encountered the *The Fabulators* in another course (taught by David Morrell before he quit to write the Rambo books), it seemed reasonable that someone who published writing textbooks would also be publishing literary theory. Little did I know.

Years later, I taught from Scholes's other textbooks. *The Practice of Writing* (with co-author Nancy Comley) was an audacious work that treated the whole range of textuality, literary to workaday, framed in three "forms of discourse": writer-oriented (expression and reflection), reader-oriented (direction and persuasion), and topic-oriented (meant in the sense of the topoi: narration, classification, analysis, and so on).

This combination of modes and aims was, if anything, somewhat old-fashioned, but the audacity came from a wild mixture of readings, from Shakespeare, Hellman, Plath, and Lawrence to magazine ads and pages of baseball statistics, and also from an astonishing array of writing exercises. Students were invited to rewrite a page from *Huckleberry Finn*, from the persona of Huck's "well educated cousin Reginald from Boston" (Scholes and Comley 1981, 8). An exercise titled "Enemy of the People" asked students to assume the role of a doctor in a beach resort town and write a speech in which you persuade the townspeople to close the beach at the height of tourist season due to dangerous sewage (Scholes and Comley 1981, 91–92). Using only the data from fourteen tables and charts, students were directed to make an argument about some aspect of the state of children in the world, both in the present and in the future (Scholes and Comley 1981, 135). As a form of "comic relief," students were challenged to write a paragraph in which they follow a strange system of classification developed in a Jorge Luis Borges essay to categorize "some appropriate set of creatures or objects" (Scholes and Comley 1981, 189). An exercise directed students to explain how to install rain gutters.

What's remarkable to me about the book is the way it invites students to exercise the full range of language, with a creative mélange of texts of all sorts with experiments whimsical and serious, at levels from sentences to self-contained texts. It challenged, already forty years ago, the kind of fractured coverage model driving English departments, not only in literary but also in writing studies. In the name of specialization and expertise, literature and writing kept genres and purposes and historical periods separate, leaving students to figure out (if they wanted, and most didn't) what any of these highly defined courses might have to do with one another—or the nonacademic world beyond. Scholes challenged those divisions and wasn't afraid to use tools of serious play to engage student writers. If students learned anything canonical, it would be an indirect effect of the main enterprise: cultivating textual power through interpretation and production intertwined.

In Introduction to English Studies at Illinois State University, I taught from *Elements of Literature* (1991), which included not only fiction, poetry, and drama but also essays and films—a groundbreaking expanse for the time. The course was a gateway to an undergraduate major that required work in linguistics, literature, and writing (composition and creative and technical), asking students to develop a theory of English studies presented in a portfolio created in a capstone senior seminar. (For a characterization of that seminar and the curriculum and goals it capstoned, see a 1993 article by then-chair Charles Harris.)

This model included ISU's doctoral program, which culminated (before comps and dissertation) in four required seminars: ENG 590: Composition, ENG 540: Linguistics, ENG 560: Literature, and ENG 510: The Teaching of English. When I taught 510 in the late 1990s, the readings included Berlin's *Rhetorics, Poetics, and Cultures*; Graff's *The Labyrinths of Literacy*; Raymond's *English as a Discipline*; Slevin and Young's *Critical Theory and the Teaching of Literature*—and Scholes's *The Rise and Fall of English (1998)*, the profound book that put everything else into conversation. The PhD additionally required a teaching internship and a dissertation that had at least one chapter dealing with teaching implications. There was a pragmatic as well as philosophical aspect to how English at Illinois State defined itself. The department was producing about half the middle school and high school English teachers in Illinois, and teaching literature was only part of their jobs. At the doctoral level, ISU was a blue-collar place that wasn't likely to compete with the other PhD programs in the state, at the University of Illinois, Chicago; Northwestern; and so on. Our graduates were destined for the vast majority of jobs in places with no doctoral programs and with significant teaching expectations, and they were successful. When I was the department's graduate director, I researched the careers of our first 120 doctoral grads and learned that 104 of them (86%) were in tenure-track positions at a time when the national rate was 40–50 percent.

I shared those statistics at the 2001 ADE Summer Seminar for English Department Chairs, and with Scholes himself, in a breakfast overlooking Monterey Bay from a beach hotel. I'd asked if he'd kept in touch with Carl Klaus, and he invited me to sit down. He thought the ISU experiment, by then nearly twenty years in, was encouraging, though he found it hard to believe various disciplinary interests could get along. He was a featured speaker at a seminar that included the theme "Future Challenges for the Humanities Faculty."

Scholes made that topic central in his 2004 MLA Presidential Address. He imagined the field's best future would be crucially concerned not with venerating beautiful objects or "sacred texts" but with developing "an understanding of textuality and ideology in a world in which people are bombarded with ideologically loaded texts from morning to night" (Scholes 2005, 732). With writing and reading at the co-equal core, Scholes urged that "we think of ourselves as humanists first and members of this or that administrative unit second."

We're fifteen years past that talk, and Scholes's vision of a unified purpose driving English departments and attracting students is diffuse at best, more likely dim. English enrollments have continued to decline.

No doubt much of this is due to the skyrocketing cost of higher education, which, in concert with popular derisions of college and a shift from education as a public good to a private one, have pressured students to choose majors perceived to return income on tuition. Traditional "life of the mind" or "critical thinking" or "skills with language" defenses no longer have much power, even as professors earnestly brandish studies of liberal arts majors' career success relative to those studying in business.

But not all areas of English studies are suffering equally. Composition studies, technical writing, and, especially, creative writing have enjoyed booms for many years now, as students can see both personal rewards and career skills in the arts of making texts. New writing majors have grown and attracted students, much in the way that the "practical" major of communication has done for years. Some of this growth occurred in writing tracks within English departments, but much has happened in newly created separate departments and programs. Weary of underclass treatment in some English departments, impatient that, even after decades, the kinds of syntheses that Scholes and others have imagined will never occur, and, empowered by university administrator perceptions that writing is a practical skill meriting actual investment, writing faculties have won divorces, sometimes as independent service programs, sometimes as full-blown departments with majors. While some English departments have tried to save marriages, especially to preserve budgets, others have welcomed separation. The English department at my university, for example, two years ago redefined and renamed itself as English and Literary Arts, ceding all "nonliterary" textual studies and production to an independent writing program with twenty-seven permanent faculty, of which I'm executive director. I'm happy to be involved in that thriving vital enterprise, but as someone also with a tenured appointment in English, I'm dismayed by its "retreat into belletrism" (Scholes 2005, 731).

Writing studies hasn't quite been blameless in these developments. My main sphere of activity is writing, so I'm especially alarmed by Emily J. Isaacs's insightful chapter in this volume. She worries that the burgeoning discipline of writing studies will "repeat the mistakes of English" by focusing less on "the workaday, applied teaching of writing" than on transmitting the scholarly content of the field itself. Isaacs's concerns are justified. I'm happy enough that writing studies is fostering the kind of interpretive work of present-day noncanonical texts that Scholes advocates. Consider Trish Roberts-Miller's *Rhetoric and Demagoguery*, for example, or David Gold and Jessica Enoch's volume on *Women at Work: Rhetorics of Gender and Labor* (2019). But my concern is that paths to field status and attention will further solidify around criticism, research, and theory, with students more important as consumers of these productions than as producers themselves, and with writing teachers who directly work on reading and writing with undergraduate nonmajors relegated in the new writing studies just as they had long been in the old literature.

Scholes's concerns in his presidential address were larger than the survival of English departments. Discussing George Steiner, John Guillory, and Terry Eagleton, he noted the utter failure of the traditional humanities to humanize (witness the Holocaust), the disappearance of whatever cultural capital literature one might have held, with the rise of a new professional-managerial class, and the insidious ways that the turn to theory could be co-opted by industrial and bureaucratic structures for a "pragmatism" that denied absolute truths or universal values. He also saw fundamentalism as deleterious as pragmatism, for which "there is only one truth, and nothing but universal values. And this is the case whether we are talking about Christian fundamentalism, Islamic fundamentalism, Marxist fundamentalism, or any other kind of fundamentalism." In a world polarized by pragmatism and fundamentalism, Scholes feared, "some of the weapons are rhetorical, taking the form of mythmaking and media domination" and "a conquered fundamentalist is likely to become a terrorist—regardless of what kind of fundamentalist he or she may happen to be" (Scholes 2005, 730–31).

As I write in 2019, fundamentalist domestic terrorism abounds, abetted by leaders who brandish rhetorical weapons with hubristic nonchalance. The results are fundamental challenges to the very possibility of public discourse and deliberation, challenges through the rhetorical weapons: denying facts, inventing histories, ignoring documents, misrepresenting events, lying. Furthermore, Christian fundamentalists have unfathomably embraced a president whose personal history and values (from paying for sex to celebrating torturers to spending Sundays on golf courses rather than in churches) contrast starkly with their espoused own. We're observing extraordinary pragmatism when achieving certain conservative "religious" values trumps doctrines and traditions. And what are those values? American Family Association broadcaster Sandy Rios has complained that "when the left is talking about white supremacism, they're talking about the roots of this country. They're talking about Christianity. They're talking about hard work, about capitalism and free-market values" (2019). If Scholes in 2004 thought "dire" a world situation in which "those who lack all conviction have joined forces with those who are full of passionate intensity," I cannot imagine the adjective he might choose to describe the state of discourse today.

Assessing how the "humanizing" aspects of English departments and writing programs have failed to shape a better-functioning reading and writing public, Scholes would be entitled to say, "I told you so," pointing to curricular and pedagogical calls he'd made decades ago, mostly dismissed. But I suspect he'd bite his tongue, partly from a sense of graciousness, partly from a sense of reassurance that we still had all sorts of possibilities for doing better. His complex menu of ideas for curricula and pedagogy remains appealing, as evidenced by the chapters Ellen Carillo has seated in this volume. Scholes himself has hosted, absent and after the fact, a marvelous intellectual dinner. He's furnished important, exciting topics for conversation—about reading, writing, teaching, the profession, the high stakes of textual power. I think he'd be pleased that those topics have generated sufficient energy around the table to ensure hosts for future dinners.

Kenny Smith's chapter, for example, offers a smart approach to teaching against the unfettered (and too-convenient) post-truth student dismissal that no journalistic source is credible. Smith uses Scholes's ideas for negotiating a middle ground between poststructuralist denials of reference and enlightenment aspirations for objective language. He has students read (in the deepest sense) and write about a range of texts diverse in genre, purpose, and political values, and if Scholes and Comley were writing a 2020 edition of *The Practice of Writing*, they'd surely supply several units fit to the task. Lynée Lewis Gaillet and Angela Christie explain how textual power might orient curricula and pedagogy at levels beyond single classrooms, to whole English departments in the context of a wider university program connecting college to career. Their chapter explains why English departments should embrace, not abjure, the test of how "what we have to teach will be useful to this society and to the individuals who study with us" (Scholes, quoted in Gaillet and Christie, chapter 12). I have to imagine that some would fault Gaillet and Christie—as they might Scholes beyond them—for a kind of collaborationist/accommodationist pragmatism that discards "tradition" for "the market." True, Scholes's work does proffer a survival strategy for English. As Thomas P. Miller notes, English departments might yet in the future find enrollments and funding by orienting toward Scholes's assertion that "the business of English departments is to help students improve as readers and writers." However, that business historically has so lacked prestige as to have been ignored except at less famous colleges or in relatively nascent disciplines like writing studies. Miller holds some optimism that a next generation will enact these changes. I fear that higher education's climate may already have changed too much, too fast.

But then I tend to pessimism, a consequence of having been long enough in the profession to see Scholes's ideas roll in, then out, like waves on Dover Beach. One virtue in reading these chapters is the refreshing spirit that there is important work to be done and there are clear (if not easy) possibilities for doing it. It's not too late! Here are the pathways! Aren't they exciting?! That, too, is the virtue of rereading Scholes years afterward, of reencountering his sense of urgency not only for English departments or the humanities, but for all students and for democracies, of reencountering his steady optimism even when there seems little occasion for it. It was an optimism born of plenitude and play, impelled by a multitude of texts to be interpreted and texts to be made, those basic yet inexhaustible activities of reading and writing. Remembering Scholes from his days at Iowa long ago, Richard Lloyd-Jones (2002, 57) noted that he "became a door by which the profession generally could enter into a larger sense of itself." That door remains inviting and open.

REFERENCES

Gold, David, and Jessica Enoch, eds. 2019. *Women at Work: Rhetorics of Gender and Labor.* Pittsburgh, PA: University Pittsburgh Press.

Harris, Charles B. 1993. "Mandated Testing and the Postsecondary English Department." *ADE Bulletin* 104 (4): 4–13.

Lloyd-Jones, Richard. 2002. "Common Cause." *ADE Bulletin* 130: 56–58.

Rios, Sandy. 2019. "What Is Causing the Outbreak of Violence in America?" *Sandy Rios in the Morning.* AFR: American Family Radio. August 8, 2019. https://afr.net/podcasts.

Roberts-Miller, Trish. 2019. *Rhetoric and Demagoguery.* Carbondale: Southern Illinois University Press.

Scholes, Robert. 1985. *Textual Power: Literacy Theory and the Teaching of English.* New Haven, CT: Yale University Press.

Scholes, Robert. 1998. *The Rise and Fall of English.* New Haven, CT: Yale University Press.

Scholes, Robert. 2005. "Presidential Address 2004: The Humanities in a Posthumanist World." *PMLA* 120 (3): 724–33.

Scholes, Robert, and Nancy R. Comley. 1981. *The Practice of Writing.* Boston, MA: St. Martin's.

Scholes, Robert, and Carl H. Klaus. 1972. *Elements of Writing.* New York: Oxford University Press.

Scholes, Robert, and Carl H. Klaus, Nancy R. Comley, and Michael Silverman. 1991. *Elements of Literature: Fiction, Poetry, Drama, Essay, Film 4e.* New York: Oxford University Press.

ABOUT THE CONTRIBUTORS

Ellen C. Carillo is professor of English at the University of Connecticut and the writing coordinator at its Waterbury campus. She is the author of *Securing a Place for Reading in Composition: The Importance of Teaching for Transfer* (Utah State University Press, 2015); *A Writer's Guide to Mindful Reading* (WAC Clearinghouse/University Press of Colorado, 2017); *Teaching Readers in Post-Truth America* (Utah State University Press, 2018); the *MLA Guide to Digital Literacy* (Modern Language Association, 2019); and editor of *Reading Critically, Writing Well*, 12th edition (Bedford/St. Martin's, 2019). Her scholarship, which focuses on the importance of teaching reading alongside writing, has also been published in many journals and edited collections. Ellen is co-founder of the Role of Reading in Composition Studies Special Interest Group of the Conference on College Composition and Communication (CCCC) and regularly presents her scholarship at regional and national conferences. She has been awarded grants from the Northeast Modern Language Association (NeMLA), CCCC, and the Council of Writing Program Administrators (CWPA).

Angela Christie currently serves as the faculty director of Georgia State University's Quality Enhancement Plan (QEP): College to Career: Career Readiness through Everyday Competencies. College to Career is a university-wide initiative that will increase students' ability to recognize and demonstrate the career competencies they are learning through their curricular and co-curricular experiences. As faculty director, Dr. Christie oversees the development, refinement, and implementation of College to Career and works with units and personnel across the university. In her home department, she is a senior lecturer of English. Dr. Christie has been the associate director of Lower Division Studies since 2007. In that capacity, she has mentored graduate teaching assistants, edited the university's Guide to First-Year Writing, served as the assessment reporter for the department's core courses and developed paired-instructor courses for the College of Arts and Sciences.

Paul T. Corrigan teaches English at the University of Tampa. He lives in the Peace River Watershed. In addition to literary scholarship, he has written about teaching in *Reader, Pedagogy, Profession, TETYC, College Teaching, Teaching & Learning Inquiry, TheAtlantic.com*, and other venues. He blogs at teachingandlearninginhighered.org. He is currently writing a book on teaching literary reading.

Lynée Lewis Gaillet is distinguished university professor and chair of the English Department at Georgia State University. Her book projects include *Scottish Rhetoric and Its Influence; Stories of Mentoring; The Present State of Scholarship in the History of Rhetoric; Scholarly Publication in a Changing Academic Landscape; Publishing in Community; Primary Research and Writing: People, Places, and Spaces; On Archival Research; Writing Center and Writing Program Collaborations; Remembering Differently: Re-figuring Women's Rhetorical Work;* and *Composing in Four Acts*. She is a past president of the Coalition of Feminist Scholars in the History of Rhetoric and Composition.

Douglas D. Hesse is professor of English and founding executive director of writing at the University of Denver, where he's been named university distinguished scholar. He is a past president of the National Council of Teachers of English, past chair of the Conference on

College Composition and Communication, and past president of the Council of Writing Program Administrators. He edited *Writing Program Administration* and held leadership roles in MLA. Hesse has published over seventy-five articles and chapters and co-authored four books, including *Creating Nonfiction* and *The Simon and Schuster Handbook for Writers*. His work focuses on writing pedagogy, narrative theory, creative nonfiction, and issues in English studies. He's won the Donald Murray Prize and been named Young Rhetorician of the Year. Hesse was educated in rural Iowa schools and holds a PhD from The University of Iowa.

Alice S. Horning is professor emerita of writing and rhetoric at Oakland University, where she held a joint appointment in linguistics. Her research over her entire career has focused on the intersection of reading and writing, concentrating lately on the increasing evidence of students' reading difficulties and how to address them in writing courses and across the disciplines. Her work has appeared in the major professional journals and in books published by Parlor Press and Hampton Press. Her most recent books include *Reading, Writing, and Digitizing: Understanding Literacy in the Electronic Age*, published in 2012 by Cambridge Scholars Publishing; *Reconnecting Reading and Writing*, co-edited with Beth Kraemer and published in 2013 by the WAC Clearinghouse and Parlor Press; *What is College Reading?*, co-edited with Cynthia Haller and Deborah-Lee Gollnitz and published by the WAC Clearinghouse; and *Literacy Then and Now*, published by Peter Lang. Her current project is titled *Literacy Heroines: Women and the Written Word*, also published by Peter Lang. She is the editor of the Studies in Composition and Rhetoric book series for Peter Lang.

Emily J. Isaacs is professor of writing studies and executive director of the Office for Faculty Advancement at Montclair State University. Isaacs specializes in writing pedagogy, writing assessment, and writing programming in higher education. Professor Isaacs's scholarship has focused on best practices for writing instruction and administration, the national state of writing instruction and support at US four-year universities, and teaching and learning in public higher education. Her articles have appeared in *Pedagogy*, *College English*, *Writing Program Administration*, *Writing Center Journal*, the *Journal of Teaching Writing*, and in several book collections. In addition, she is the author of three books, including, most recently, *Writing at the State U* (Utah State University Press).

Christopher J. La Casse is an assistant professor and director of the Hewitt Writing and Reading Center at the US Coast Guard Academy. His primary research interest focuses on how the economic, political, and cultural pressures of the First World War shaped the development and dissemination of modernism(s) in literary magazines and modern periodicals. His publications have appeared in *Criticism* (2016), *American Periodicals* (2016), *The Edinburgh Companion to the First World War and the Arts* (2017), *Women's Space: Essays on Female Characters in the Twenty-First Century Science Fiction Western* (2019), and *The Routledge Companion to the Literary Magazine* (forthcoming). He serves as secretary of the Research Society for American Periodicals and is a principal faculty member of the NEH Summer Institute, City of Print: New York and the Periodical Press (2015 and 2020).

Robert Lestón is an associate professor of English and chair at the New York City College of Technology, CUNY. He has published widely in a number of different journals and co-authored *Beyond the Blogosphere: Information and Its Children* (2012). Recent work includes "The Politics of Recognition in Building Pluriversal Possibilities" in *Decolonial Conversations in Posthuman and New Material Rhetorics* (forthcoming), edited by David Grant and Jennifer Clary-Lemon. He is working on a book that investigates the relationship between decolonial rhetorics, autonomous communities, and social movements in the Global South.

Kelsey McNiff is associate professor of English/composition at Endicott College. She received her MA and PhD in history from Princeton University. Prior to joining Endicott, she spent eight years on the faculty of the Harvard College Writing Program and two years as the first director of academic partnerships at the Harvard Art Museums. At Endicott, she primarily teaches the required first-year critical reading and writing course sequence, which she helped design, as well as courses in composition, history, and history and memory. Her work has appeared in *Currents in Teaching and Learning*, *Art as Research* (2013), and the *Journal of Interactive Technology and Pedagogy*. Her current research focuses on supporting students in the transition to college-level reading and writing.

Thomas P. Miller is a professor of rhetoric and composition in the English Department at the University of Arizona, where he served as vice provost for ten years. He has won awards for his research, teaching, mentoring, diversity leadership, and advocacy for shared governance. He has published five books and over fifty articles, chapters, and reviews on political rhetoric, writing programs, the history of literacy and English studies, and theories of rhetoric. He is currently working on a book entitled "Leadership as a Liberal Art and Integrative Discipline" that argues that collaborative models of leadership can help strengthen coalitions of faculty and staff to resist corporatization, expand undergraduate majors, and achieve the potentials of the engaged university

Jessica Rivera-Mueller is an assistant professor of English at Utah State University. Her teaching focuses on teacher development processes in multiple classroom contexts, including English-teacher education, secondary education, and college composition. Within this focus, she advocates for pedagogical inquiry, teacher agency, and social justice. As a teacher educator, she teaches English teaching methods courses for undergraduate students and composition theory courses for graduate students. She also serves as her university's supervisor for English concurrent enrollment courses throughout the state of Utah. In this role, she sponsors teacher development for practicing English teachers. Her scholarship on teacher development has also appeared in *Teaching/Writing: The Journal of Writing Teacher Education* and *Journal on Empowering Teaching Excellence*.

Christian Smith is an associate professor in the Department of English at Coastal Carolina University, where he teaches composition and rhetoric and coordinates the MA in writing program. His work has appeared in *College Composition and Communication*, *Computers and Composition*, *Literacy in Composition Studies*, and a number of edited collections.

Kenny Smith is a lecturer in the writing program at the University of California, Santa Barbara. His research focuses on how literacy skills transfer from the classroom to the outside world, particularly in regard to the interpretation of scientific texts and journalism. He is currently working on a project that examines the rhetoric of biologist memoirs.

INDEX

Abejas, Las, 215
academia, 235; discourse in, 153–54; program development in, 193–94; and real world, 232, 233; research goals, 107–8
access, accessibility, 178; of writing, 12–13
ACT, reading comprehension, 45
Acteal Massacre, 215
activism, 207
ADE. *See* Association of Departments of English
Adler-Kassner, Linda, *Naming What We Know,* 48, 193
advertising, 65, 66
advocacy, in English as discipline, 93–94
After Theory (Eagleton), 241
Agassiz, Louis, "fish" exercise, 148–49
Akyol, Mustafa, "Away in the Manger . . . Or Under a Palm Tree?," 124
Althusser, Louis, 214, 218, 219
Amazing Stories, 66
"American Language" (Mencken), 87
annotation strategy, 50
anthologies, 57; scholarly curated, 58–59
antioppression classrooms, 141
antioppression pedagogies, 134, 140
antiracist classrooms, 141
Appadurai, Arjun, 147
appropriation, 140
archives, 4, 61; student use of, 68–69
Ardis, Ann, 58
argument, 117; and rhetoric, 129–30; Rogerian, 120, 121; in texts, 162, 163
argumentation, argumentative practices, 67, 140
Aristotle, 101
Armer, Frank, 65
Armstrong, Sonya, 55
Arnold, Matthew, 235, 246; *Culture and Anarchy,* 244–45
"Ars Poetica" (MacLeish), 161
artifice, levels of, 218
ArtMag, 61
assessment, student, 220–21
Association of American Colleges and Universities, 179, 202

Association of Departments of English (ADE), 14, 209, 256; "A Changing Major," 7, 196, 197–98, 199; recommendations, 207–8; survey by, 169–70, 177
Atlanta Writers Club, 208
Atlantic, The, digital repository, 61
Auden, W. H., 99
audience, 67, 121; determining and evaluating, 124–25; in invitational essays, 123, 126–27; self-awareness, 128–29
author(s), 172; death of, 167, 168; intention of, 158–59
authority, textual, 27, 101
"Away in the Manger . . . Or Under a Palm Tree?" (Akyol), 124

Bad Blood (Carreyrou), 151–52
baccalaureates, in humanities, 170–71
Barthes, Roland, 87; "Death of the Author," 167, 172
Bartholomae, David, 214, 218, 223; "Inventing the University," 190; on Quentin Pierce, 220–24; *Ways of Reading,* 6; "The Tidy House," 6, 219–20
Bayard, Pierre, 168, 172, 173; *How to Talk about Books You Haven't Read,* 167, 180
Bazerman, Charles, 50
Bazin, Victoria, 9
Bean, John, 55, 59, 68
beliefs, and discourse, 148–49
Believing/Doubting Game, 6, 119
belles lettres, 161, 243
Benjamin, Walter, 101
Berila, Beth, 134, 140, 141
Berlin, James, 138, 139–40, 168
Bernays, Eddie, 65
Bérubé, Michael, 169, 170
Between the World and Me (Coates), 141–42
biliteracy, 50
binary literature, 98
Black Lives Matter, 215
Black Nationalism, 223
Black Orpheus (Sartre), 222
Black Panther Party, 223
Blau, Sheridan, *Deep Reading,* 42

Booth, Wayne, 7, 9
boyd, danah, 147
Boyer, Ernest, on integrative learning, 179–80
Brooks, Cleanth, 91
Brown, Michael, 141–42
Brown University, 13, 169
bumper stickers, textuality of, 103–4
Burkean identification, 140
Bush administration, 148, 160
business, 35, 178

CAE. *See* Critical Art Ensemble
canon of methods, 25–26, 34; English studies, 88–94, 200; tree of reading metaphor, 35–36
canon of texts, for writing studies, 194
career competencies, 203; *National Association of Colleges and Employers*, 202; QEP, 204–5
career literacy, 206
Carreyrou, John, *Bad Blood*, 151–52
Castiglione, Baldassare, 244; *Il libro del cortigiano*, 243
CCC (journal), reading and literacy articles, 43, 44(table)
CCCC. *See* Conference on College Composition and Communication
CE (journal), reading and literacy articles, 43, 44(table)
Center for Contemplative Mind in Society (CMind), 133
"Changing Major: The Report of the 2016-17 ADE Ad Hoc Committee on the English Major, A" (ADE), 7, 196, 197–98, 199
Chao, Elaine, 152
Chapman, David, 183
Churchill, Suzanne, 58
Citation Project, The, 39–40, 45–46, 55, 68
citations, student use of, 45–46
citizenship, 6, 16, 18; empathy and, 117–18; and rhetoric, 160
civic literacy, 145
civic virtue, empathy as, 16, 119, 129
Clifford, John, *Making Literature Matter*, 190
close reading, 157
Clueless in Academe (Graff), 160
CMII. *See* Creative Media Industries Institute
Coates, Ta-Nehisi, *Between the World and Me*, 141–42
cognition, empathy and, 130
Cole, Jean Lee, 58
Coleridge, Samuel Taylor, 244

collaboration, in reader-led classrooms, 64
college, reading in, 4, 41–42
College Board, 176
College to Career: Career Readiness through Everyday Competencies (GSU), 199
College to Career (CTC) QEP (Georgia State University), 198, 202, 207–8; critical thinking through writing, 200–201; curricular map, 203–4; student learning outcomes, 204–5; student success initiatives, 199–200
Collier, Patrick, 58
Columbia University, 75
Comley, Nancy, *Text Book*, 8, 32, 188
communication(s), 18, 171, 204; listening and understanding, 120–21
composition, 98, 170, 243; first-year, 184, 186; and literature, 9, 197, 231
Composition and Literature: Bridging the Gap (Horner), 196, 197
composition and rhetoric studies, compositionists, 3, 182, 191, 192, 214, 219–20, 257; and literary studies, 16–17
composition-literature (comp-lit) war, 9, 184
Composition, Rhetoric, and Disciplinarity (Malenczyk et al.), 192, 193
comprehension, transmediation and, 125
Conference on College Composition and Communication (CCCC), 186; conferences, 42, 253–54; reading and literacy as issue for, 40, 41, 43; "The Students' Rights to Their Own Language," 213
conflicts, teaching, 160
Conrad First, 61
consciousness, 249
consumer culture, 65
consumption, 192; of non-literature, 229–30; production within, 216, 231–32
contemplative practices, 34, 136, 139, 141, 142–43; reading aloud and, 133–34
Contemplative Practices in Higher Education: Powerful Methods to Transform Teaching and Learning (Barbeza and Bush), 139
context, reading in, 28, 29
conversation, 108–90
Corrigan, Paul T., 143
Council of Writing Program Administrators (CWPA), 15; conference sessions, 40–41, 42–43
counterpublics, 178
craft, reading as, 13–14, 24, 25, 49
Craft of Reading, The (Scholes), 4
Crafty Reader, The (Scholes), 12–13, 15, 24, 28, 32, 38–39, 49

Creative Media Industries Institute (CMII), 208
creative reading, 34, 179
creative writing, 205, 229; in English departments, 99–100, 170
Critical Art Ensemble (CAE), 215
critical reading, 4, 24, 34, 38, 48, 56, 117
critical reflection, 51
critical thinking, 34, 67–68, 129, 202, 210, 257
critical thinking through writing (CTW), 200–201
"Critical Thinking, Reading, and Composing" (WPA), 68
criticism, 31, 162, 175, 236; schools of, 172
crowd sourcing, 193
CTW. *See* critical thinking through writing
Cultural Capital (Guillory), 174, 241, 242
cultural studies, 171, 175
cultural-studies approach, *Textual Power* as, 138–39
culture, 31, 91, 173, 237, 244; technobureaucratic, 246–47, 249
Culture and Anarchy (Arnold), 244–45
Cultures of Reading (*PMLA*), 54
Currell, Sue, 9
curriculum, 77, 89, 168; English, 87–88, 206, 212–13, 219; knowledge building in, 96–97; 224
CWPA. *See* Council of Writing Program Administration
cynicism, 109, 147, 155

D'Anastasio, Cecilia, "Inside the Culture of Sexism at Riot Games," 153
Death of a Discipline (Spivak), 250
"Death of the Author" (Barthes), 167, 172
debate, reading for, 31–32
de Certeau, Michel, 216–17, 221; *The Practice of Everyday Life*, 213
deconstructionism, 89, 136, 137–38, 171, 228, 230–31, 247; reading in, 28–29
decontextualized reading, 56, 60–61
Dedalus, Stephen, 249
Deep Reading (Sullivan et al.), 42
de Man, Paul, 136, 137
democracy, 129, 140, 155; empathy and, 117–18
democracy fatigue, 147
Department of Religious Studies (GSU), and WellStar Health System, 208
Derrida, Jacques, 31, 109
detective novels, 33
dialectic, 190, 250
dialogue, invitational essay and, 126

diaries, 33
DiCenzo, Maria, 64
differentiation, in English, 229
digital environments, 147; humanities in, 3, 13; literacy in, 16, 174, 179; repositories, 61; technology, 204, 205; text in, 50
directed self-placement (DSP), 186
Dirty Hands (Sartre), 222
discourse, 151; academic, 153–54; and beliefs, 148–49
discussion, parameters of, 124
disinformation, 16, 147
dispositions, problem-exploring, 55
Divergent (novel), 80
Dominguez, Ricardo, 215
Donahue, Patricia, 9
"Doubting/Believing Game" (Elbow), 6
Douglass, Frederick, "The Meaning of July Fourth for the Negro," 133–34
Downs, Doug, 194
drama, 33
DSP. *See* directed self-placement
dynamic reading practices, 67

Eagleton, Terry, 136, 137, 242, 246; *After Theory*, 241
EDT. *See* Electronic Disturbance Theater
Educating for Democracy (Shulman), 118
education, 16, 18, 139, 140, 222. *See also* higher education
Educational Testing Service (ETS), 176
egocentrism, cognitive, 59
Elbow, Peter, 7, 9; "Doubting/Believing Game," 6
Electronic Disturbance Theater (EDT), 215
Elements of Criticism (Karnes), 243
Elements of Fiction (Scholes), 171
Elements of Literature, 255
Elements of Poetry (Scholes), 171
Elements of Writing (Klaus), 254
emotions, and textual meaning, 141
empathy, 51, 124, 125, 130, 150; and citizenship, 117–18; as civic virtue, 16, 129; as imaginative process, 118–19
empathy experiment, 153
empiricism, 136, 140
Encyclopedia of Communication Theory, The, 123
engaged university, 180
English, English studies, 3, 10, 15, 17, 54, 83, 85–86, 169, 170, 187–88; advocacy in, 93–94; canon of methods, 88–92; curriculum, 4, 7, 98–100, 146; as discipline, 13, 87–88, 112–13; graduate-

level, 106–7, 109–10; literary history, 92–93, 94–98; literature and, 100–101; as professional unconscious, 228–29; research in, 107–8; restructuring, 110–11, 233–34; teaching, 7–8; values of, 35, 202–3
English After the Fall: From Literature to Textuality (Scholes), 4, 13, 24, 27–28, 54, 69, 176
English departments, 7, 8, 17, 86–87, 92, 107, 112, 182–83, 191, 200, 208, 230, 259; curriculum design, 212–23; decline and reform of, 168–69, 175–78; enrollment in, 169–70, 184, 256–57; future of, 99–100
English majors, 202, 209; decline in, 197–98; marketability of, 205–6; writing tracks, 184–85
Enlightenment, 243, 244, 246
Enoch, Jessica, *Women at Work*, 257
enrollments, in English, 169–70, 184
equity, increasing, 178
essays, 161; argument-based, 120; invitational, 122–24
ethics, of reading, 16, 30, 135–36
ETS. *See* Educational Testing Service
evaluation, 43, 111; academic discourse, 153–54; of journalistic articles, 152–53
Everett, Justin, *A Minefield of Dreams*, 185
Everything's an Argument (Lunsford and Ruszkiewicz), 120–21, 126
experience, reading as, 23–24
experienced curriculum, 224
experiential learning, 179
"Experiment in Computer-Based Education Using Hypertext, An," 13

Fabulators, The (Scholes), 12, 254
fact checking, 46
faculty, composition and rhetoric, 186, 187, 191; teaching reading, 46–47, 50
faenix culprit, 85
Faigley, Lester, 138, 168
"fake news," 135, 137, 138, 148
Fanon, Frantz, 222
fantasy, 33
fashion, political and cultural, 90
Faulkner, William, 234
fiction-writing workshops, 202
Fields of Writing to Fields of Reading (Comley et al.), 29, 40
Fight Stories, 66, 67
film, 33, 99
Finnigan's Wake (Joyce), 85
first-year composition, 184, 185, 194; teaching, 186, 192

Fish, Stanley, 170; *Professional Correctness*, 113
Fish/Rorty solution, 108
Fitzgerald, F. Scott, 105
FLC. *See* freshman learning communities
FloodNet program, 215
Flower, Linda, 6
fortunate fall, 85; "A Fortunate Fall?" (Scholes), 85–113
Foss, Sonja K., 121
Foucault, Michel, 172, 190, 227; "What Is an Author?," 172
"Framework for Success in Postsecondary Writing, The," 16, 67
Fraser, Nancy, 214
freedom, 124
freshman learning communities (FLC), 198
Frye, Northrop, 88, 90, 91, 235
Fulfilling the American Dream: Liberal Education and the Future of Work (Association of American Colleges and Universities), 202
fundamentalism, 247–48, 249, 251, 258

Gaillet, Lynée Lewis, archival projects, 68–69
Geertz, Clifford, *The Interpretation of Cultures*, 228
Genesis of Secrecy (Kermode), 234
genre(s), 174, 226–27; reading, 33
Georgia State University (GSU), 208, 209; College to Career QEP, 198, 202, 203–4; student body, 206–7; student success initiatives, 199–200
Gibson, Walker, 254
Ginger (magazine), 65–66
Goffman, Erving, 232
Gold, David. *Women at Work*, 257
graduate programs, 106–7, 109–10; reading theory and pedagogy, 47–48
Graff, Gerald, 168, 170; *Clueless in Academe*, 160
grammar, 190, 207, 250
Gravity's Rainbow (Pynchon), 95
Green, Martin, 12
Griffin, Cindy L., 121
Guggenheim fellow, 14
"Guide to the News" (Reddit), 152–53
Guillory, John, 246, 247; *Cultural Capital*, 174, 241, 242
Guttenberg Galaxy (McLuhan), 167

Haas, Christina, 6
Habermas, Jürgen, *The Structural Transformation of the Public Sphere*, 214
habits of mind, 16, 118, 120

Hananu-Bresch, Cristina, *A Minefield of Dreams*, 185
Hand, Learned, 130
Hayden, Wendy, 68
hermetic positions, on texts, 137–38
Hesse, Doug, 7
higher education, 139, 178, 222; reforms, 208–9
high school course, Schole's proposal for, 175–76
Hirsch, E. D., 89
historiances, literary, 234
history, 64; literary, 94–98
Hockney, David, 99
Hogarth, William, 99
Hollrah, Matt, 8
Holmes, Elizabeth, 151
Horner, Winifred Bryan, *Composition and Literature*, 196
Howard, Rebecca Moore, Citation Project, 45
How to Talk about Books You Haven't Read (Bayard), 167, 180
Huffman, Debrah, 43
humanism, 73, 245; concept of, 242–43; importance of, 248–49; Steiner on, 239–40
humanities, 3, 72, 107, 118, 169, 183, 209, 250, 258; in academia, 242–43; role of, 240–42
"Humanities in a Posthumanist World, The," 14, 17
Hume, David, "On the Standard of Taste," 243
Hunter, Duncan, 152
hypertext, in teaching poetry, 13

Idea of a University, The (Newman), 245
identities, identity, 65, 140; textual, 66–67
ideology, 256; and journalism, 148
Illinois State University, 255; doctoral program, 256
image-text analysis, 65–66
imagination, primary and secondary, 244
individual, freedom of, 161
information literacy, 16, 179
Inoue, Asao, 40, 214, 219
"Inside the Culture of Sexism at Riot Games" (D'Anastasio), 153
institution: language of, 223; as site of power, 214–15; standardization, 221–22
insurrection, January 6, 2021, 7
integrative learning, 179–80
"Integrative Learning" (*Peer Review*), 179
intellectual engagement, ways of reading in, 26, 27–29, 30

intention, 105; author, 158–59
interactive literacies, 174
interdisciplinarity, 10, 17
International Literacy Association, 41
interpretation, 162, 236–37
Interpretation of Cultures, The (Geertz), 228
intertextuality, 168, 178–79
"Inventing the University" (Bartholomae), 190
invitational essays, 122; audience in, 126–27; class assignment, 124–26; revision in, 127–28; rhetoric in, 123–24
invitational rhetoric, 121, 123–24
Iowa Writers Workshop, 229
Iraq invasion, journalist response to, 148
Islamophobia, 135

Jakobson, Roman, 91
James Joyce Quarterly, 12
Jameson, Frederic, *The Political Unconscious*, 237
Jamieson, Sandra, 45, 193
job market, English graduates, 107, 111, 169, 205–6, 256
journalism, 33, 150–51, 154; source and text evaluation, 152–53; texts, 147–48
journalistic discourse, 146; on Theranos, 151–52, 153
journals, academic, 153–54
Joyce, James: *Finnegan's Wake*, 85; *Ulysses*, 94–95
"Justice Denied in Massachusetts" (Millay), 162

Karnes, Henry, *Elements of Criticism*, 243–44
Katz, Tamar, 55, 158, 161
Keats, John, on reading as process, 101–2, 104–5
Kellogg, Robert, *The Nature of Narrative*, 12
Kermode, Frank, *Genesis of Secrecy*, 234
Kirsch, Gesa, 143
Klaus, Carl, 256; *Elements of Writing*, 254
Knight Foundation, 147
Knoblauch, Abby, 130
knowledge(s), 67, 80, 104, 192, 237; in literary history, 96–97; standardized, 221–22
Krebs, Paula, 199
Kress, Gunther, 253
Kuhn, Thomas, 112

language, 4, 139, 149, 163–64(n3), 190, 207, 213, 223, 250; secular and hermetic positions in, 135–36; subaltern public, 218–19
language practices, literature and, 189–90

Lanham, Richard, 160, 168, 177
lateral reading, 46
Latham, Sean, 5
Laurence, David, 177
Leahy, Mark, 220
learning, 15, 17, 78, 80, 130; historical, 97–98; integrative, 179–80
"Learning and Teaching" (Scholes), 15, 72, 73
learning theory, 125
learning-to-teach process, 83
Lectio Divina, 134, 141, 142
lecturing, 4, 50, 55
liberty, 130
Libro del cortigiano, Il (Castiglione), 243
life, and literature, 30
listening, 120–21, 126, 159; to other, 160–61; rhetorical, 140
literacy, 7, 145, 172, 183, 206, 213; changes in, 173–74, 176–77; development, 54; instruction, 135, 141, 185; media, 16, 147, 179; reading and, 42–43
literae humaniores, 243
literariness, 91, 98
literary analysis, 192
literary criticism, 175, 212; anthropological analysis, 227–28
literary fiction, Empathetic Reading, 51
Literary Review, 12
literary studies, 3, 91–92, 187, 192; and composition studies, 16–17; history of, 94–98
literary texts, 236
literary theory, 31–32, 89, 188, 228
literature, 30, 92, 158, 161, 162, 174, 175, 239, 241, 243; and composition, 9, 197, 231; as cultural artifact, 189–90; prestige of, 234–35; reading vs. critical editions, 58–59; as sacred and secular texts, 100–101; as secular scripture, 235–37
Lockhart, Tara, 9
Lunsford, Andrea, 7; *Everything's an Argument*, 120–21, 126
Lynch, Paul, 143

MacLeish, Archibald, "Ars Poetica," 161
magazines, 5, 33, 57
Mailloux, Steven, *Rhetorical Power*, 172
"Making Composition Matter" conference (CCCC), 253–54
Making Literature Matter (Schilb and Clifford), 190
Malcolm X, 214, 215, 222
Mantegna, Andrea, 242
manufactured consent, 51

Man Who Shot Liberty Valence, The, 33
marginalized communities, literacy and, 213
mass media, 101
mastery, research as, 106–7
materiality, 62; commonsense, 136
Mathieu, Paula, *Tactics of Hope*, 215
Maxwell, Jason, 9
McCluhan, Marshall, *Guttenberg Galaxy*, 167
McComiskey, Bruce, 138
McGann, Jerome, 58, 61
McGuffey's *Fifth Eclectic Reader*, 159
meaning, 39, 56, 217
"Meaning of July Fourth for the Negro, The" (Douglass), reading aloud, 133–34
media, 145; literacy, 16, 147, 179; manipulation of, 237–38
media and cultural studies, 169
Media Insight Project, 147
media studies, 3, 10
medium(s), 33; scholarly curated, 58–59
Mellon Foundation, Andrew W., 14, 209
Mencken, H. L., "American Language," 87
metacognition, 32, 63, 128, 193
metaphor, tree as reading, 24, 35–36
meta-thinking, 76
methods: canon of, 25–26; for reading, 14–15
Millay, Edna St. Vincent, "Justice Denied in Massachusetts," 162
Milton, John, 236, 239
mindfulness, 122
mindful reading, 24, 34
Minefield of Dreams: Triumphs and Travails of Independent Writing Program, A (Everett and Hananu-Bresch), 185
MLA. *See* Modern Language Association
MJP. *See* Modernist Journals Project
Modern Culture and Media, Department of (Brown University), 13
modernism, 57; literary, 3, 4
Modernism in the Magazine (Scholes and Wulfmann), 15, 61–62, 64
Modernist Journals Project (MJP), 13, 61, 62–64
Modernist Magazines Project, 61
Modern Language Association (MLA), 14, 40, 169, 170, 175, 177, 196
monologues, 125
Moody, Stephanie, 9
morale, in graduate programs, 107
Morrell, David, 254
motivation, student, 122
multimedia texts, 178

Index   271

multiple choice instruments, reading for, 45
"Muses' Farewell, The" (Steiner), 239–40

Naming What We Know (Adler-Kassner and Wardle), 48, 193
National Association of College and Employers (NACE), competencies, 204, 205
National Association of Colleges and Employers, 202
National Council of Teachers of English (NCTE), 14, 15, 43; conference sessions, 40, 41
national curriculum, 89
National Endowment for the Humanities (NEH), 14, 209
National Writing Project, 15
Nature of Narrative, The (Scholes and Kellogg), 12
NCTE. *See* National Council of Teachers of English
negotiations, rhetorical, 140
NEH. *See* National Endowment for the Humanities
New Critics, 90, 92, 102, 158, 171
New Humanists, 246
Newman, John Henry, *The Scope and Nature of University Education*, 245–46
Newman, Mary, 55
news sources, evaluating, 152–53
Newton, Huey, 223
New Yorker, digital repository, 61
New York Times, 153
Nietzsche, Friedrich, 109
Nilson, Linda, 50
nonfiction prose, 51
non-literature, consumption of, 229–30
nonreading, nonreaders, 167, 168
Nussbaum, Martha, 65

Oakland School Board, AAVE, 213
Obama, Barack, 155
objectivism, 139
objectivity, journalism and, 150
Occupy protests, 215
Ohmann, Richard, 138
online environment, 46, 47, 50. *See also* digital environment
opera, 33
oral interpretation, 159–60
oratory, 243
Organisation for Economic Cooperation and Development (OECD), Programme for International Student Assessment, 45

Orlando (Woolf), 94
Orthodoxy, 226
others, otherness, 117, 135, 159; listening to, 120–21, 160–61; understanding, 31, 154
"Outcomes Statement for First-Year Composition" (WPA), 67

Pacesetter course, 150
paintings, 33
Palmer, Parker, 139
Panasonic, and GSU Creative Media Industries Institute, 208
Pedagogy: Critical Approaches to Teaching Literature, Language, Composition, and Culture (journal), 9, 47
Peer Review, "Integrative Learning," 179
performance, 34, 178
periodicals, 58, 64; student use of, 68–69; study of, 62–63; textuality of, 57, 60, 69–70
periodical studies, 9, 15
Persona (Gibson), 254
persuasion, 129
persuasive texts, 119, 162, 163
Petrosky, Anthony, *Ways of Reading*, 6
PhD degrees, program, 107, 110–11, 169, 170, 256
Phelps, Louise Wetherbee, 183
Phillips, Stephanie, 220
Pierce, Quentin, 214, 218, 219–20, 221, 222, 223–24
PISA. *See* Programme for International Student Assessment
Plato, 101, 250
PMLA (journal), *Cultures of Reading*, 54
poaching, 217
poetry, 13, 32, 34, 92, 101, 161
Politico, 152
politics, 31, 93, 130, 137
Pope, Alexander, 149
postcolonialism, 212
postliterate society, 167
postmodernism, 172, 212
postpositivist theories, 140
poststructuralism, 16, 136, 148, 149, 171, 190, 212, 227, 231
post-truth era, 16, 135, 147, 148; politics, 137, 138
power, 31; rhetorical, 101, 102; textual, 160, 169
practice(s), 14, 39, 210, 232, 233, 234
Practice of Everyday Life, The (de Certeau), 213
Practice of Writing, The (Scholes, Comley, and Peritz), 29, 40, 254–55, 259

pragmatism, 248
preservice teachers, research-scholarship heuristic, 75–83
prestige, of literature, 234–35
privilege, 141, 214
process, 67, 173; reading as, 101–6
production, 192; consumption within, 216, 231–32
Professional Correctness (Fish), 113
professionalism, anti-professional, 170
Programme for International Student Assessment (PISA), 45
Protestant tradition, 161
Protocols of Reading (Scholes), 26, 31, 38, 49, 216
prototactician, Scholes as, 216, 218
psycholinguistics, 18
public agencies, 178
publication, academic, 108
Pulp Magazine Archive, The, 61
Pulp Magazine Project, 61, 65–66
Pulp Making of America Collection, 61
purpose, and ways of reading, 29–32
Pynchon, Thomas, *Gravity's Rainbow*, 95

quality enhancement plan (QEP), 18, 207–8, 210; college-to-career, 17, 198–202; student learning outcomes, 203–5
quote mining, 39, 55

racism, locating, 141
"radial reading" process, 58–59
Radical Americas (open-access journal), 9
Rake's Progress, The (Stravinsky), 99
Ransom, John Crowe, 113
Ratcliffe, Krista, 140
reader-led classroom, 64
reader-response theories, 171
readers (books), 57–58
reader-text interactions, 56
reading(s), 9, 29, 30, 33, 40, 117, 125, 155, 161, 178, 179, 217; college-level, 41–43; contemplative, 133–34, 142–43; as craft, 13–14, 25; critical, 4, 6, 10, 34; decontextualized, 60–61; ethics of, 16, 135–36; as experience, 23–24; habits, 51, 55; methods for, 14–15; non-literature, 229–30; pedagogy, 3, 47–48; practicing, 25, 39; as process, 101–6; as productive activity, 231–32; rhetorical, 56–57; teaching, 46–47, 49–50, 159; and writing, 157–58. *See also* ways of reading
reading aloud, 34, 163–64(n3); contemplative pedagogy, 133–34; as rhetorical exercise, 159–60; role of, 134–35

reading brain, 54
reading comprehension, ACT, 45
reading editions, 60–61
"Reading Frederick Douglass Contemplatively" session, 133
Reading Special Interest Group (CCCC), 40
reading theory, graduate training in, 47–48
Reaffirmation Leadership Team (GSU), 199
real world, and academy, 232, 233
recitation, values of, 202–3
recontextualization, 59
Reddit, "Guide to the News," 152–53
relativism, 109
Renaissance humanism, 243, 245, 246
repositories, digital, 61
research: goals of, 107–8; graduate-level, 106–7; and scholarship, 73–74; teacher-learning and, 75–83
research papers, traditional, 68
research-scholarship heuristic, in teacher-learning, 75–83
Research Society for American Periodicals Book Prize, 14
Research Society for Victorian Periodicals, 61
resistance, 141, 161
Rethinking Racism: Emotion, Persuasion, and Literacy Education in an All-White High School (Trainor), 141
revision, in invitational essays, 127–28
rhetoric, 3, 32, 101, 140, 141, 146, 160, 243; and argument, 129–30; invitational, 121, 123–24
rhetorical capacity, of students, 11
rhetorical context, 56
rhetorical exercise, reading aloud as, 159–60
Rhetorical Power (Mailloux), 172
rhetorical theory, 188
Rhetoric and Demagoguery (Roberts-Miller), 257
Riche, David, 138
Ricoeur, Paul, 235
Rios, Sandy, 258
Rise and Fall of English: Reconstructing English as a Discipline, The (Scholes), 4, 7, 13, 15, 149–50, 170, 175–76, 189, 190, 196–97, 213, 217
Roberts-Miller, Trish, *Rhetoric and Demagoguery*, 257
Rockwell, Norman, 14
Rogerian argument, 120, 121
Romanticism, 244, 245

Rosenblatt, Louise, 10, 31
Rowling, J. K., 14
RTE (journal), reading and literacy articles, 43, 44(table)
Russia Today, 153
Ruszkiewicz, John J., *Everything's an Argument*, 120–21, 126

Sackey-Milligan, Rose, 142; "Reading Frederick Douglass Contemplatively" session, 133–34
sacred texts, 32–33, 100, 161
SACSCOC. *See* Southern Association of Colleges and Schools Commission on Colleges
SAE. *See* Standard American English
Salvatori, Mariolina Rizzi, 9
Sanchez, Claudio, 254
Sánchez, Raúl, 136, 140
Sandel, Michael, 130
Sartre, Jean-Paul, 214, 221, 222
Schecter, Laura, 9
Schilb, John, *Making Literature Matter*, 190
scholarship: integrative learning and, 179–80; and research, 73–74; teacher-learning, 74–78
science, and media, 145
science fantasy, 33
science fiction, 4, 5, 12, 33
Scope and Nature of University Education, The (Newman), 245–46
Seale, Bobby, 223
secularism, 101, 137
secular scripture, literature as, 235–37
Securing a Place for Reading in Composition: The Importance of Teaching for Transfer (Carillo), 47
self-awareness, audience and, 128–29
self-government, 130
self-reflection, 136; critical, 134, 174
semiotics, 3, 13, 169; of language, 11–12
Semiotics and Interpretation (Scholes), 11, 12, 174
September 11, 2001, 5–6, 154, 159
Shakespeare, William, reading plays of, 104–5
Shareblue, 152
Shaughnessy, Mina, 220
Shulman, Lee S., *Educating for Democracy*, 118
Skerrett, Allison, 82–83
skills-building pedagogy, 205
Smith, Adam, *The Wealth of Nations*, 244
Smitherman, Geneva, *Talkin and Testifyin*, 6
social identity, 65

socialization, readerly, 60
social justice, 25
social media, 154; information from, 146–47
Society for the Scientific Study of Reading, 41
Society of Professional Journalists, 152
Soliday, Mary, 9
source material, student use of, 45–46, 58–60, 69
Southern Association of Colleges and Schools Commission on Colleges (SACSCOC), 199
Special Interest Group for Reading in Composition Studies (CCCC), 41
specialization, in English major, 8, 95–96
speeches, 161
Spenser, Edmund, 236
Spivak, Gayatri, *Death of a Discipline*, 250
stakeholders, research and scholarship, 79
Standard American English (SAE), 212, 213; production of, 221–22
"Standard of Taste, On the" (Hume), 243
Stanford History Education Group, 46
statistics, quantitative literacy, 145
Steiner, George, 242, 244, 245, 247; "The Muses' Farewell," 239–40
STEM programs, 200
Storri website, 75
Stravinsky, Igor, *The Rake's Progress*, 99
Structural Fabulation: An Essay on Fictions of the Future (Scholes), 12
structuralism, 3, 11–12, 226–27, 231
Structuralism in Literature, An Introduction (Scholes), 12, 174
Structural Transformation of the Public Sphere, The (Habermas), 214
student-learning outcome measures, 200, 204–5
student-researchers, and periodicals, 62–63
students, 6, 32, 51, 55, 80, 207; archival projects, 68–69; reading abilities, 15, 43; rhetorical capacity, 10–11; specialization, 95–96; as subaltern public, 218–19; use of source material, 45–46, 59–60
"Students' Rights to Their Own Language, The" (CCCC), 213
student success initiatives, 199–200
style, 174, 227
subaltern counterpublic, 214
subaltern publics, language and, 218–19
Sullivan, Patrick, *Deep Reading*, 42
surface reading, 55

tactical strategies, 213–14; in writing studies, 215–16
Tactics of Hope: The Public Turn in English Composition (Mathieu), 215
Talkin and Testifyin (Smitherman), 6
Tate, Allen, "Tension in Literature," 162
teacher-learning, 72–73; research-scholarship heuristic, 74–83
teachers, 48, 55, 234; preservice, 76–83
teaching, 5, 111, 190, 234; English, 7–8; first-year composition, 186, 192; problems in, 72–73, 79–80; reading, 46–47, 49–50, 159; and research, 106, 108
Teaching Literature course, research-scholarship heuristic in, 75–83
technobureaucracy, 246–47, 249, 251
technological literacy, 16, 179
television, 99
"Tension in Literature" (Tate), 162
testing, high stakes, 55
TETYC (journal), reading and literacy, 43, 44(table)
Text Book: An Introduction to Literary Language (Scholes, Comley, and Ulmer), 188
Text Book: Writing through Literature (Scholes, Comley, and Ulmer), 4, 8, 29, 32, 174, 175, 188, 190
textbooks, 57–58, 168, 190
texts, 28, 50, 58, 59, 172, 189; aesthetic vs. rhetorical, 117, 161; evaluating, 43, 55; hermetic understandings, 137–38; journalistic, 147–48; reading of, 104–5; reverence before, 6, 27; studying, 175, 238; types of, 26, 32–33
Textual Identities (course): periodicals used in, 65–66; purposes, 64–65, 66–67
textuality, textual studies, 3, 4, 8, 15, 59, 61, 112, 136–37, 146, 160, 169, 172, 173, 174, 187, 188, 191, 192, 251, 255, 256; of bumper stickers, 103–4; canon of methods, 88–94; comparative, 33; periodical, 60, 69–70; purpose of, 189–90; and rhetorical reading, 56–57
Textual Power: Literary Theory and the Teaching of English (Scholes), 4, 7, 8, 13, 14, 17, 24, 27, 40, 63, 69, 135, 148, 149, 174, 176, 189, 216; as cultural studies approach, 138–39; on textuality, 136–37
theory, 241; failure of, 247, 249–50
Theranos, reporting on, 151–52
thinking, 190; critical, 6, 34, 67–68, 129, 202, 210, 257
"Tidy House: Basic Writing in the American Curriculum, The" (Bartholomae), 6, 219–20

Tinberg, Howard, *Deep Reading*, 42
Tough, Sweet, and Stuffy (Gibson), 254
Trainor, Jennifer, *Rethinking Racism*, 141
"Transition to College Reading, The" (Scholes), 4, 117, 134, 135
transmediation, 125
tree, as metaphor, 23–24, 35–36
Trump, Donald, 135, 155
truth, truthfulness, 82, 109, 148, 149, 235, 242; pursuit of, 130, 151
Tumblr, 202
Two Cultures of English: Literature, Composition, and the Moment of Rhetoric, The, 7, 8–9

Ulmer, Gregory, *Text Book*, 8, 32, 188
Ulysses (Joyce), 94–95
undergraduates, in humanities, 170–71
understanding, 120–21
unionization, 107
UC Davis sit-ins, 215
University College of London, *Radical Americas*, 9

value, in invitational rhetoric, 123–24
van Dam, Andries (Andy), 13
verbal texts, 91
video games, 5
videos, 33
violence, epistemological, 139
virtual libraries, 167, 180
Virtual Newsstand of 1925, 61
virtue, and taste, 246
vocabulary, reading for, 39
vocationalism, antivocational, 170
Vox, 153

Wardle, Elizabeth, 55; *Naming What We Know*, 48, 193
Washington, Amber, 82–83
ways of reading, 15, 26; intellectual moves, 27–29; Modernist Journals Project, 63; purpose and, 29–32; types of text, 32–33
Ways of Reading (Bartholomae and Petrosky), 6, 220
Wealth of Nations, The (Smith), 244
websites, 215, writing on, 162–63
WellStar Health System, 208
WellStar Religion and Public Life Fellowship, 208
West, E. James, 9
"What Is an Author?" (Foucault), 172
white supremacy, eradication of, 222
Williamson, Thea, 82–83
Wingard, Joel, 7
Wolf, Maryanne, 50

women, objectification and representation, 65, 66
Women at Work: Rhetorics of Gender and Labor (Gold and Enoch), 257
Woolf, Virginia, *Orlando*, 94
Wordsworth, William, 244
WPA. *See* Writing Programs Administrators
WPA (journal), reading and literacy articles, 43, 44(table)
WPA-L (writing program administrators' listserve), 7, 47
Writer's Guide to Mindful Reading, A (Carillo), 143
writing, 25, 120, 125, 175, 179; accessibility of, 12–13; critical, 6, 10; online programs, 47; and reading, 157–58; scaffolding, 190–91
writing-about-writing (WaW), 194
Writing about Writing (Wardle and Downs), 193
Writing Programs Administrators (WPA), "Outcomes Statement for First-Year Composition," 67
writing studies, 257–58, 259; development of, 193–94; as discipline, 191–92; future of, 16–17; hierarchy in, 192–93; independence of, 182–83; as movement, 186–87; and reading, 40–43; tactical in, 215–16; theme-based courses, 64
writing studies departments, 8, 10, 17; formation of, 184–85; independent, 183–84; university status of, 185–86
Wulfman, Clifford, *Modernism in the Magazine*, 15, 61–62, 64

xenophobia, challenging, 5–6

Yale School of Deconstruction, 137
Yeats, William Butler, 248, 250
Young, Vershawn Ashanti, 42

Zajonc, Arthur, 139
Zapatista uprising, 215
Zedillo, Ernesto, 215

www.ingramcontent.com/pod-product-compliance
Lightning Source LLC
Chambersburg PA
CBHW031100080526
44587CB00011B/757